IMAGES
of Modern America

Los Gatos

I0806367

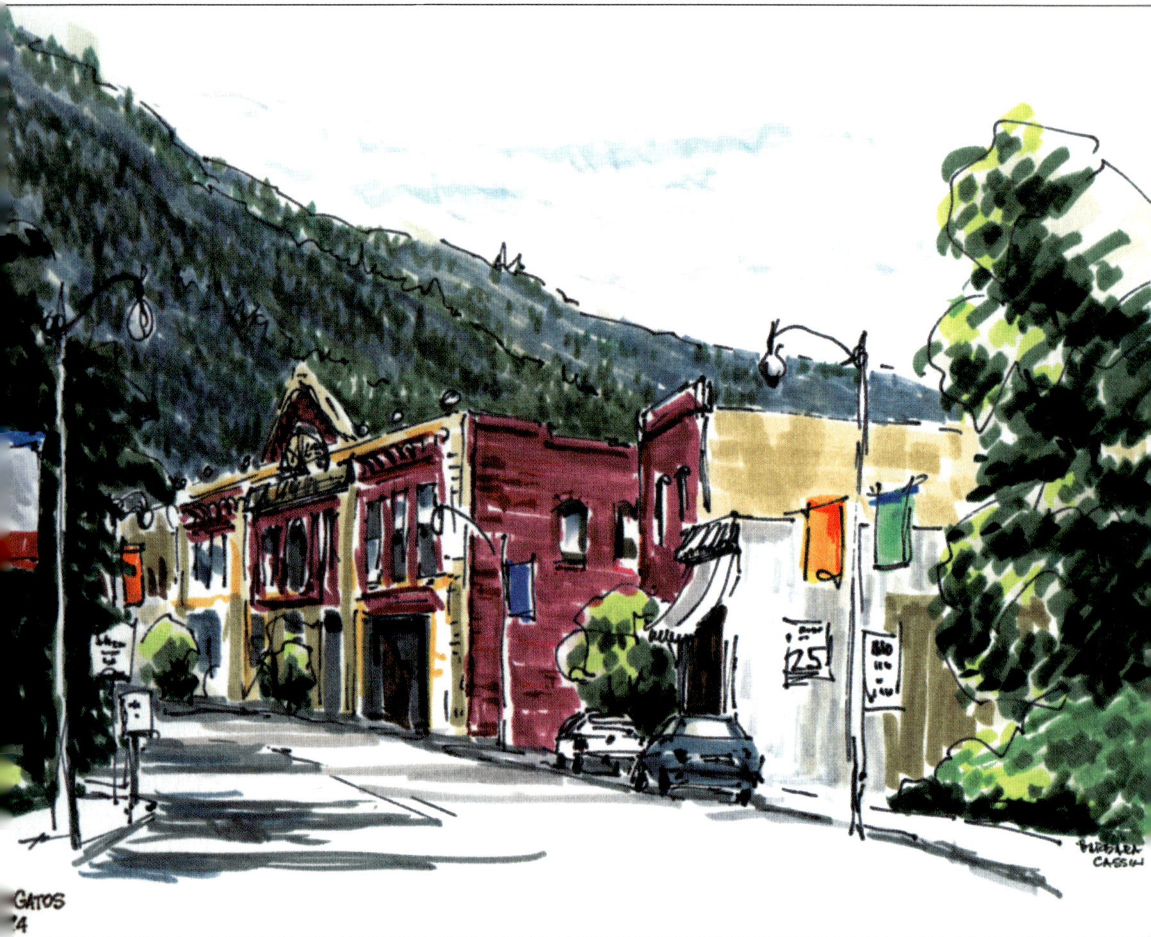

East Main Street. Barbara Jones Cassin (1919–2010) was a 1937 graduate of Los Gatos High School. Daughter of Elizabeth Ann McSwain and California state senator Herbert C. Jones, she painted watercolor scenes of Los Gatos, including the one shown here. Her endowment to Los Gatos Public Library provided funding for an enhanced "opening day" collection for the new library. (Los Gatos Public Library.)

On the Front Cover: Clockwise from top left: The 1894 La Cañada Building has survived two earthquakes (courtesy of Brian Bergtold); buildings at 37–45 East Main Street were shattered during the 1989 Loma Pieta earthquake (see page 61); the new Los Gatos Public Library is the pride of the community (see page 91); attractions at Vasona Lake include rental sailboats, kayaks, and a one-third-scale railroad (see page 85); the Strawberry Festival was a summertime tradition for 36 years (see page 38).

On the Back Cover: From left to right: Los Gatans have been going to the movies at 43 North Santa Cruz Avenue for nearly 100 years (see page 9); the "2-Spot" steam engine was rescued from a scrap heap by Billy Jones in 1939 (see page 87); Los Gatos High School was constructed in 1925 (see page 92).

IMAGES
of Modern America

Los Gatos

Peggy Conaway Bergtold

ARCADIA
PUBLISHING

Copyright © 2015 by Peggy Conaway Bergtold
ISBN 978-1-4671-3421-7

Published by Arcadia Publishing
Charleston, South Carolina

Printed in the United States of America

Library of Congress Control Number: 2015942248

For all general information, please contact Arcadia Publishing:
Telephone 843-853-2070
Fax 843-853-0044
E-mail sales@arcadiapublishing.com
For customer service and orders:
Toll-Free 1-888-313-2665

Visit us on the Internet at www.arcadiapublishing.com

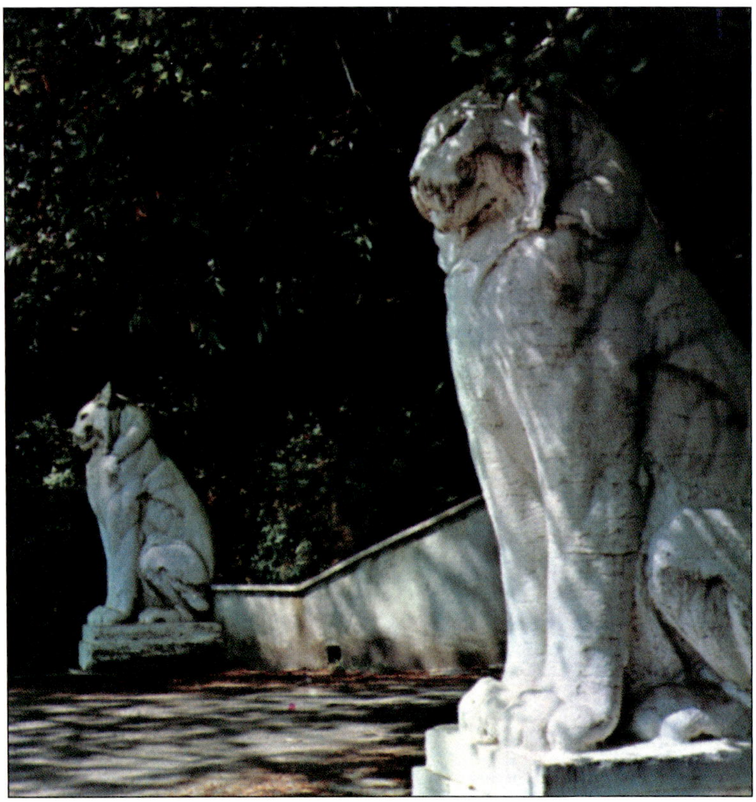

Colossal Cats. Charles Erskine Scott Wood built the Cats Estate south of town and commissioned artist Robert Treat Paine to create two eight-foot-tall cats to guard the entrance to his property. The iconic cats were completed in 1922. Wood had recently returned from Europe and found Los Gatos bereft of public art. He considered the cats "a sort of missionary work in culture in California." (Courtesy of the author.)

Contents

Acknowledgments

While visiting the California History Room at the California State Library in Sacramento a few years ago, I came upon the first issue of the *Placer Times*, a little newspaper published in "Upper California" in 1849–1850. A quote in one of the articles has stayed with me ever since: "History is only a repetition of the workings of human nature in a somewhat modified form and shape." With the writing of this, my fifth photographic history of Los Gatos for Arcadia Publishing, I have learned that things change but they also tend to stay the same. Los Gatos has always worked hard and played hard. People with ideas find their way into town. The community is generous in helping people who fall ill or experience a tragedy. The weather is great, the parking not so much, and multistory buildings are often knocking at the door. Los Gatans are fiercely protective of their town and value where they live.

That said, I hope you enjoy this brief look at the past 60 years of Los Gatos history. There have been many high points and a few low points. My goal is to provide a representative collection of images, as a comprehensive view is not possible in these pages.

I owe great thanks to many, including Dick Sparrer, who made the archives of the *Los Gatos Weekly-Times* (LGWT) available to me. Many of the photographs in this book come from that source, and they were often taken by skilled photographer George Sakkestad.

Codes at the ends of captions indicate other sources: Charles Bergtold (CB), Los Gatos Public Library (LGPL), Brian Bergtold (BB), and the US Geological Survey (USGS). Some photographs are from private collections, as noted, and some are from the author's collection (AC). I owe special thanks to a cadre of talented photographers, including Ken Benjamin, Ed Lucey, Greg Stepovich, Ron Horii, and especially George Sakkestad and Brian Bergtold.

INTRODUCTION

Los Gatos was a great place to grow up. Anyone who had the opportunity to do so will tell you that without hesitation. What made it such a special small town, and how has it changed from the 1950s to now?

The simple physical beauty of the place has always been a factor. The town, never called a "city," snuggles into a sweet spot at the base of the majestic Santa Cruz Mountains, which sometimes appear nearly close enough to touch. Los Gatos is where the urbanism of Silicon Valley meets rugged mountain terrain, under an open sky. The town does not have the closed-in feeling of some communities to the north, on the crowded San Francisco Peninsula.

Back in the 19th century, Los Gatos weather was often described as "salubrious," an old-fashioned term that means "making good health possible." The town's magnificent Mediterranean climate still provides a pleasant, sunny, and invigorating milieu most days of the year.

Whether it was fishing and wading in Los Gatos Creek, riding on the Billy Jones steam railroad, cutting 'cots, traveling on the newly-opened Highway 17, enjoying Thanksgiving dinner at the Hotel Lyndon, watching one of more than fifty annual Christmas parades, or standing in awe as a Southern Pacific train barreled into the downtown station, each generation and each person has a unique set of precious memories.

Some people remember the Sunshine Market, the numerous car dealerships with shiny new automobiles, a Shakespearean play at Old Town Theater, dancing to a live rock 'n' roll band in the amphitheater at Old Town, or eating too many strawberries at the annual summer festival. Some rode the Peerless Stage to San Jose or Santa Cruz, had drinks at Mt. Charley's or a hot dog at the Happy Hound. Some lunched at Mimi's Rooftop Café or the Red Lantern Restaurant. Many succumbed to the temptation of a butter-baked pastry at Polly Prim's. Nearly everyone marveled at the success of a Los Gatos invention, the Pet Rock, all the while eagerly purchasing one for the sock drawer, where it still resides. People shopped for antiques, worried about the Mediterranean fruit fly, and turned out to football games to cheer for the Los Gatos High School Wildcats.

Perhaps you rode your bicycle around the Almond Grove to deliver the *Los Gatos Times-Observer* newspaper, celebrated St. Patrick's Day at C.B. Hannegan's, or ventured across the street from the high school for a cheeseburger and malt at Foster's Freeze. Maybe you watched or played in the Turkey Day football game against rival Campbell High School and wondered how someone was able to kidnap—apparently on more than one occasion—the huge and weighty steel statue of "El Gato" from Los Gatos High School's inner quad. You may have wished you could scramble up the steep road to the Cats Estate and have a look around or explore the old railroad tunnels south of town. Conceivably, you took a walk on the flume—despite being told not to—and met a bobcat on your way. You might have stopped by the Town Plaza to watch talented artists paint *en plein air*. Or perhaps you are one of a dedicated band of people who worked for decades to bring about the dream of a new public library for Los Gatos, one which illustrates and illuminates the pride that Los Gatans have in their community.

The dramatic transformation of Los Gatos from a small agricultural village to an upscale Silicon Valley community took place during the years documented in this book. The orchards disappeared and landmark buildings were demolished in the 1960s. The raucous 1970s arrived with cultural unrest and growing pains. Homeowners' groups wanted to preserve the town as it had always been, while the owners of new bars, restaurants, and boutiques encouraged growth. Both the citizenry and the council were divided. Also during this era, older homes in town began to be restored, and real estate prices soared.

Throughout its history, Los Gatos has had its share of sorrow, tragedy, and natural disaster. Fires in 1985 and 1997 threatened the town. Landslides have occurred during wild and wet winter storms. Crime has increased, and Los Gatans have been shocked by several murders in recent decades. The Loma Prieta earthquake, which struck with a magnitude of 6.9 on October 17, 1989, at 5:04 p.m., shook all of Northern California but hit Los Gatos especially hard. Buildings were broken and shaken from their foundations, people fled their homes, and one-third of the downtown district was shut down.

With gigantic effort, Los Gatos was rebuilt, and the preservation of historic buildings took on new importance. In some ways, the earthquake brought the town together, as everyone struggled to preserve what was best about Los Gatos. All in all, Los Gatos today is a town where old meets new in a charming manner. Nostalgia runs deep in the veins of native Los Gatans, while newer residents celebrate and embrace the vitality and beauty of the place they have chosen to call home. Los Gatos was a magical place to grow up, and it is an exceptionally nice place to live today.

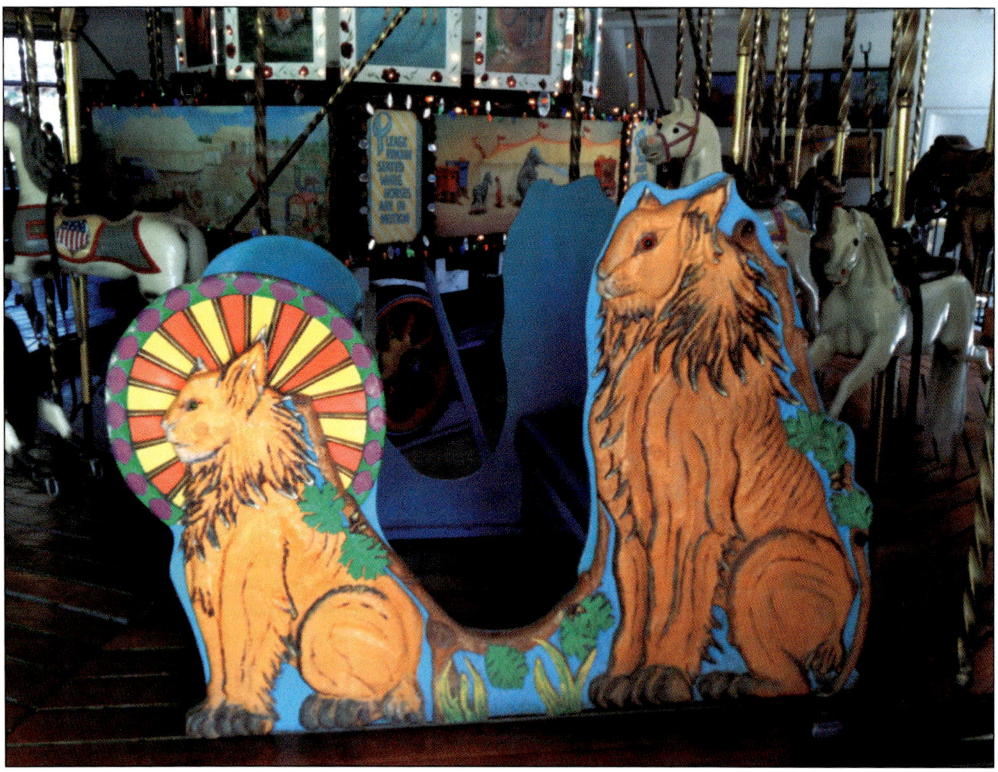

CAROUSEL CATS. Echoing their larger brethren at the Cats Estate, these two wildcats are current residents on the historic W.E. "Bill" Mason Carousel at Oak Meadow Park. The carousel was manufactured for use at the 1915 Panama-Pacific International Exposition and shipped around the Horn from England. After 10 years of restoration, the ride opened to the public in 1990. (BB.)

One

MID-CENTURY MODERN

THE 1950s

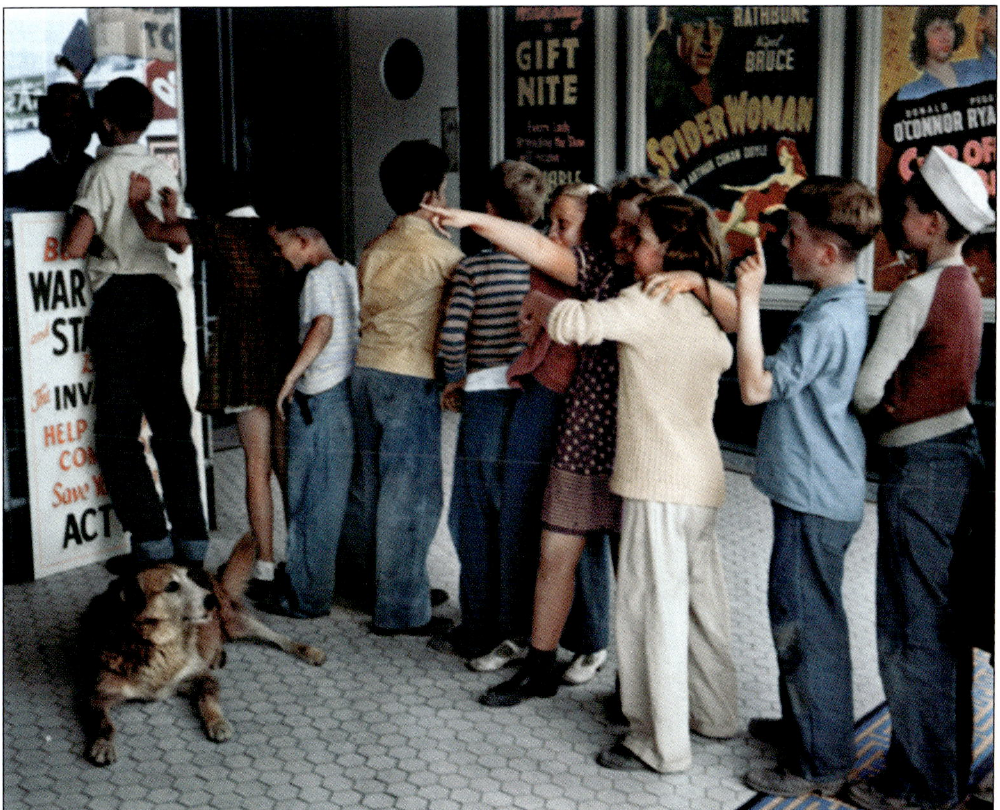

MOVIE TIME LINEUP. Going to the movies at 43 North Santa Cruz Avenue has been a popular pastime in Los Gatos for nearly 100 years. The Strand, the Premier, and the Gatos all preceded the deluxe remodeled venue that opened in 2014. This photograph dates to 1944. (LGPL.)

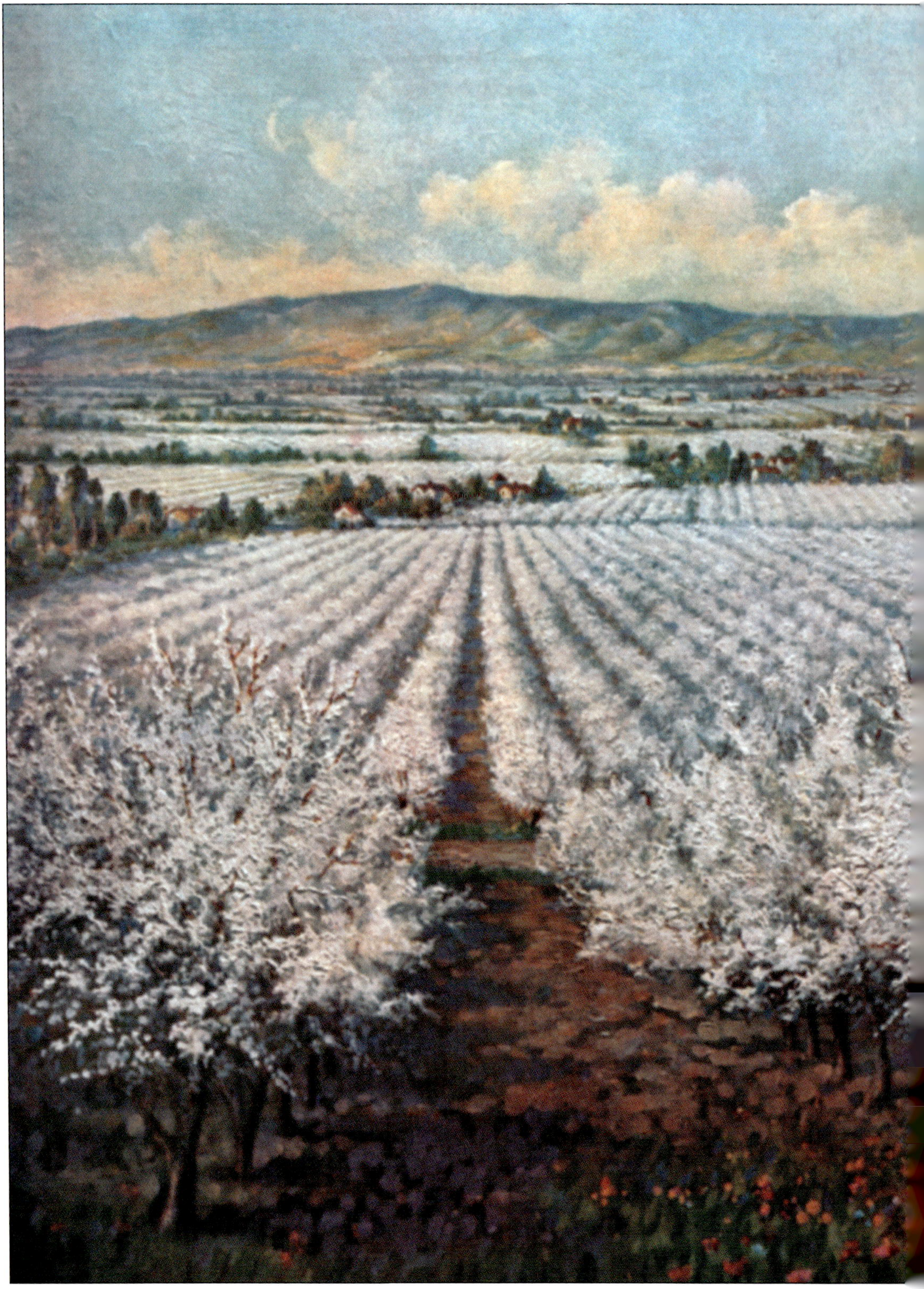

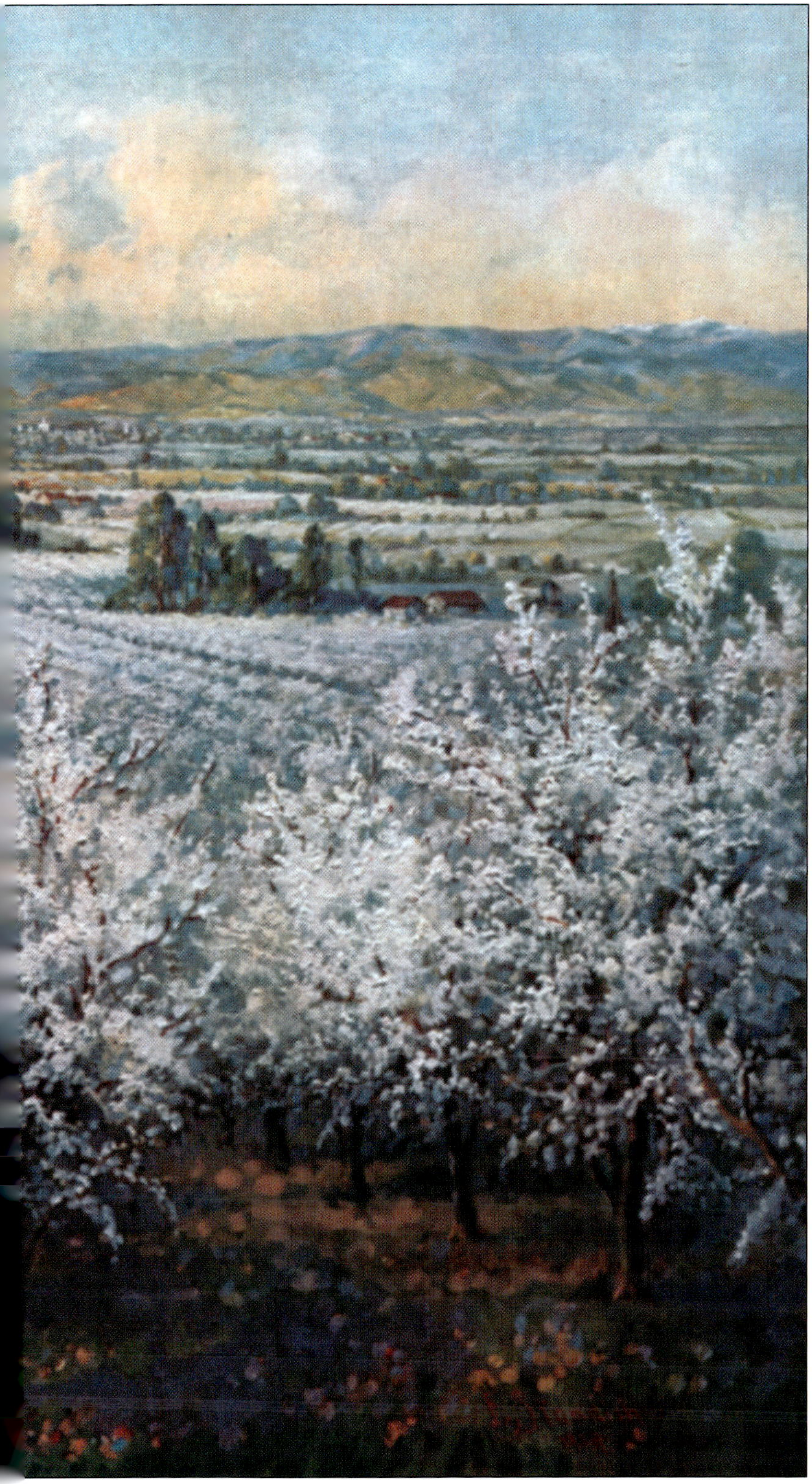

The Way We Were. Los Gatos crowns the southwestern foothills of the Santa Clara Valley and is blessed with fertile soil, a mild climate, a long growing season, and abundant sunshine. French prunes, apricots, cherries, peaches, pears, grapes, all types of vegetables, walnuts, and almonds grew in profusion. This enchanting scene depicts the springtime view across the valley from Los Gatos toward San Jose. The balmy air would have held a subtle, sweet perfume. Most local orchards disappeared by the 1960s. (AC.)

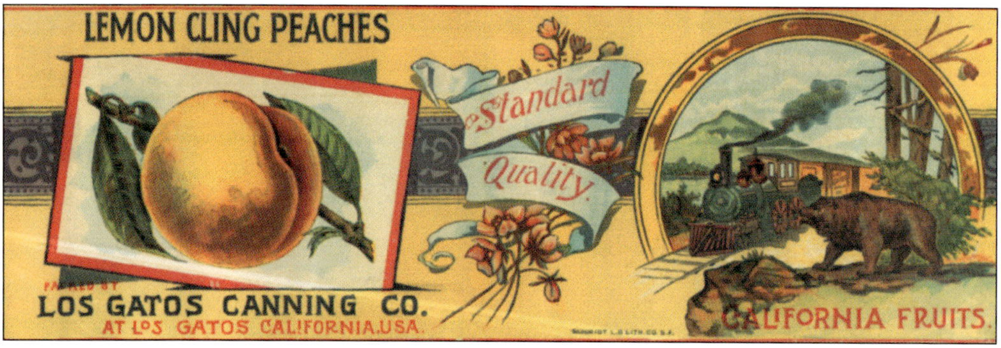

A Feast of Fruit. In 1882, soon after the railroad began hauling fruit out of the Santa Cruz Mountains, 14 investors built the Los Gatos Canning Company near where the movie theater now stands. Los Gatos exported tons of fresh, canned, and dried fruit each year during the heyday of its agricultural era. (CB.)

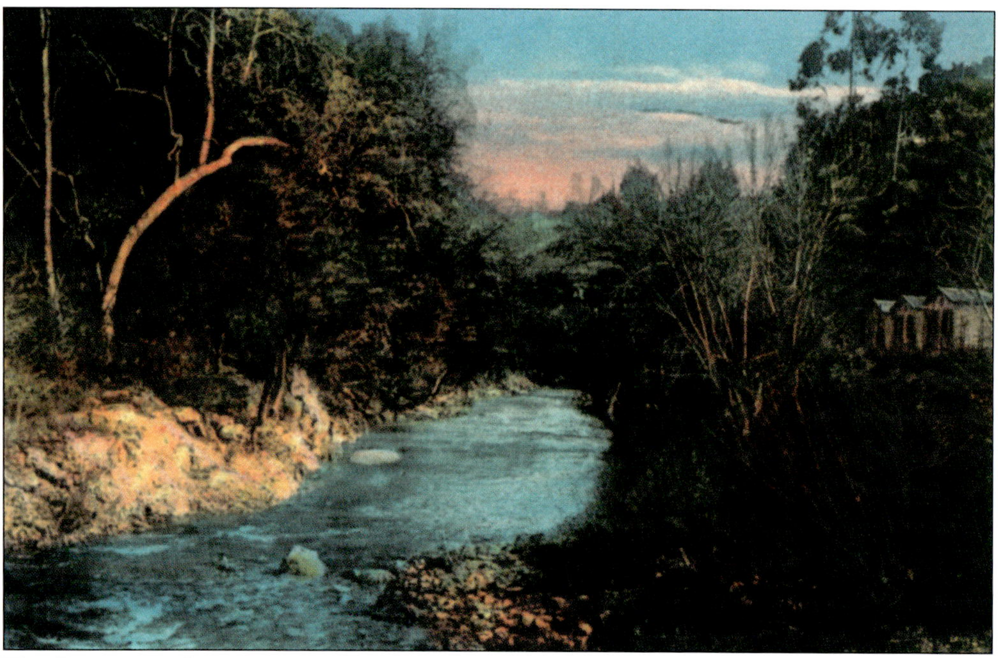

The Beautiful Creek. Los Gatos Creek sparkled with crystal-clear water and was the home of abundant speckled trout. With winter rains, it could turn into a raging torrent and cause serious flooding. But it usually served as a tranquil spot to picnic or cool off on a hot summer's day. Everything changed in the 1950s when the creek was dammed and the freeway came through town. (LGPL.)

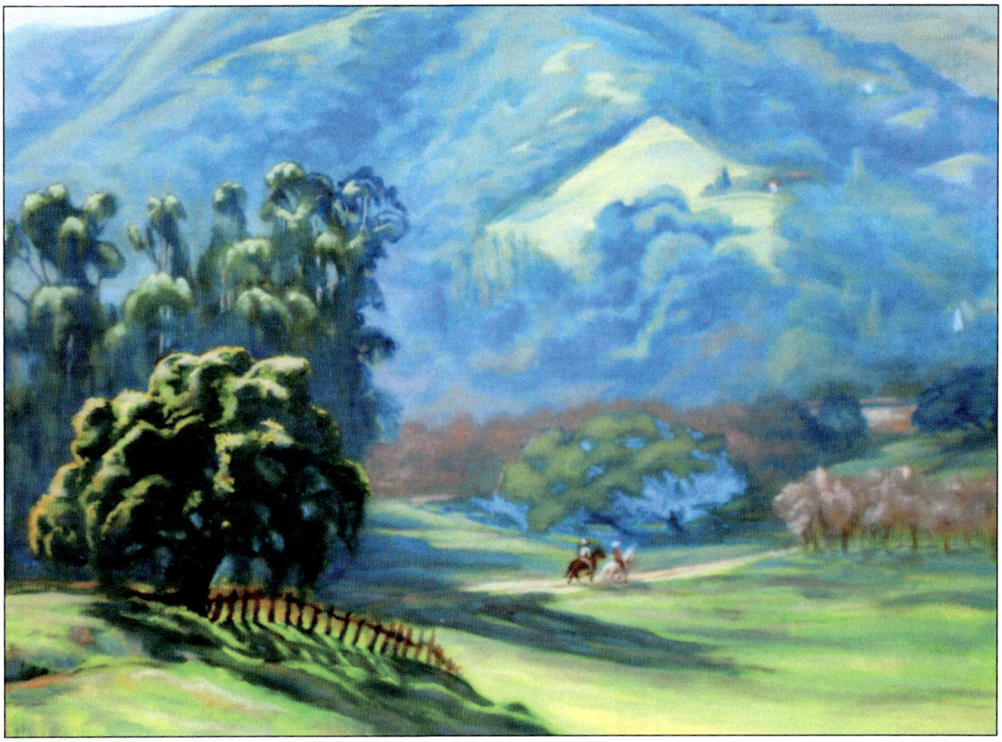

CONTROVERSY. The exquisite natural setting of Los Gatos encourages artists to step outside and paint *en plein air*. In 1947, Bella Vista Avenue resident Mildred Kaucher captured the scene above, a vista that would soon disappear in favor of Highway 17. Planning and preparation for the complex dam and reservoir project was years in the making. However, the earth-filled dam was built in only 34 weeks, between May and December 1952. The below photograph is dated September 19, 1952. An editorial in the August 21, 1952, *Los Gatos Daily Times* stated, "We are still skeptical of the wisdom of placing a dam adjacent to an earthquake fault." (Above, CB; below, LGWT.)

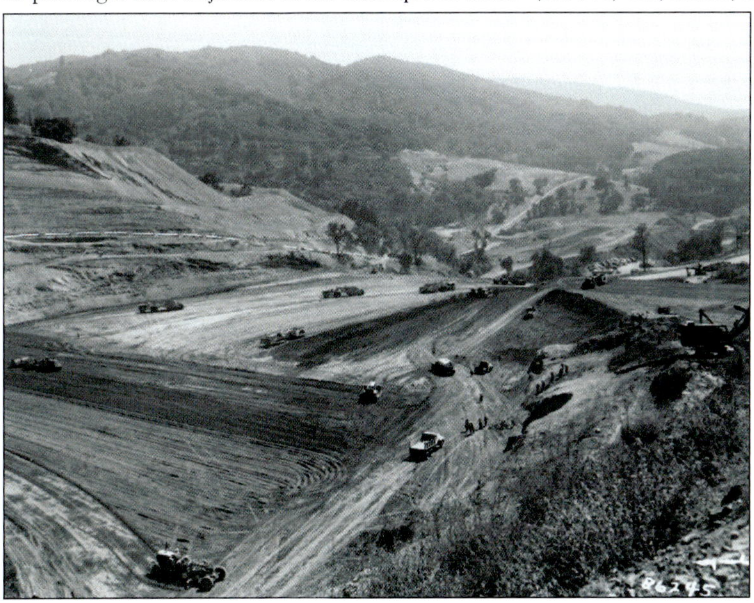

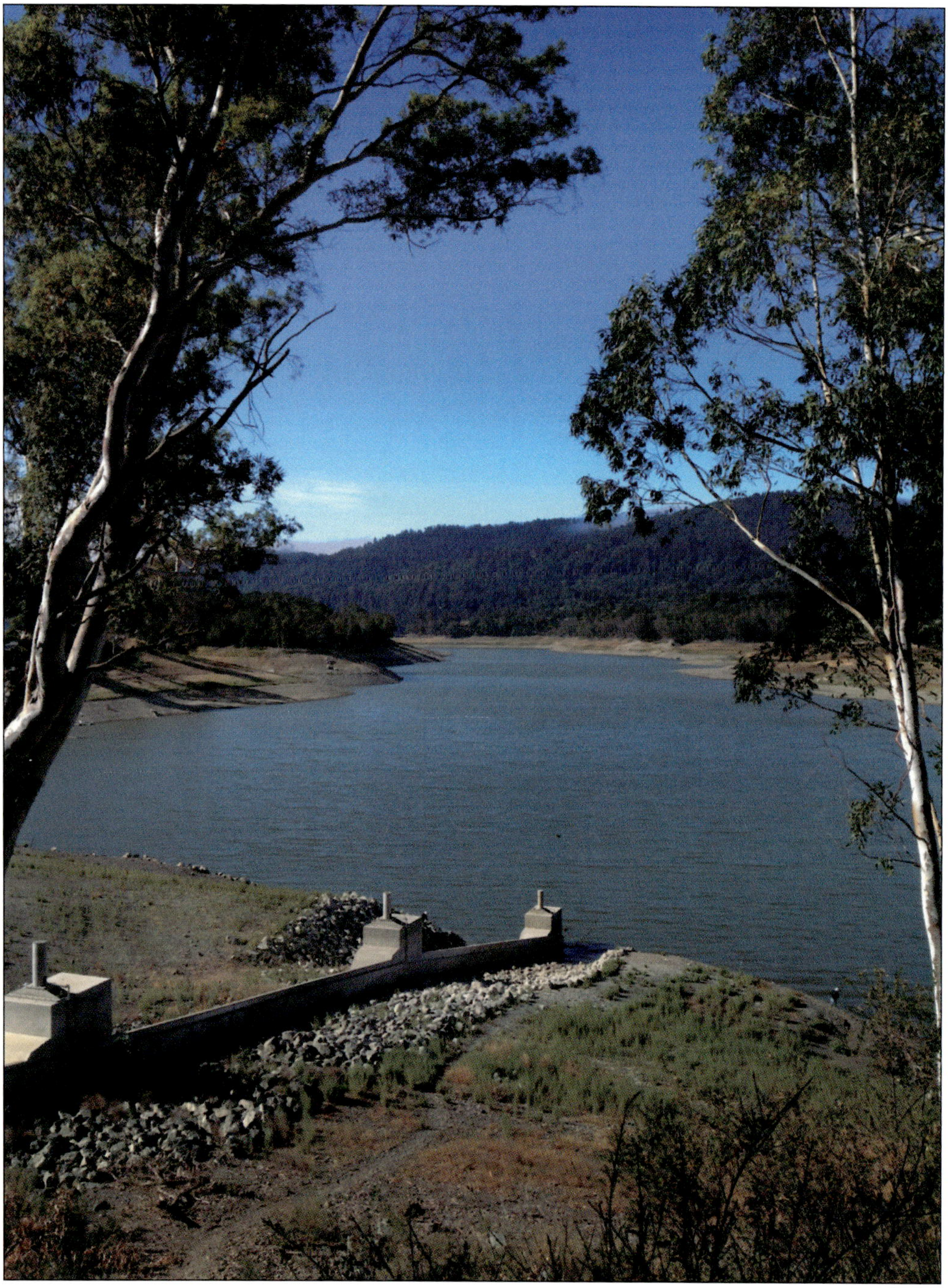

Lexington Reservoir. Built to conserve water and help manage flooding, the Lexington Dam and resulting reservoir submerged two historic small towns, Lexington and Alma, much to the consternation of hundreds of people living in the early settlements. This 2014 photograph of the reservoir shows the effects of a protracted California drought. In 1996, Lexington Dam was renamed for James J. Lenihan, a longtime director of the Santa Clara Valley Water District. (BB.)

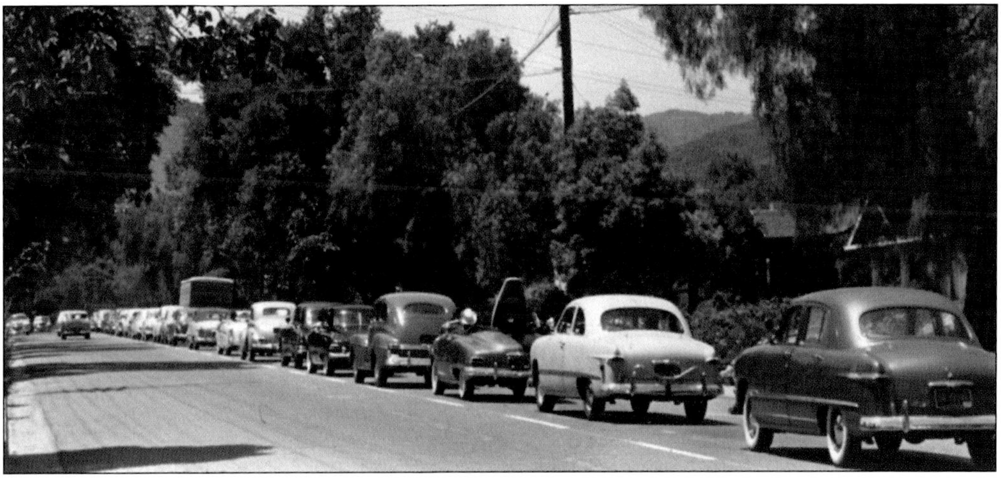

Terrific Traffic. The construction of the Lexington Dam and Reservoir caused a short section of Highway 17 to be moved to the west, to skirt around the dam, but did nothing to alleviate an aggravating traffic bottleneck at Los Gatos. Weekends, holidays, and warm summer days produced what Mayor Charles Gamble described as an "iron curtain of automobiles," all headed to or from the beach, along Main Street and Santa Cruz Avenue. In late 1951, the state highway commission approved further work on Highway 17. This time, the highway would be diverted (below) to travel along the bed of Los Gatos Creek, passing under the Main Street Bridge, and on to Campbell. Delayed by storms, landslides, and miscalculations, the new "by-pass" opened in November 1956. Traffic was relieved in town. However, the bucolic, meandering creek was placed into concrete-lined channels, and Memorial Park and the old stone Main Street Bridge were demolished in the process. (Above, LGPL; below, LGWT.)

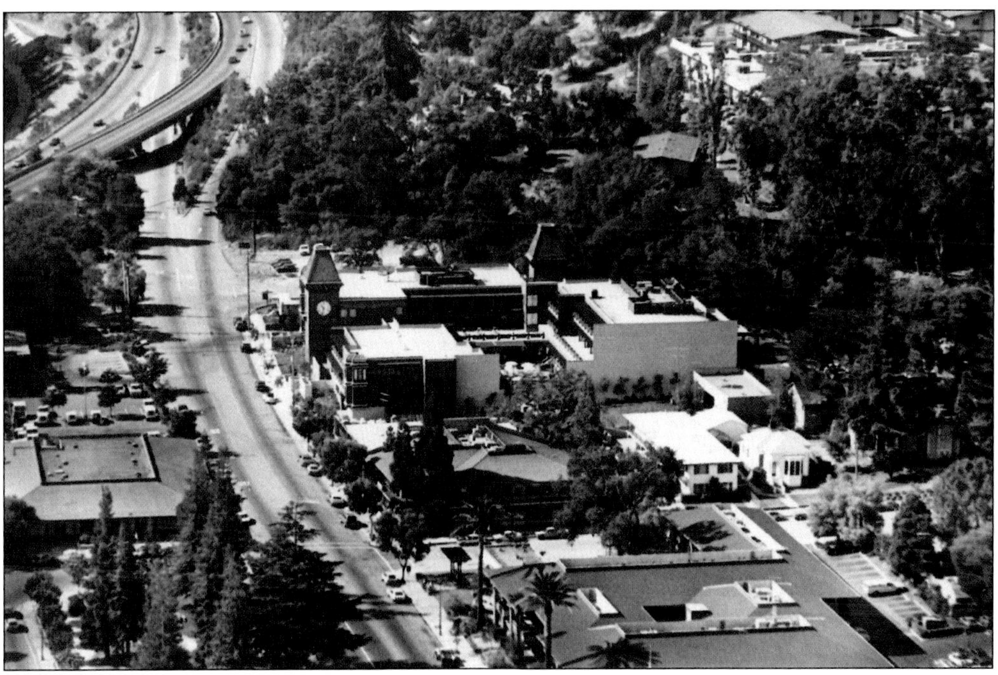

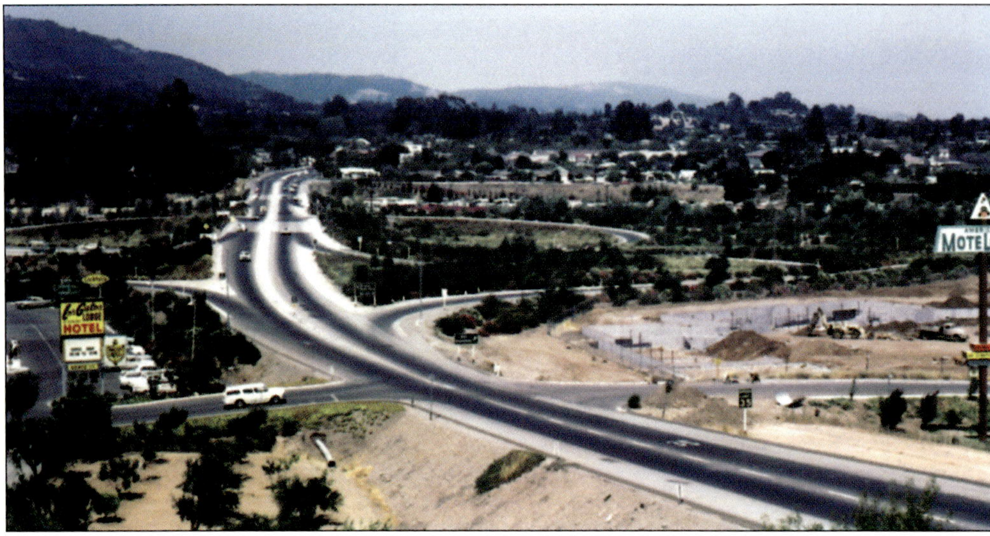

CROSSTOWN FREEWAY INTERCHANGE. The late 1950s were a time of large road projects in California. In 1957, contracts were let to construct a highway from Highway 9 (Saratoga–Los Gatos Road) to Los Gatos Boulevard. The Highway 17–Highway 9 two-level cloverleaf interchange was completed in 1959. A dedication ceremony was held on April 30, 1959, at the newly completed Los Gatos Lodge, which appears at left. (LGPL.)

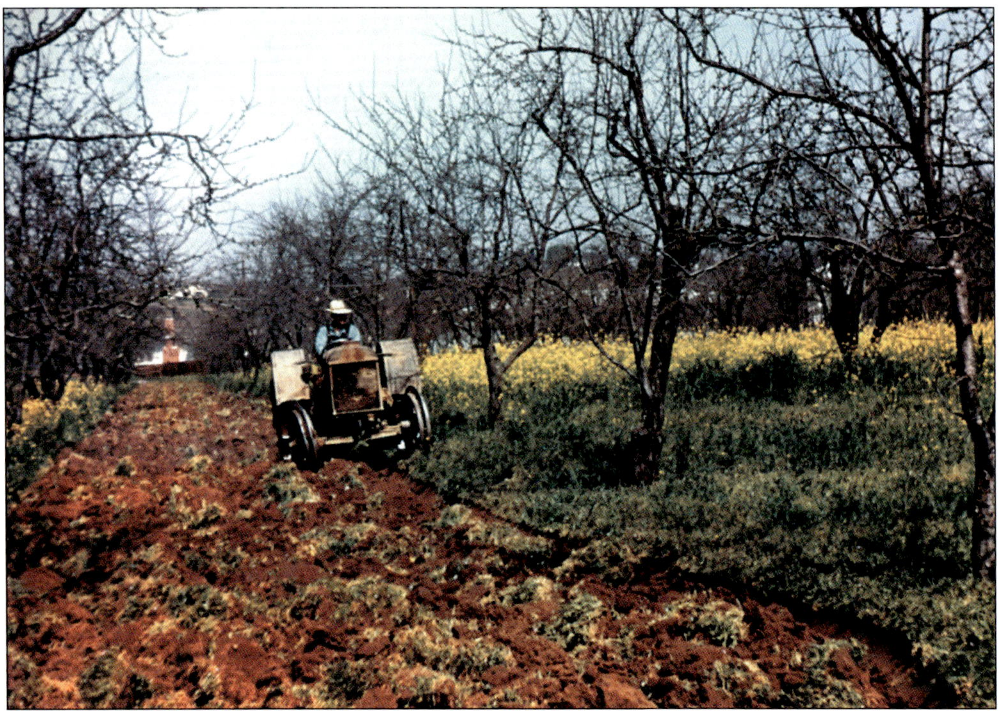

BACK AT THE RANCH. Los Gatos was beginning to feel the effects of population growth and a booming postwar economy, but prune orchards—like the one shown here being cultivated by railroader Billy Jones—still dotted the landscape. Jones assembled a one-third-scale steam railroad on his Daves Avenue ranch and provided rides for countless children. The railroad was later relocated to the Vasona–Oak Meadow Park complex. (Billy Jones family.)

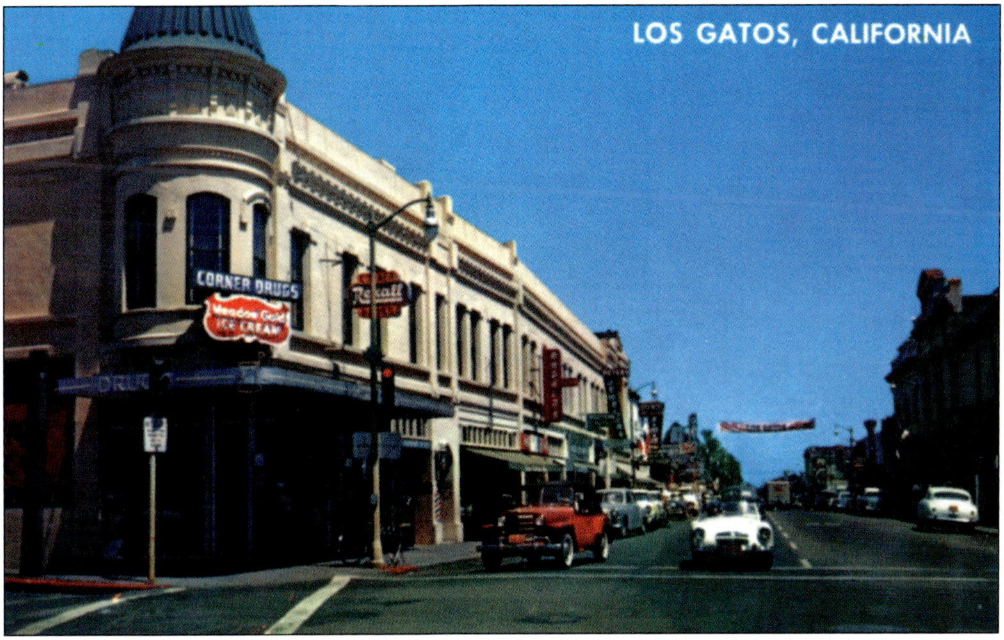

TOWN HUB. Earthquakes in 1906 and again in 1989 severely damaged the La Cañada Building. But with each disaster, the town was unwilling to sacrifice this treasured structure to the wrecking ball. Built in 1894 at Main Street and Santa Cruz Avenue, and pictured here around 1958, it housed the town's corner drugstore for years. (AC.)

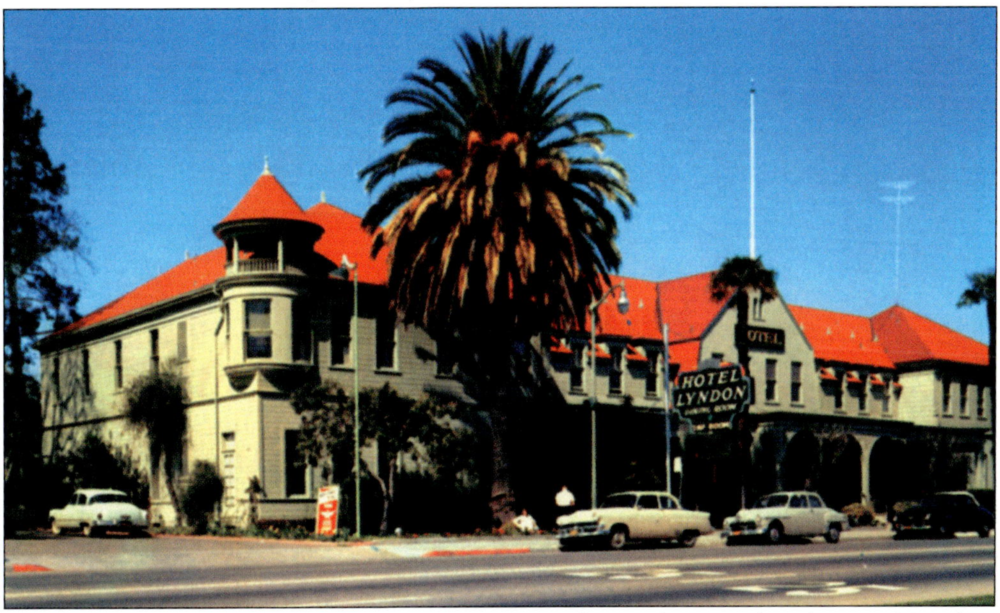

TOWN HEART. Anything that could happen in a small town happened at the Hotel Lyndon, pictured here in the mid-1950s. Flower shows, ballroom dances, banquets, lodge luncheons, political demonstrations, and family holiday dinners were all held here, across from the train depot. Some people lived at the Lyndon, and a few died there. Over the years, historic hotels at this location were remodeled, renamed, burned down and rebuilt. Hotel Lyndon (1899–1963) is remembered fondly. (AC.)

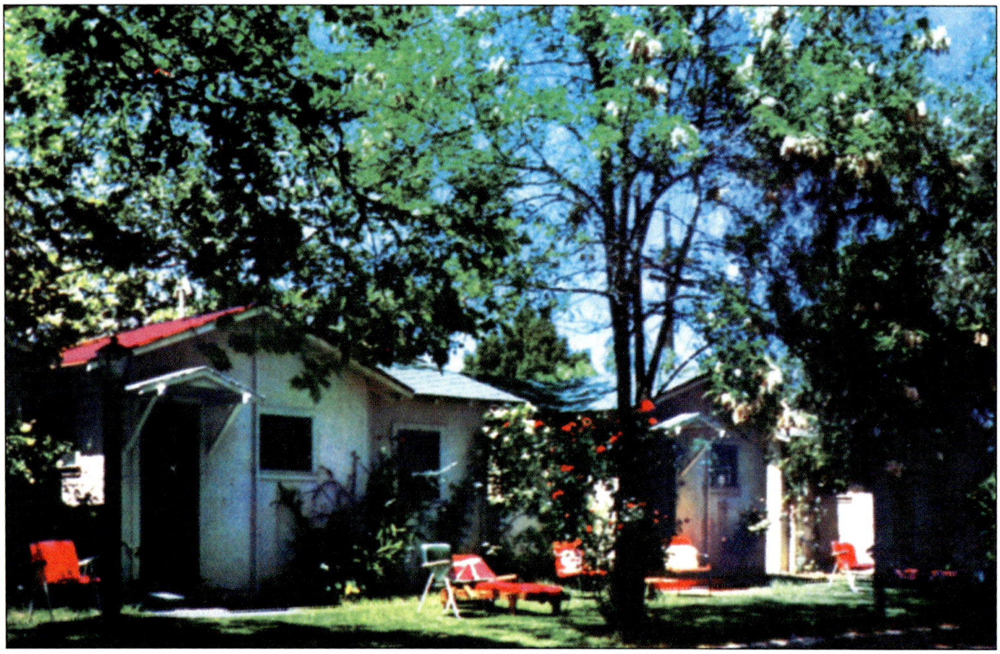

Rest and Relax at Fanning's. Los Gatos had a population of about 5,300 people when Carol Fanning issued this postcard, advertising her motor court in the early 1950s. Car-loving Californians had money to travel after World War II, and many enjoyed the separate cabins available at 214 Saratoga Avenue. (AC.)

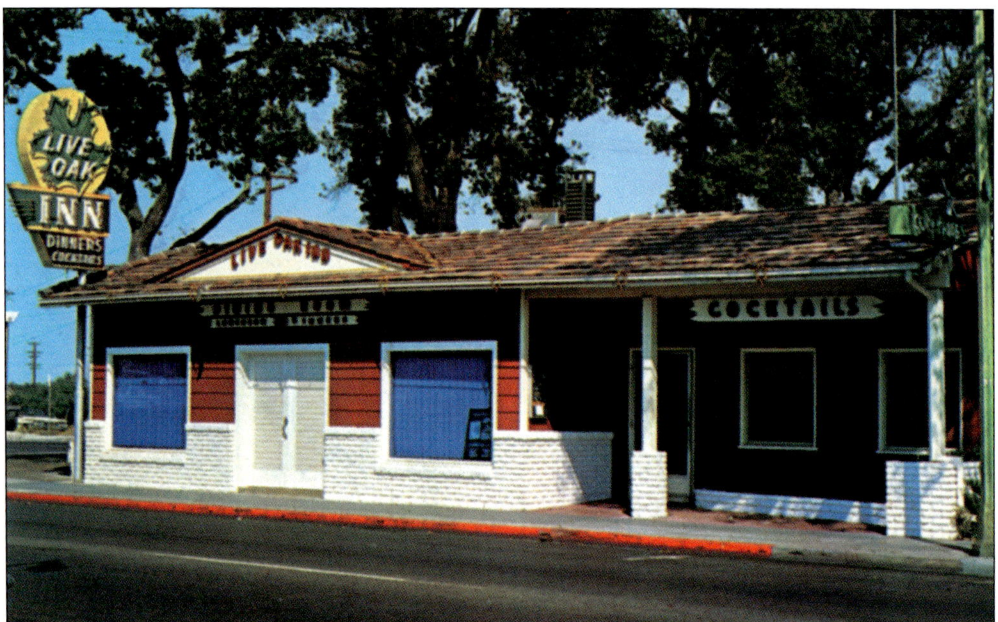

Floyd and Ruby's Place. Floyd "Bus" Benson and his wife, Ruby, operated the Live Oak Inn for decades; it was a favorite spot to dine, dance, and have a cocktail. The business was located in the Little Village shopping center developed by Effie Walton in the 1950s. After the Bensons retired in 1978, the site became the Grog and Sirloin, and it is now Double D's. (AC.)

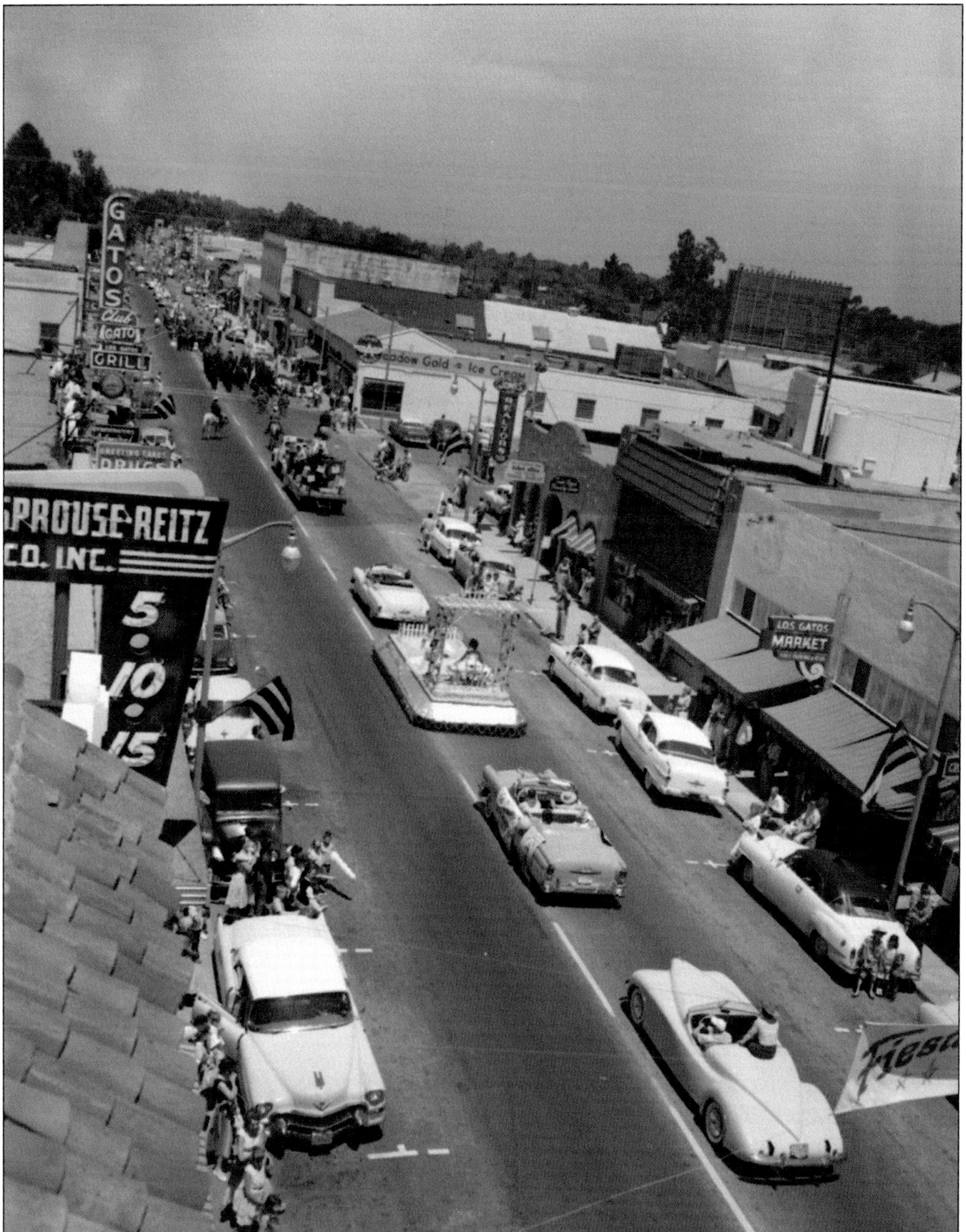

THE TOWN MADE A PARADE. An estimated 15,000 spectators lined the route of the Fiesta de Los Gatos parade on May 26, 1956. Rep. Charles Gubser served as grand marshal, mounted on horseback and waving his Stetson to the crowds. Joyce Brunetto was crowned queen for the day after selling more 50¢ fiesta buttons than the other five candidates. (LGWT.)

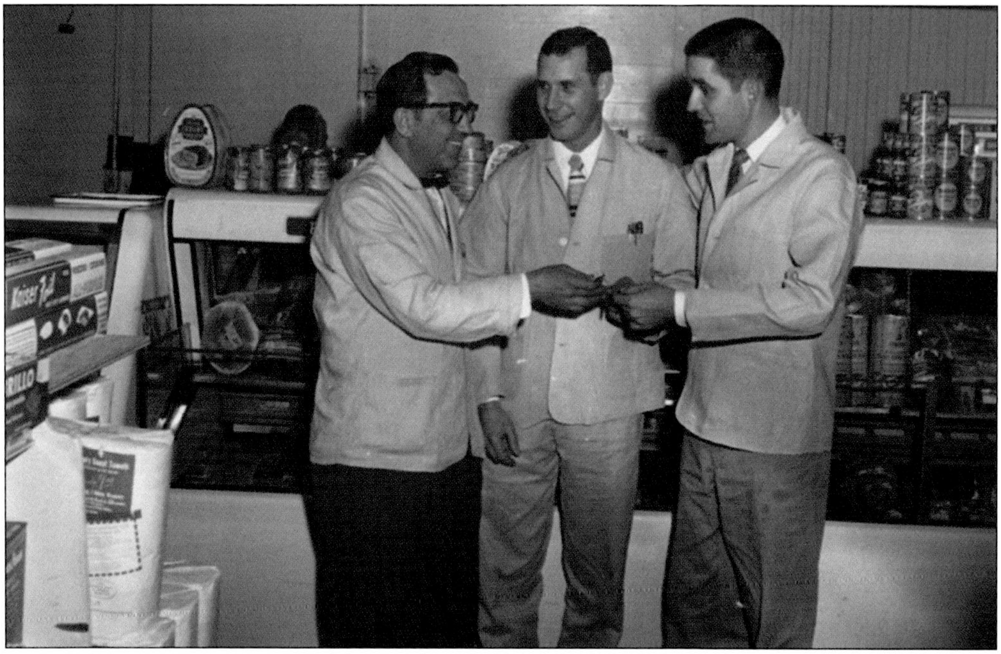

Eddie's Northside Market. Eddie Goulart (left) worked in the canneries as a boy but jumped at a chance to buy his own grocery store at 551 North Santa Cruz Avenue in 1944. For the next 30 years, he offered the best cuts of meat and the freshest produce. Eddie and his wife, Marie, extended credit to their regular customers and invited them to an annual Christmas party. (LGWT.)

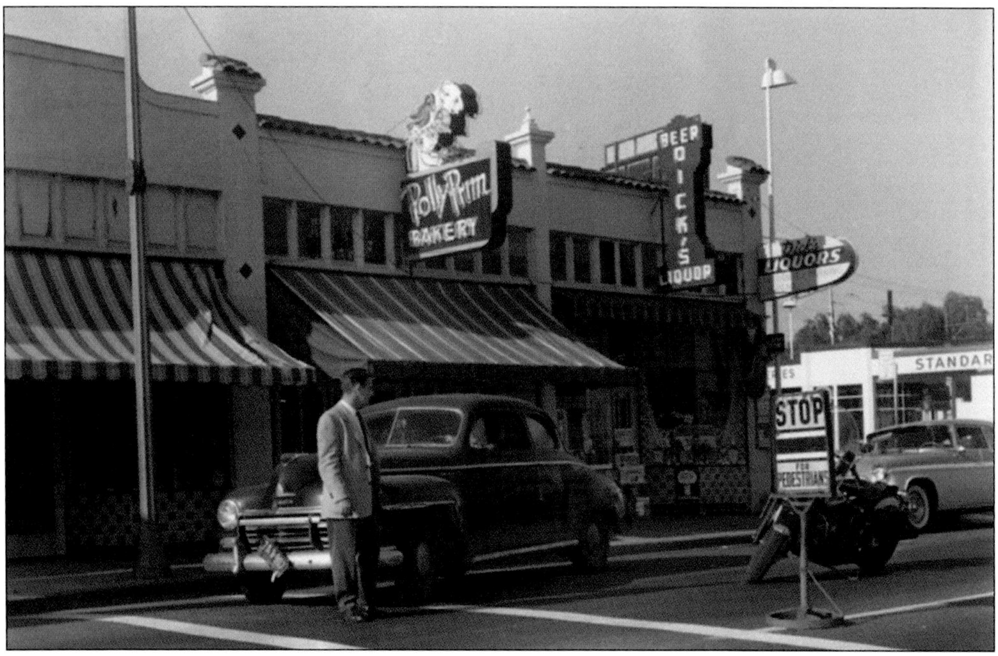

Polly Prim Bakery. Everyone loves a great bakery, and for years the aroma of butter-baked pastries, cakes, and tarts in the oven made it hard to just walk on by 55 North Santa Cruz Avenue. Ray Robertson was the baker in residence before he founded Los Gatos Office Equipment & Supply. His son Jon and Jon's wife, Alicia, are now successful publishers and printers in town. (LGWT.)

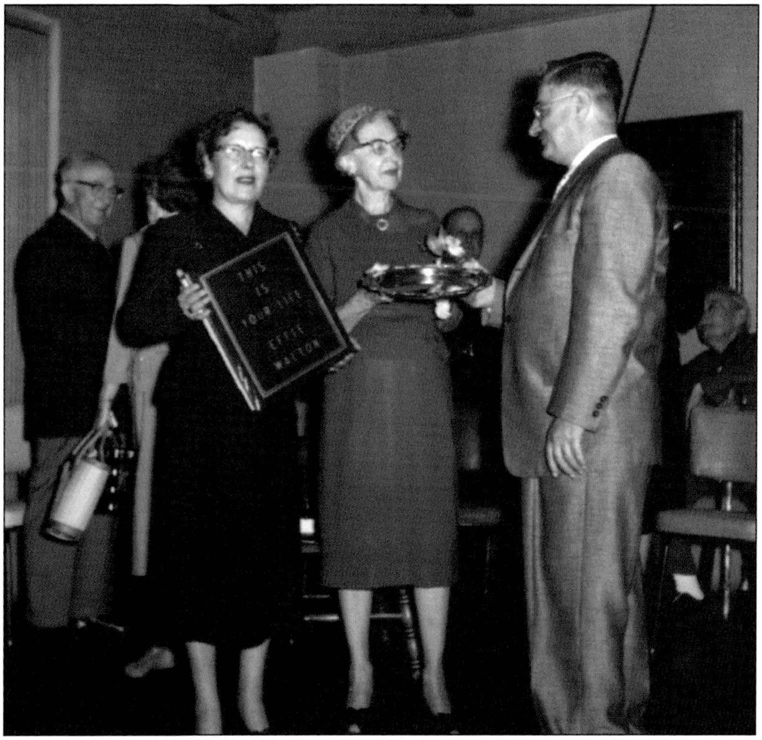

THIS WOMAN MEANT BUSINESS. When Effie Viola Stapp Walton (center) retired from her successful career in real estate, her colleagues presented her with a "This Is Your Life" scrapbook. Remembered for selling lots in the mountains and then developing the Little Village shopping center, Walton urged women to embrace opportunities and help equalize "an overbalance of masculine thought" in the world. (LGWT.)

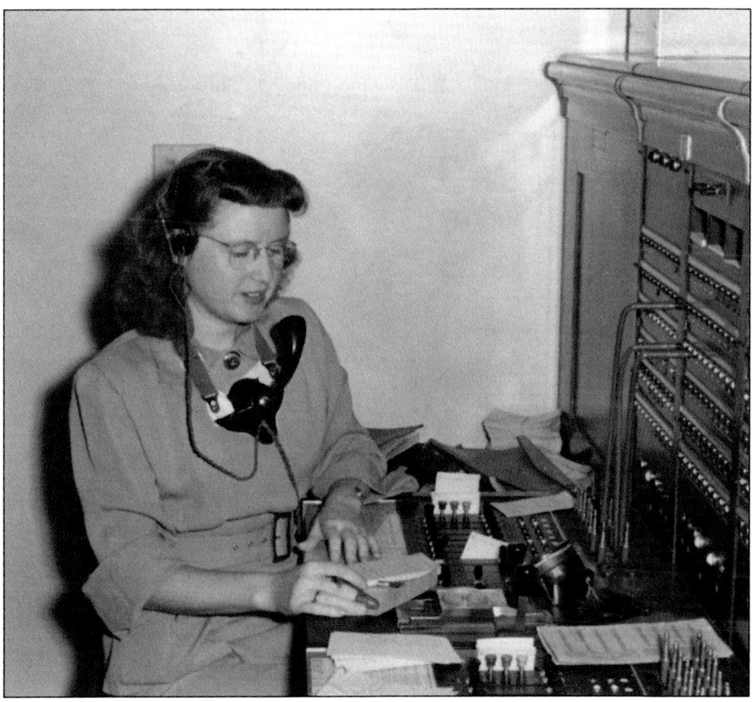

END OF THE LINE. After midnight on August 1, 1952, the 4,437 telephone subscribers in Los Gatos were able to place calls to surrounding towns by dialing the numbers themselves. The 17 operators employed by the Los Gatos Telephone Company had to be let go, including the young woman pictured here. General manager Lyndon Farwell announced that the operators would receive termination pay. (Farwell family.)

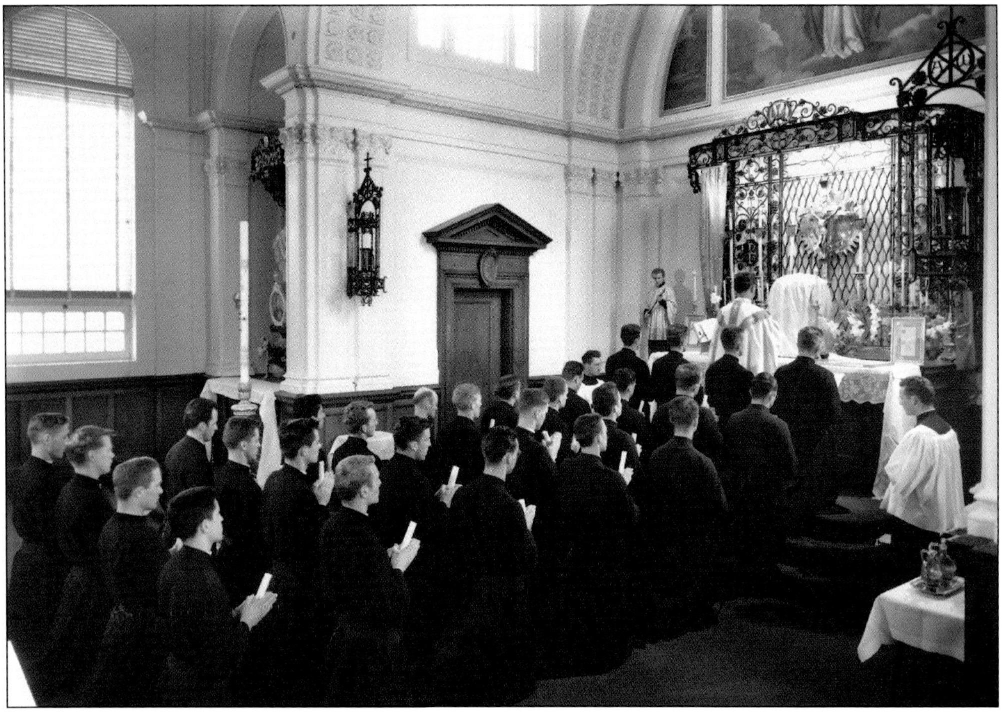

TAKING VOWS. Sacred Heart Novitiate, at the top of College Avenue, was founded in 1888 for the purpose of training men for the priesthood. Priests who had recently taken their vows gathered for this photograph, taken in 1950, which appeared in a publication called *The Western Jesuit*. (Jesuit Center.)

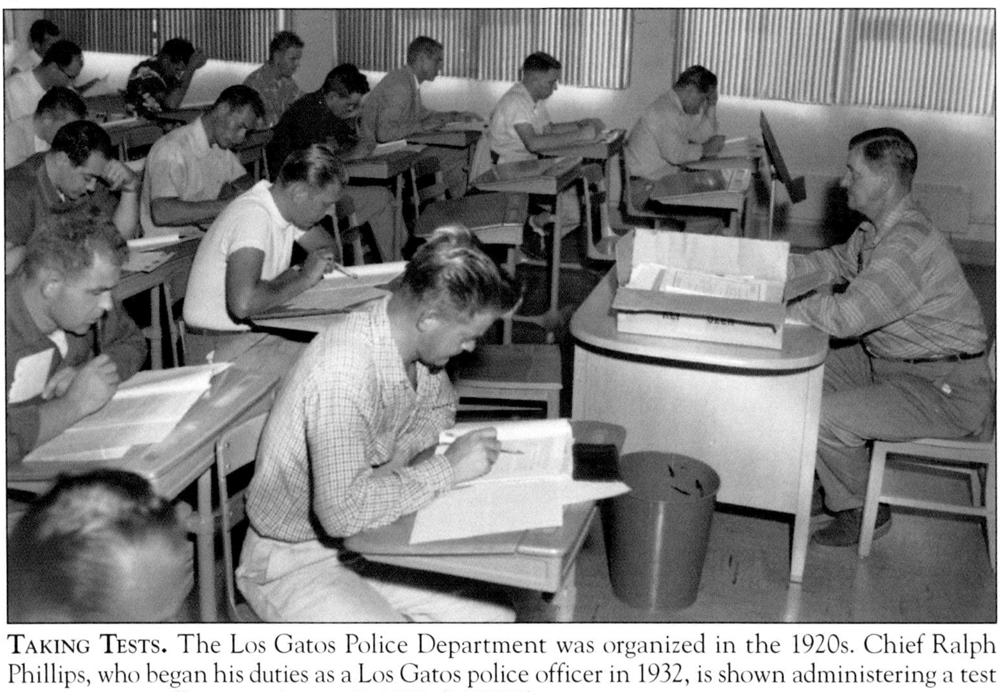

TAKING TESTS. The Los Gatos Police Department was organized in the 1920s. Chief Ralph Phillips, who began his duties as a Los Gatos police officer in 1932, is shown administering a test to prospective officers on August 2, 1955. (LGWT.)

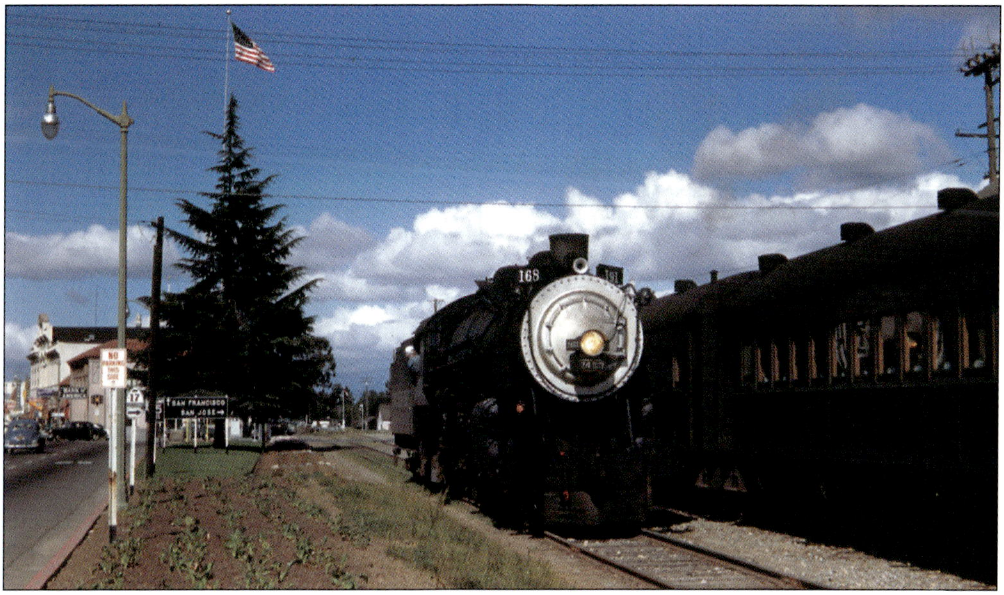

Railroad Town. The railroads of Los Gatos, an 80-plus-year tradition, ceased operation in 1959. This view, captured on a Saturday afternoon near the depot, was enjoyed by many locals who were saddened when the sights, sounds, and excitement of the railroads disappeared from town. (Charlie Givens.)

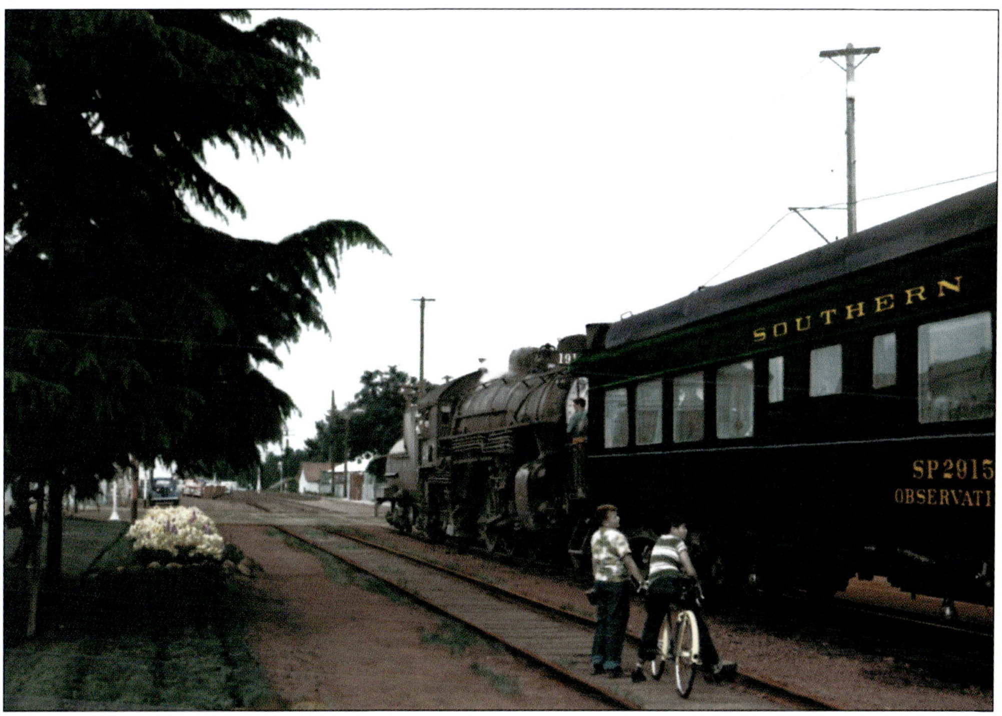

Captivated. These two Los Gatos boys appear mesmerized at the sight of Engine 2477 about to depart from the Los Gatos station. While searching for parking spaces in present-day Los Gatos, some people may not realize that the lengthy parking strips that run between North Santa Cruz and University Avenues constituted the original railroad right-of-way. (Eddie Chase.)

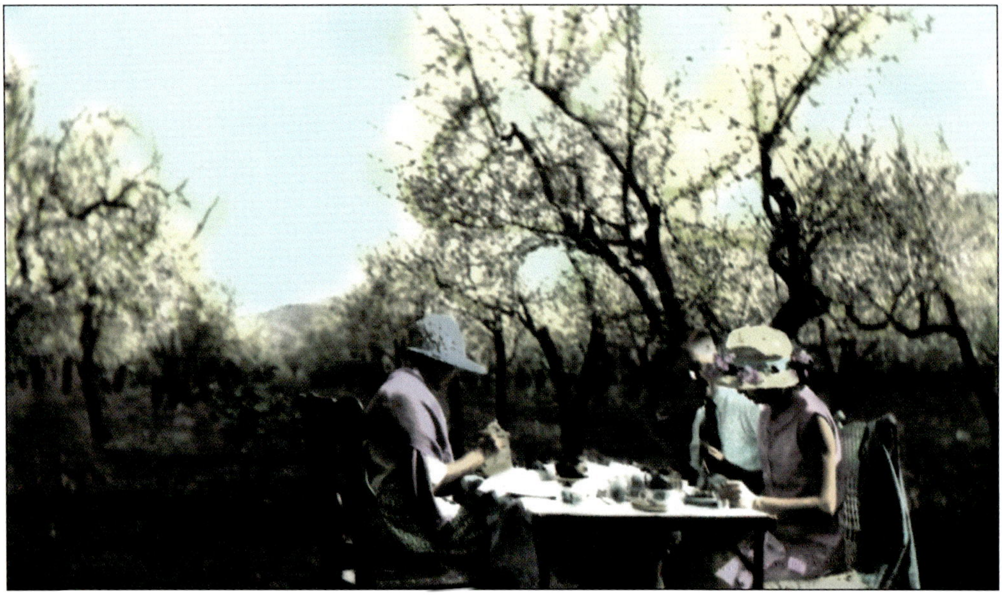

Seasons Passing. Life changed irrevocably for many Los Gatans when Highway 17 was rerouted along the Los Gatos Creek bed through the center of town in the mid-1950s. Tranquil scenes, such as this one on the Bergtold family's Placer Oaks Ranch, were fractured when earthshaking equipment moved hills to fill the roadbed. Construction lights on towers glared late into the night, and the Bergtold family home had to be moved. Soon, the sounds of traffic commenced. (CB.)

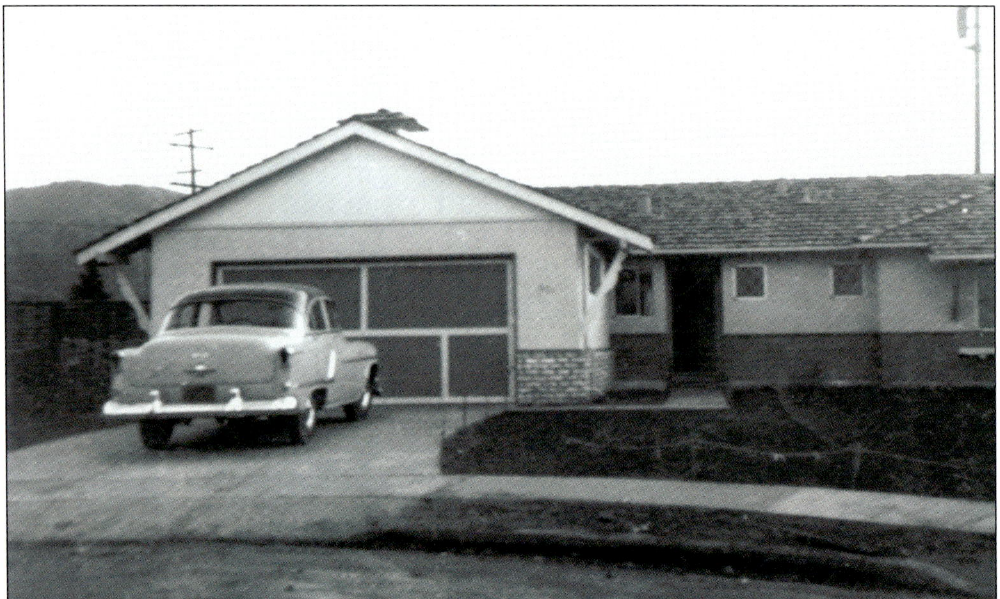

From Ranch to Ranch House. Near the end of the 1950s, town life settled into a new rhythm. Simple one-story ranch houses that nicely met the needs of young and growing families became the ideal, especially in California. An attached garage and an American-made car completed the picture. This home on Nob Hill Way was purchased by Joe and Kathy Cusick in 1958. (Kathy Cusick.)

Two

Out with the Old, In with the New

The 1960s

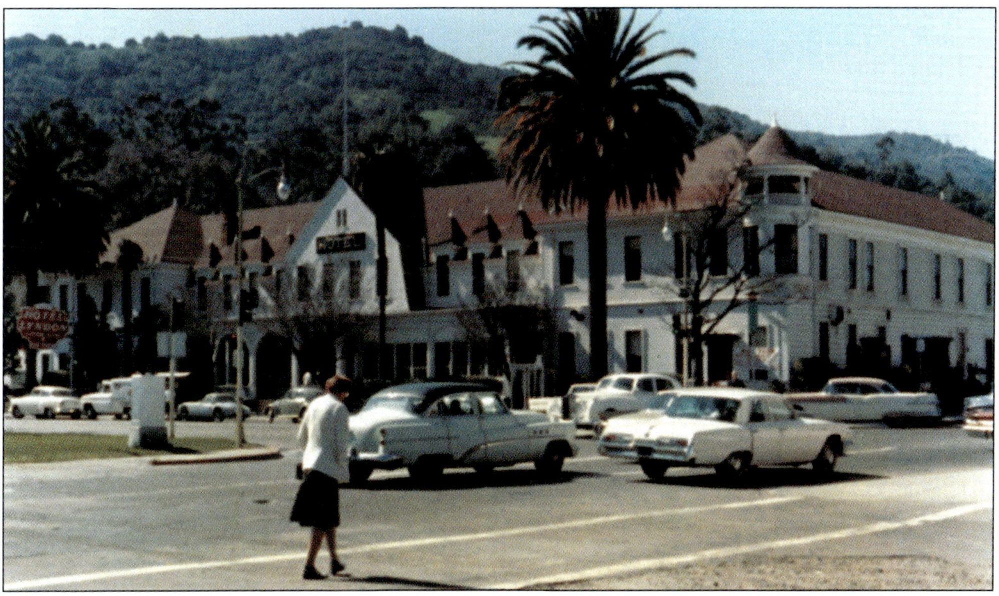

A Grand Lady's Final Days. A demolition permit was issued for the Hotel Lyndon on March 13, 1963. The job was quickly accomplished, with little comment from the community. Weeks later, the town's planning commission approved—by one vote—a replacement building, six stories high. The plan called for retail and office space, large "hotel apartments," and a bar and restaurant at the top. Townsfolk objected, and the plan was defeated. (Elinor Spencer.)

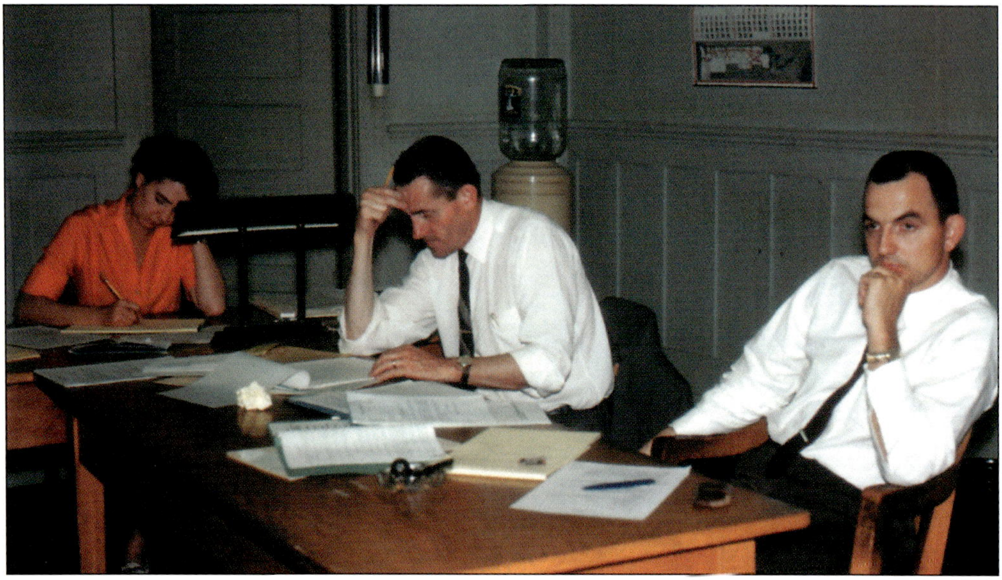

THE HIGH-RISE PROPOSAL. The early 1960s found downtown deteriorating and vacancies increasing. Nearby shopping malls pulled business away from locals. Town Manager Donald McIntyre outlined proposals for a new general plan, suggesting that the 25 small homes occupying land bounded by Tait, Bean, Massol, and Nicholson Avenues be replaced with two high-rise apartment complexes. The apartment-dwellers—prosperous professional people—would pay more property taxes and have few children to impact local schools. The plan projected a population of 90,000 people by 1985. Councilman Egon Jensen (1926–2010) remembered how the proposal created a storm at town hall in 1963, and the council made a hasty retreat. In the above image, Town Engineer Emmett Brady (center) sits next to McIntyre (right), and Town Clerk Beverly Blatnick is at left. One high-rise apartment house, the El Gato Penthouse (pictured below), did appear on East Main Street in 1963–1964. (Above, Egon Jensen; below, BB.)

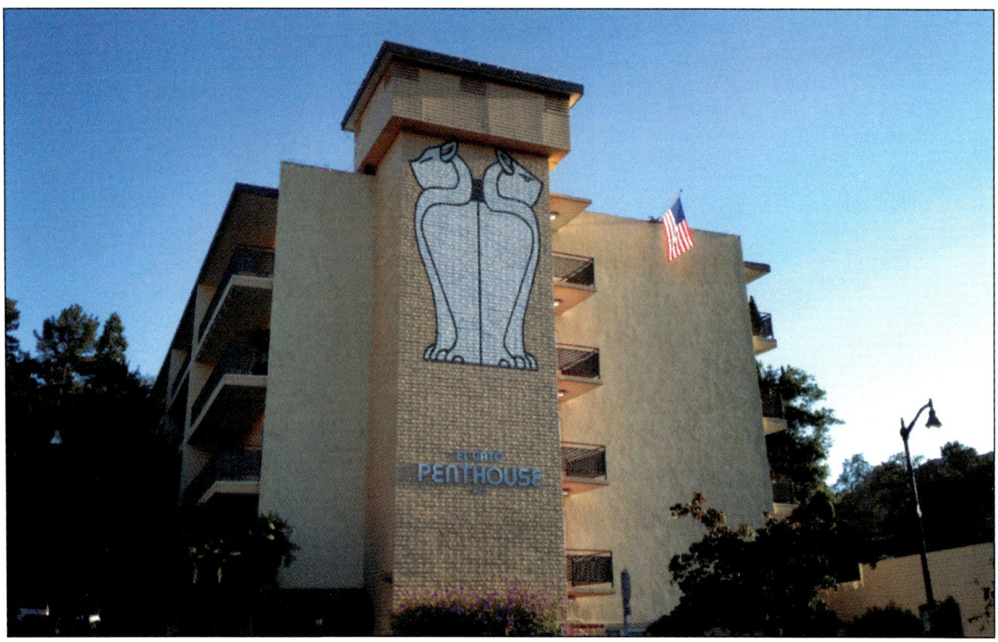

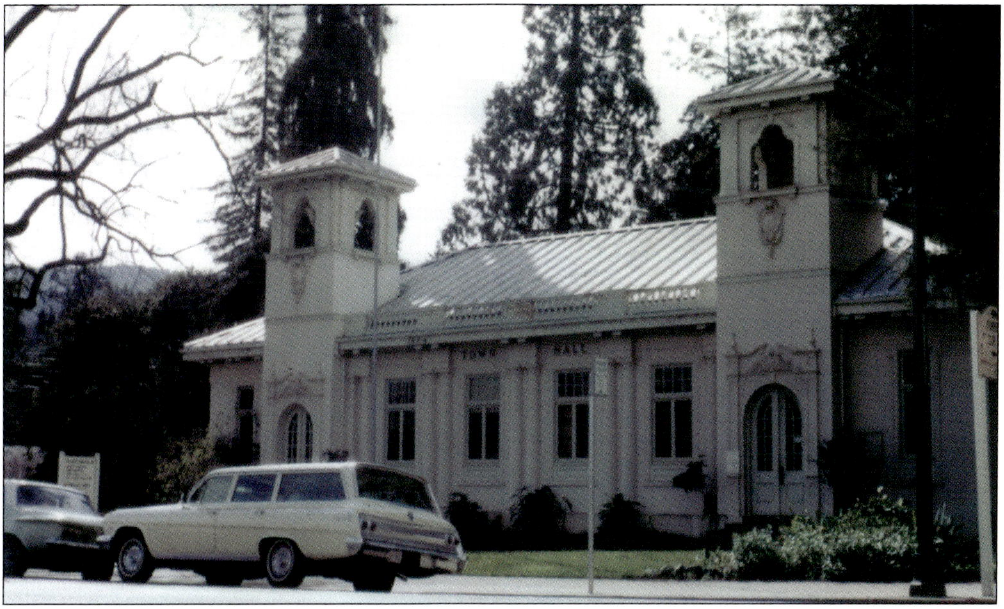

YE OLD TOWN HALL. Built in 1913, the town hall, pictured here with picturesque double belfries, was situated on the current Civic Center grounds. This building met a wrecking ball in 1965, but it did not go easily. Arguments over its fate were heated. Many Los Gatans were saddened to see it replaced by the modern complex that stands today. (Egon Jensen.)

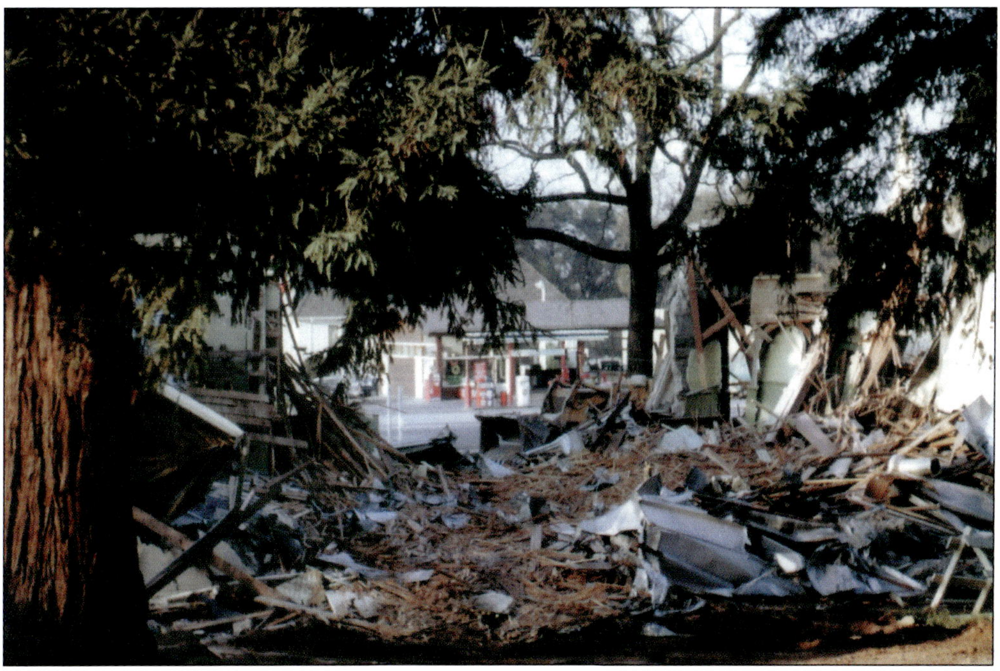

MISSING LANDMARKS. With the old town hall demolished, a Chevron station was visible across Main Street. Between 1954 and 1969, other landmarks disappeared: Carnegie Library (in 1954); the Main Street stone bridge (in 1955); the First Baptist Church on Main Street (in 1958); the Hotel Lyndon (in 1963); the Southern Pacific Railroad Depot (in 1964); the 1889 Methodist Episcopal Church (in 1968); and John W. Lyndon's home, Lyndon Heights (in 1969). (Egon Jensen.)

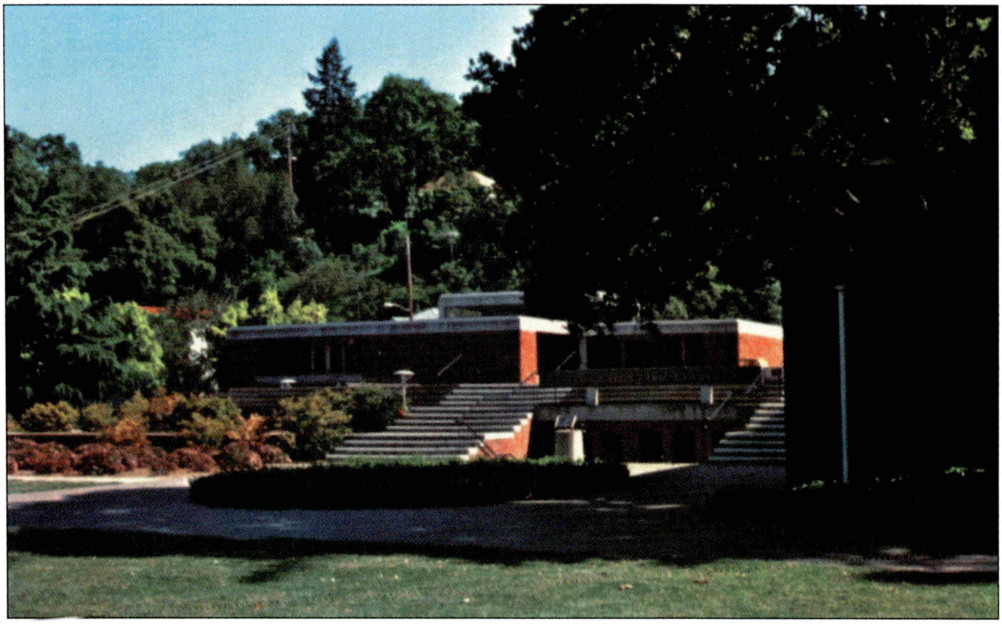

THE CIVIC CENTER. Built at a cost of just over $1 million, the new Civic Center was dedicated in April 1966. Efforts were made to preserve existing trees on the building site, including many stately and ancient redwoods. Although the building won an award for design, its bunker-like appearance is not considered especially attractive by many in the community. (AC.)

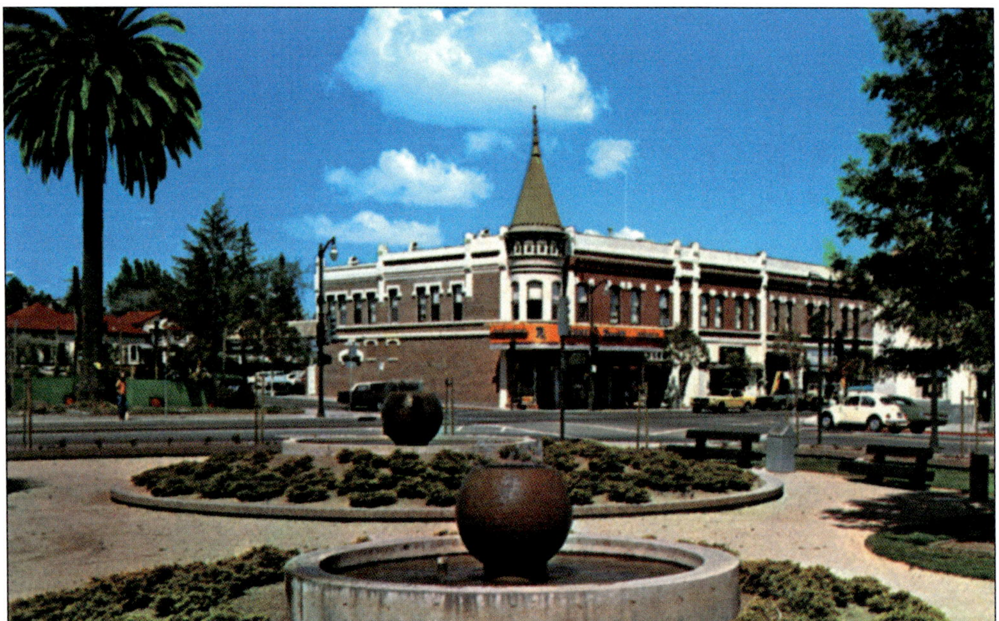

THE TOWN PLAZA. Once a railroad town, service to Los Gatos ended in 1959, followed by removal of the tracks and demolition of the depot. Until that time, the town plaza had consisted of a narrow strip of land that accommodated the town's lofty Christmas tree, a flagpole, and little else. This c. 1969 postcard provides an view of the expanded and refurbished plaza. (AC.)

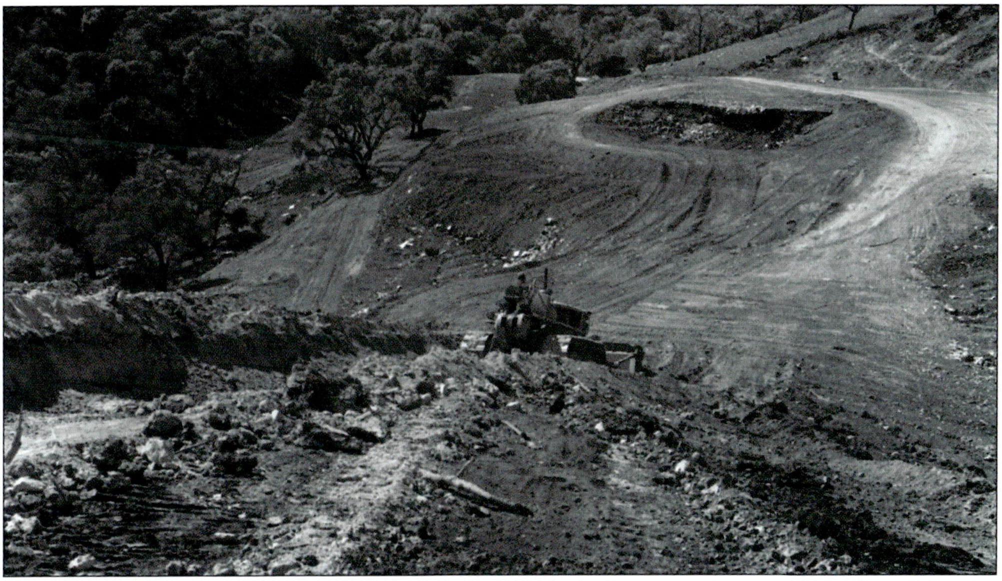

FUTURE PARK. With Memorial Park lost to Highway 17, the town dump was purchased for the development of Oak Meadow Park. Residents worked together, and on August 11, 1962, they celebrated the 75th anniversary of the town's incorporation at the new park. Games, pony rides, a little midway, exhibits, speeches, and a band made the day. (LGWT.)

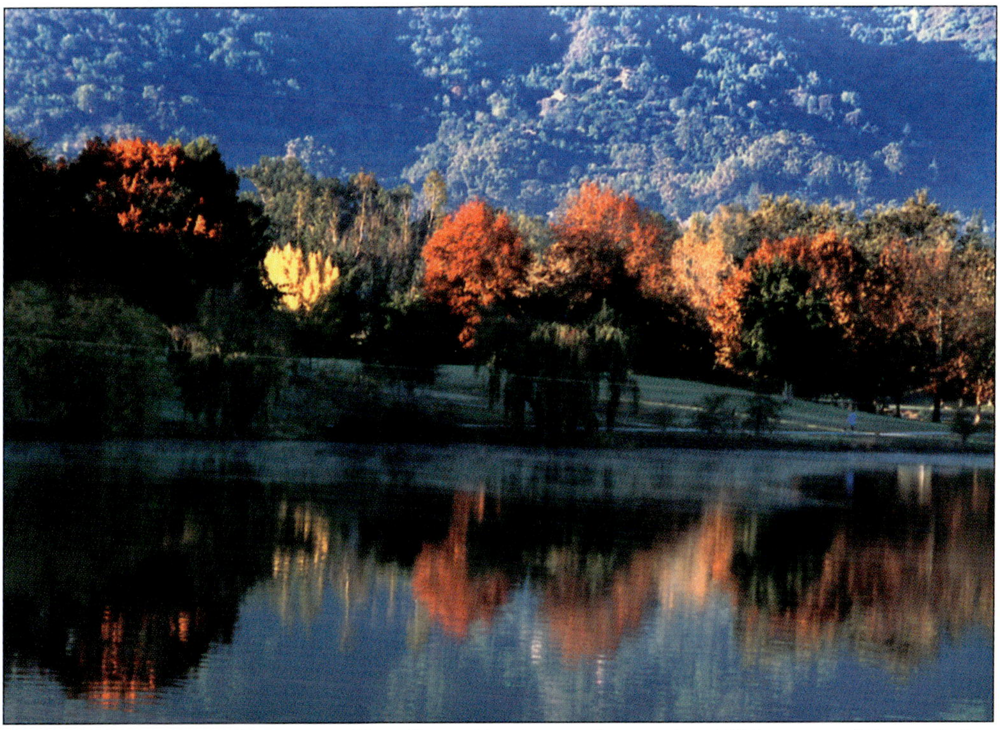

BEAUTIFUL VASONA. The waters of Los Gatos Creek were dammed in 1935 to create Vasona Lake. The dam cost $100,913 and stretched 1,000 feet across the creek, backing up 400 acre-feet of water over a 70-acre gravel percolation area. Vasona Lake County Park opened to the public in 1962. This 21st-century image shows how beautifully the lake has evolved. (Ken Benjamin.)

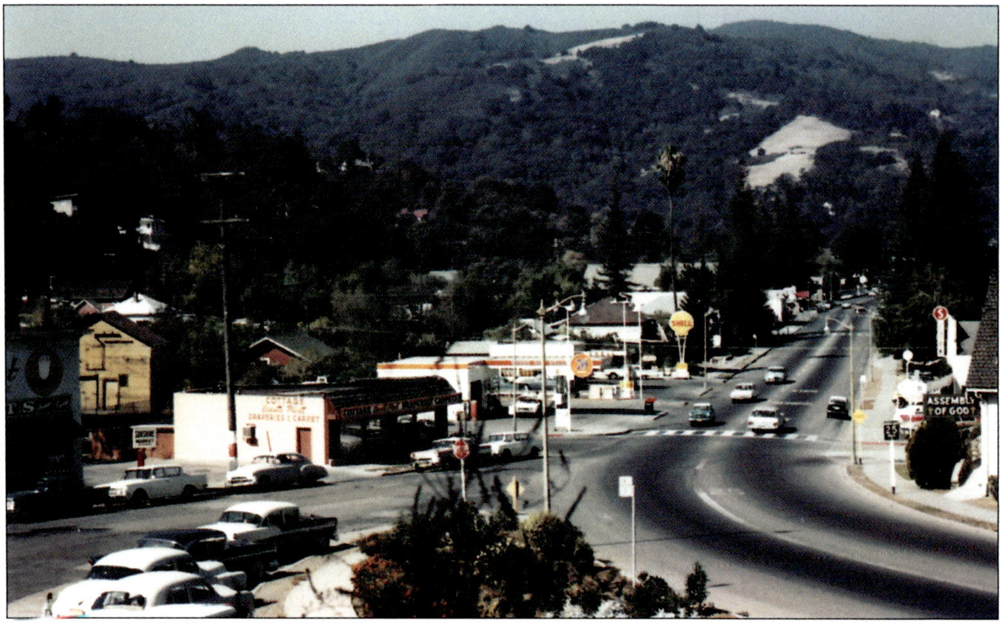

Street Scene, 1961. In this view looking west on Main Street, the popular Sunshine Market is located at far left. Built in the 1890s, the tall brown building behind the market is the barn of village blacksmith John Erickson. Two service stations in a row are indicative of the number of people who passed through Los Gatos on the way to Santa Cruz, despite the opening of the bypass in 1956. (LGPL.)

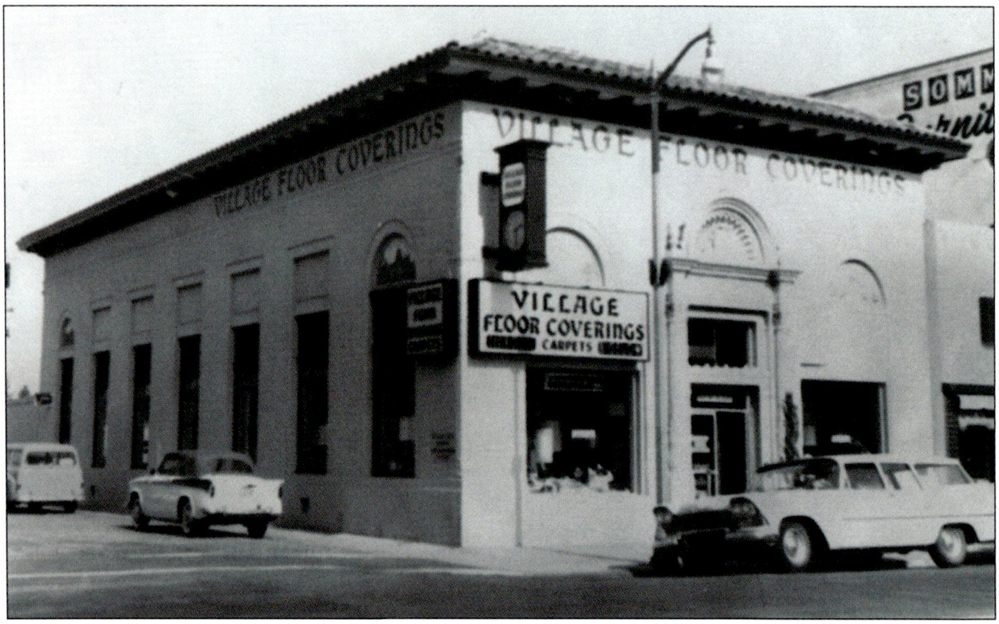

Still Standing. In November 1967, the *Los Gatos Times* reported that 26 dilapidated and unsafe buildings, mostly in the central business district, had been demolished, and 9 more demolitions were underway. One surviving structure was the Renaissance Revival First National Bank building constructed around 1920 on West Main Street. Serving as a bank until 1955, it has housed various businesses since that time; it is pictured here in 1962. (LGWT.)

FOX MOTORS. Brothers Ed and Fred Fox sold Imperial, Chrysler, Plymouth, and Valiant automobiles at 16203 Los Gatos–San Jose Road (Los Gatos Boulevard). In 1961, they advertised for a few hardworking men, promising that they would make more money and enjoy greater security than any other salesmen in the area. They wanted men with ambition to get to the top. (LGWT.)

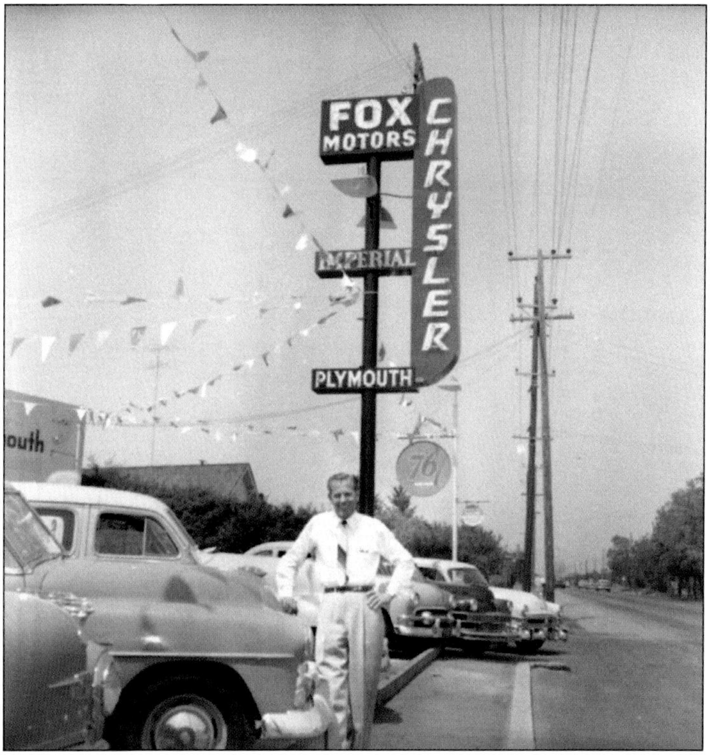

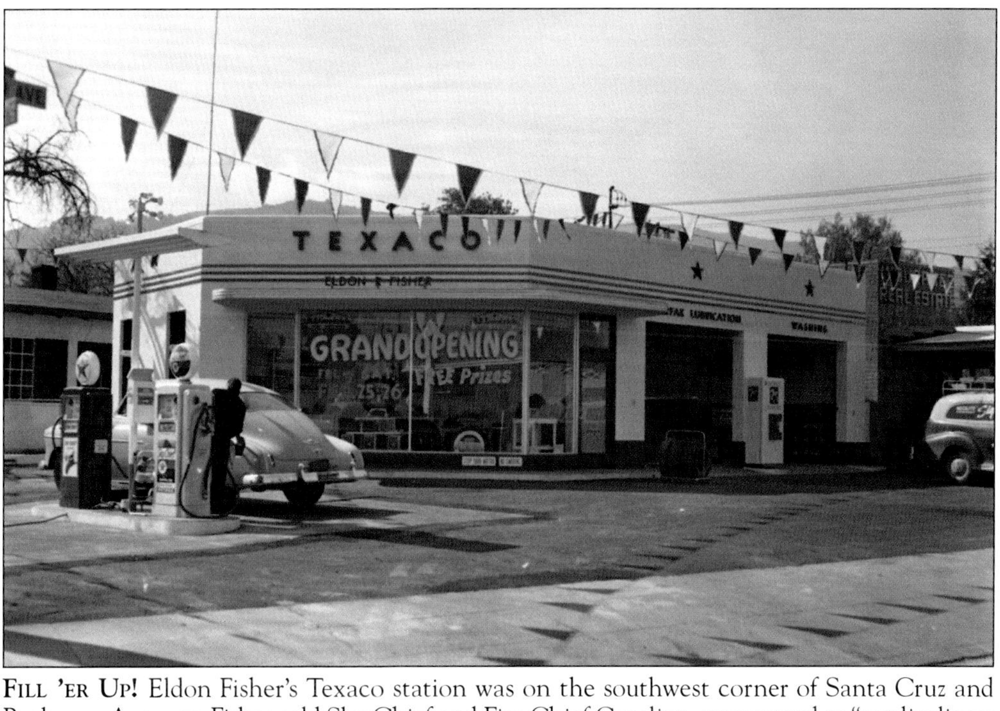

FILL 'ER UP! Eldon Fisher's Texaco station was on the southwest corner of Santa Cruz and Bachman Avenues. Fisher sold Sky Chief and Fire Chief Gasoline, guaranteed to "put liveliness back into your driving." He offered lube services and full tire recaps and also sold the newer tubeless variety. (LGWT.)

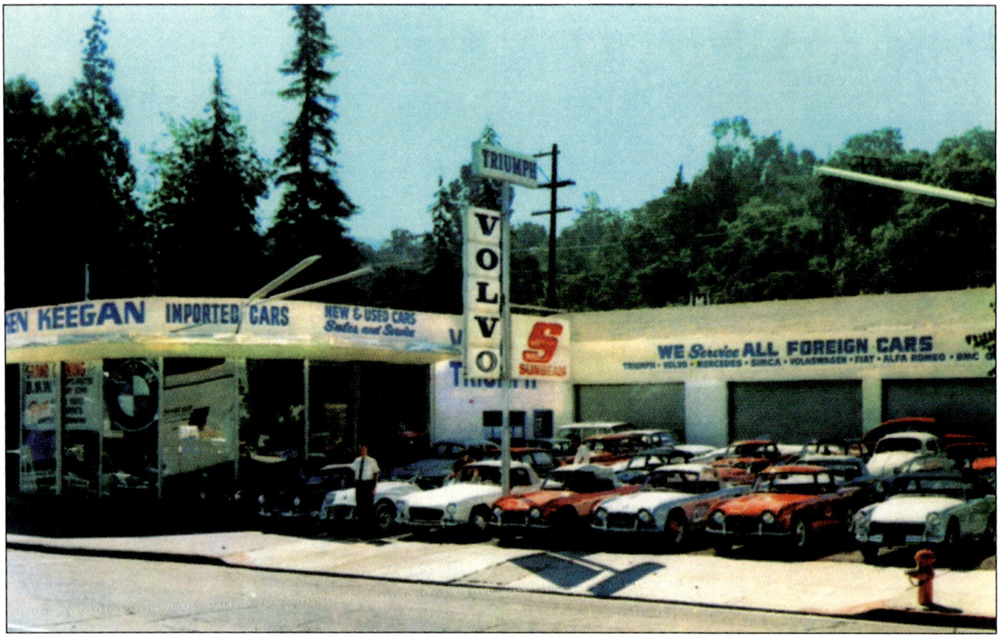

Ken Keegan's Imported Cars. For decades, Los Gatos was a mecca for car dealerships. Plymouth, Dodge, Buick, and other brands were sold on this site at 66 East Main Street. Foreign cars, including Triumphs, Sunbeams, MGs, Simcas, and Volkswagens, had become popular by the time of this photograph, taken around 1967. Ferrari of Los Gatos occupied this address from 1976 to 2003. (AC.)

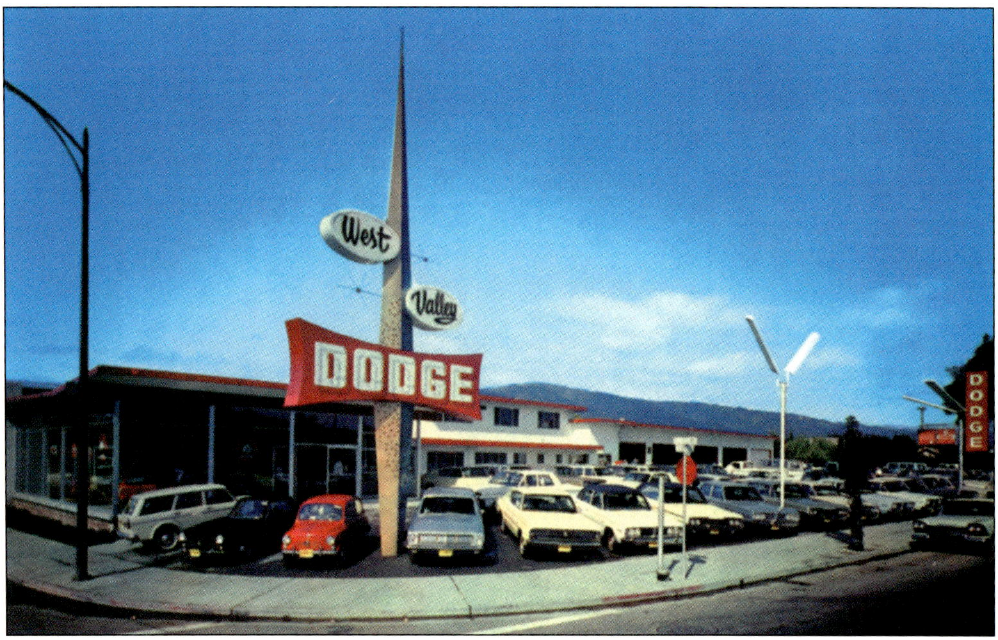

Klepinger's West Valley Dodge. During the "golden age of autos" in Los Gatos, the town depended on about a dozen automobile dealerships to provide more than half of its tax revenue. Founded in 1963 and located at 16212 San Jose Road (Los Gatos Boulevard), West Valley Dodge also sold Fiats and Jeeps. "You'll like the way you are treated," they promised. (AC.)

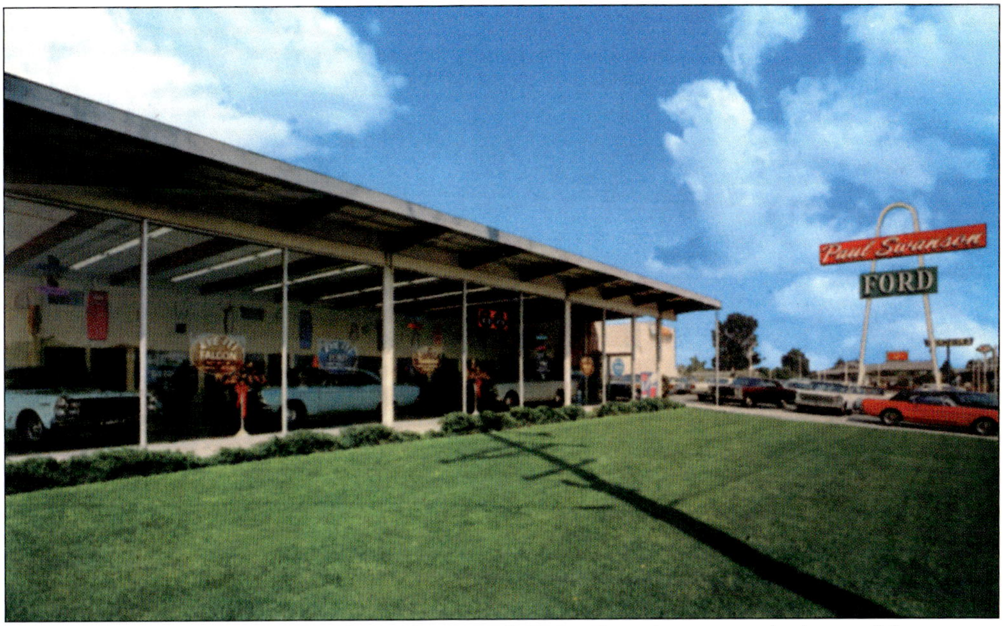

Paul Swanson Ford. Originally located on North Santa Cruz Avenue, in the heart of downtown, Paul Swanson Ford moved to the northwest corner of Blossom Hill Road and Los Gatos Boulevard in 1959. When new models arrived in the fall, the dealership windows would be covered in paper before klieg lights in the night sky would alert townsfolk to gather for the unveiling of new automobiles. (AC.)

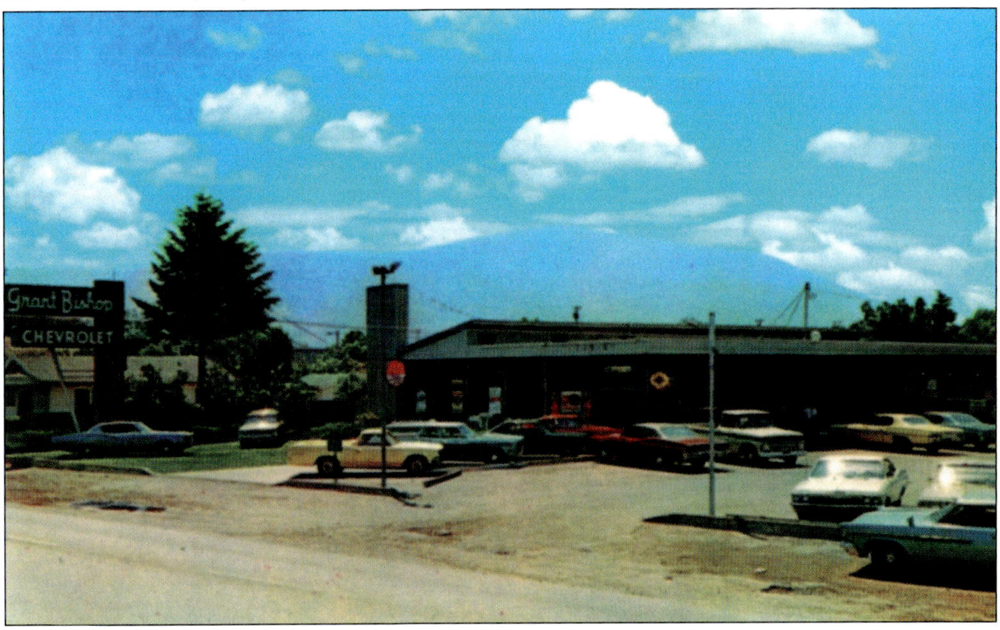

Grant Bishop Chevrolet. Grant Bishop Chevrolet incorporated in 1955, a watershed year for the manufacturer, when the first of the "Tri-Fives" were introduced. In automobile parlance, "Tri-Fives" refers to 1955, 1956, and 1957 Chevrolets, particularly the Bel Air, which was considered revolutionary in its day and is still enthusiastically collected. The dealership is pictured here in the 1960s. (AC.)

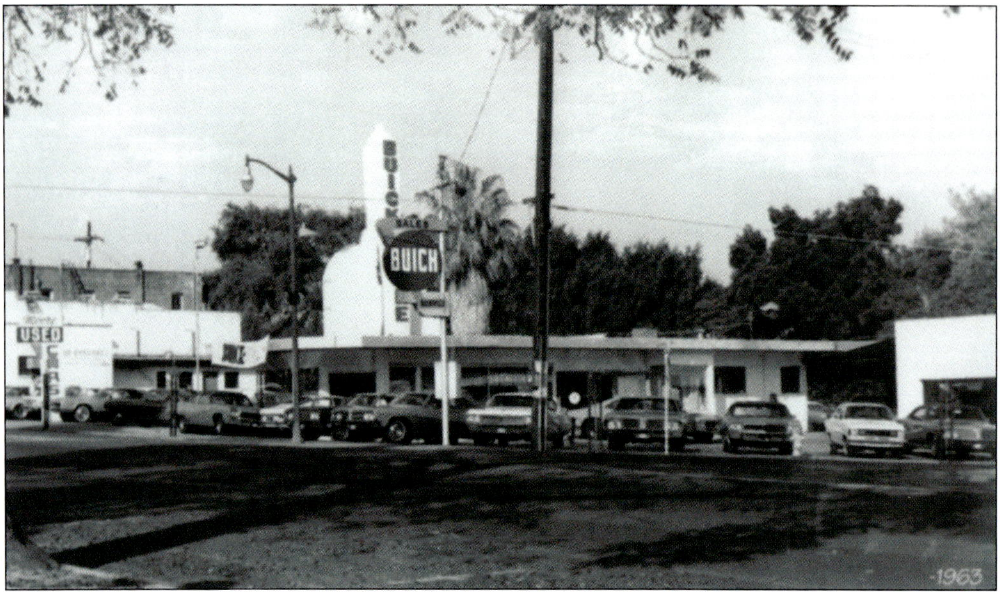

MOORE BUICK, 1963. In 1951, Edward Moore bought Danforth Buick at 11 Church Street and began a three-generation tradition. The business moved to Los Gatos Boulevard in 1967 and continues to operate today. It is the longest-standing Los Gatos dealership and the only domestic car outlet in Los Gatos to survive the economic downturn. "We own the dirt," they proudly say, allowing for lower operating costs. (CB.)

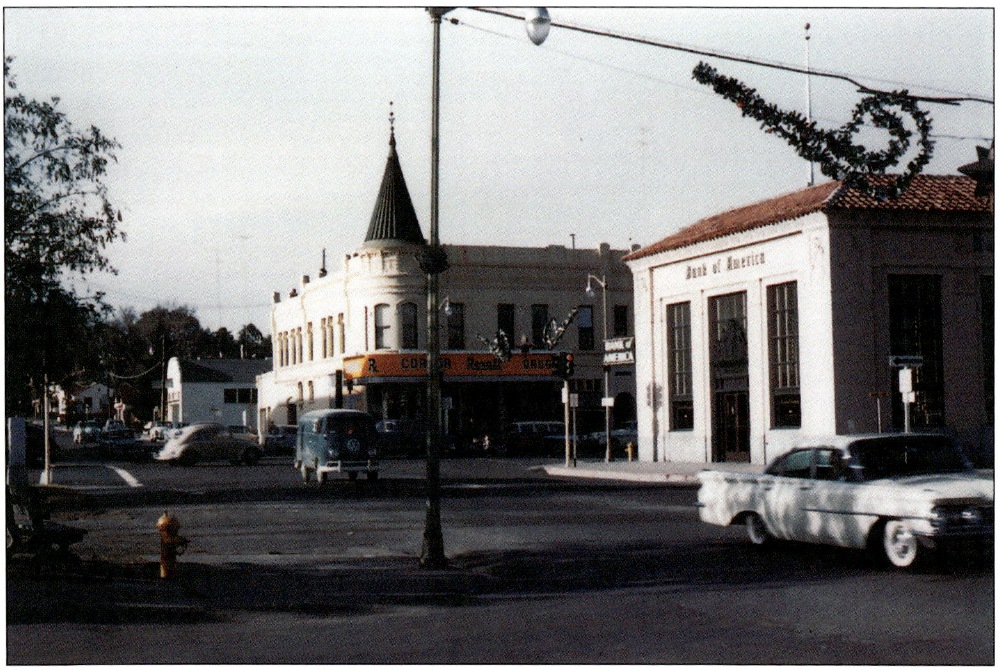

COUNTRY TOWN. With a population of about 9,000 people in 1960, Los Gatos was still a countrified small town. By 1970, the census counted nearly 23,000 residents. In 1955, the Chamber of Commerce asked local merchants for $5,500 to be used to purchase Christmas decorations. Twenty-nine strings of overhead electric lights decorated the streets for many years. (James Stoops.)

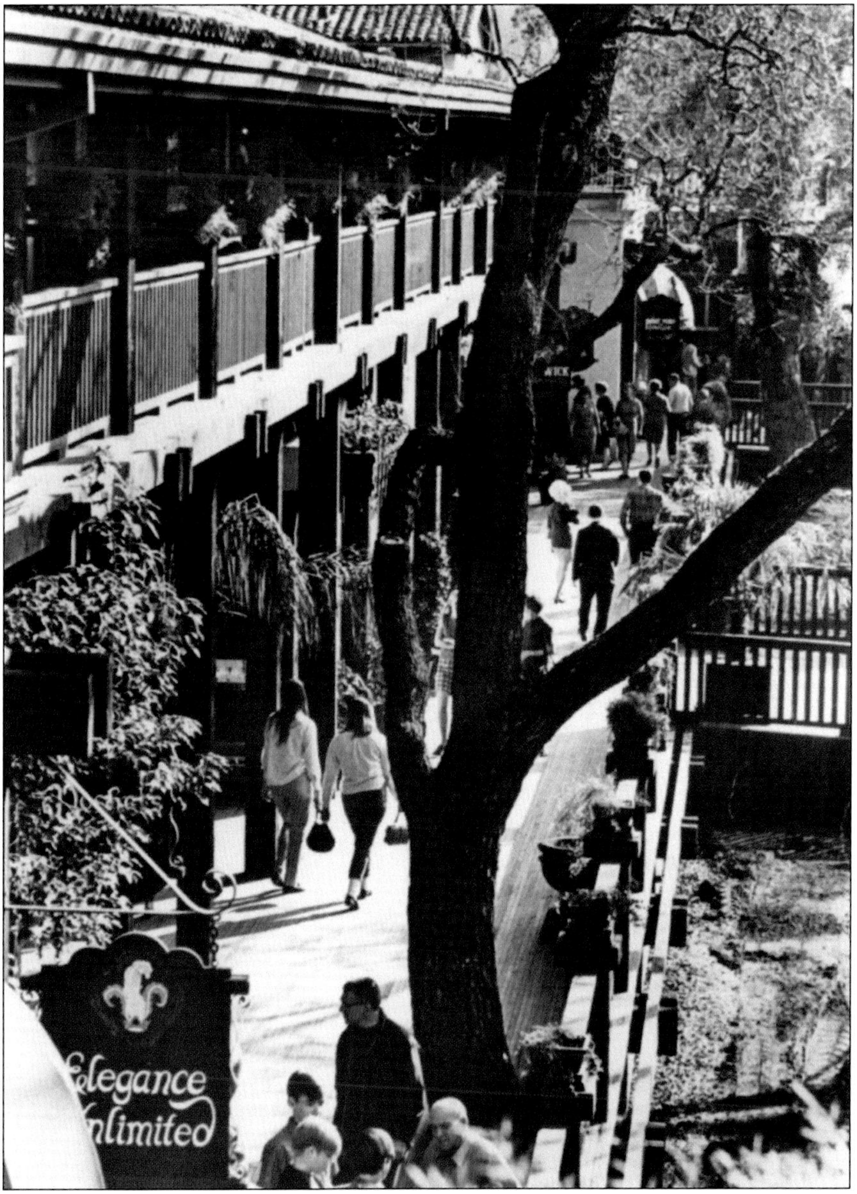

WHEN OLD TOWN WAS NEW. Already a bit down-at-the-heels in the early 1960s, downtown Los Gatos suffered another blow when University Avenue School closed in 1961 due to seismic concerns. In 1964, entrepreneur Max Walden came to the rescue. As principal owner of the derelict property, he called for a "fix-up and paint-up" of the buildings. No structures had to be razed, he said, and no streets widened. Working closely with local architect Frank Laulainen, he took a three-year and $3-million commercial and cultural gamble. The refurbished complex opened with a bang in July 1967, when the Los Gatos Fine Arts Center, later called Old Town, hosted a nine-day festival designed to present "all the creative activities and forms of expression of mankind." The intent was to focus national attention on Los Gatos as a major arts center. The first tenants included two restaurants (The Deck and El Gordo's), two potters, a woodcarver, a sculptor, a weaver, jewelry-makers, dress shops, an art photographer, and a candle-maker. This photograph dates to 1969. (CB.)

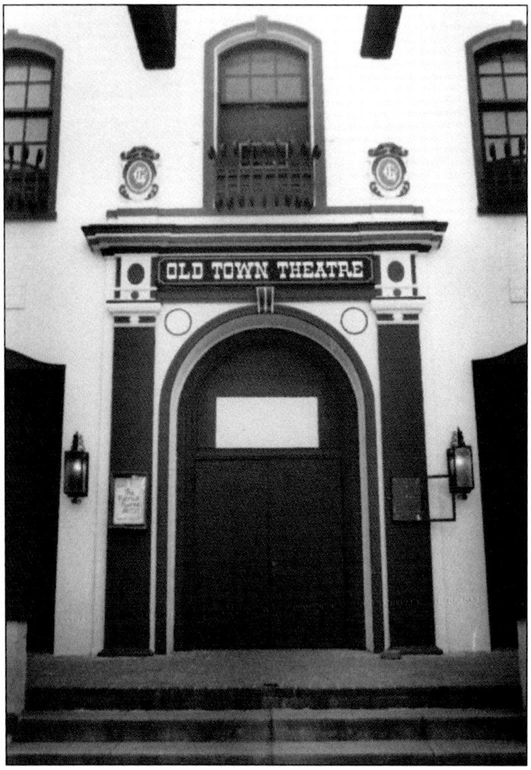

OLD TOWN THEATER. Old Town Theater was created from what had been the auditorium of University Avenue School. Once home to both the California Actors Theater and the California Shakespeare Festival, the 410-seat venue was popular for many years. When the Old Town complex underwent renovation and updating in the 1990s, restoration of the theater was deemed too costly. A Borders bookstore opened at this site in 1998. (LGWT.)

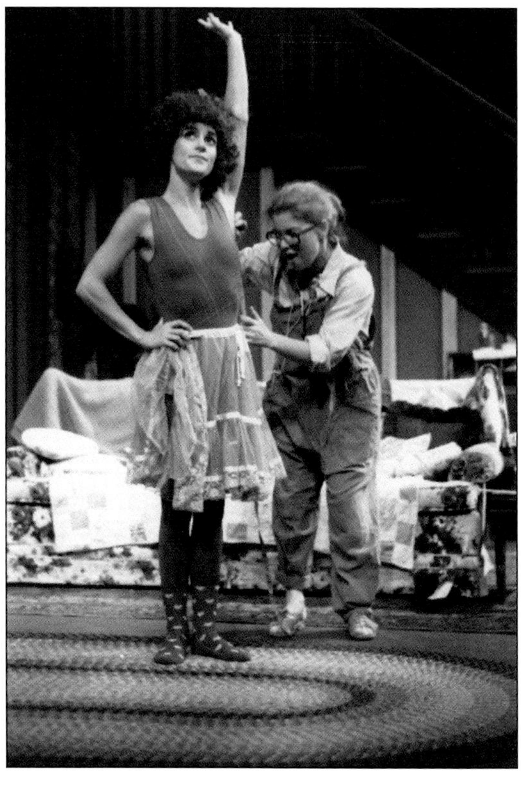

THE MISS FIRECRACKER CONTEST. In this play presented at the Old Town Theater, Marlene Shapiro (left) played the part of Carnelle Scott, a young woman struggling with her identity and the cultural expectations of her small Mississippi town. In this image, Carnelle's friend, Popeye Jackson (Reina Woodyard), is helping her prepare for the Miss Firecracker Contest. (LGWT.)

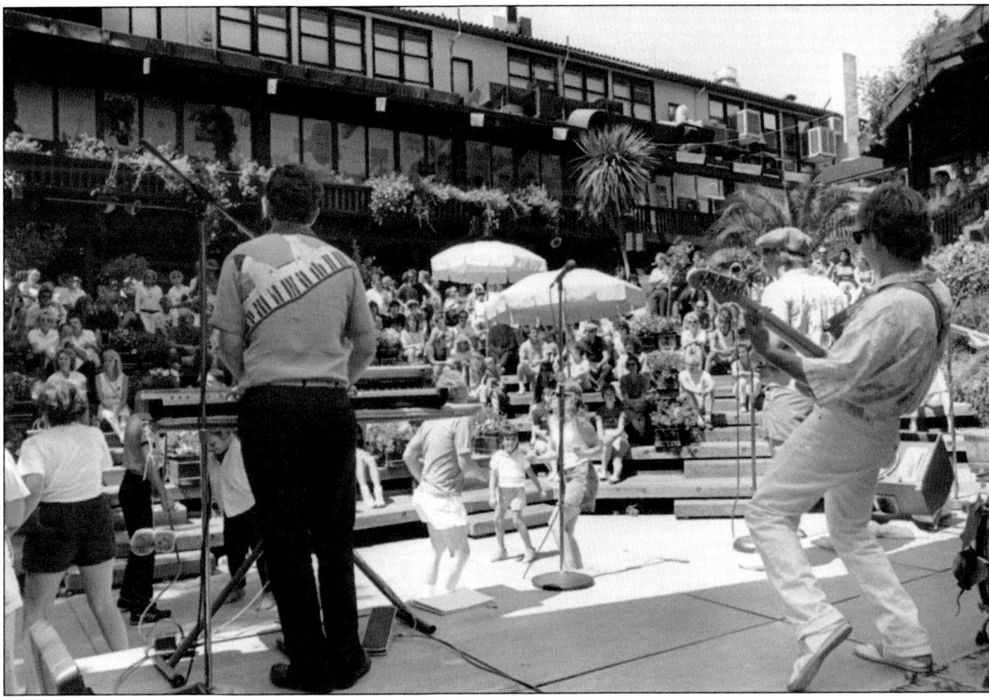

Old Town Amphitheater. Old Town brought new energy and excitement to Los Gatos, as well as economic benefits. The amphitheater behind the complex featured local bands and other entertainment. On June 16, 1990, a section of balcony overlooking the amphitheater, packed with people listening to the band Cool Jerks, collapsed and slid down on top of spectators sitting on the steps below. Fourteen people were injured. (LGWT.)

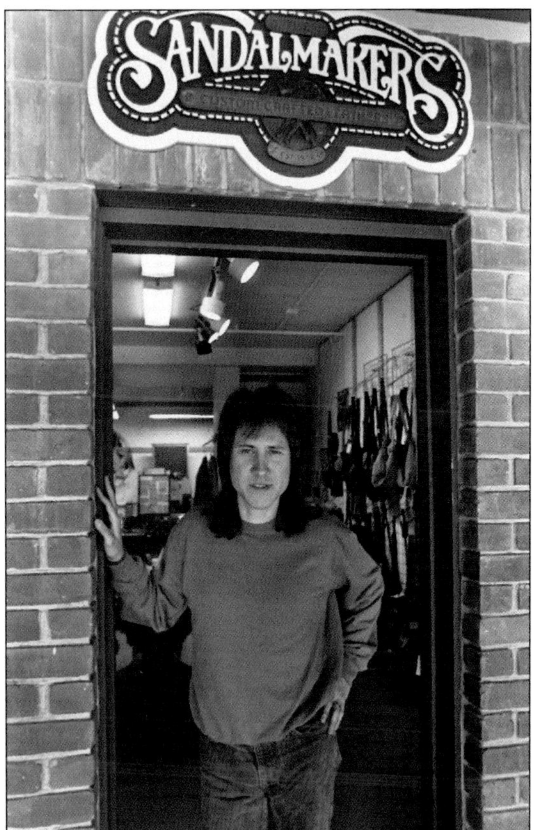

Collective Memory. Vanished businesses from the early days of Old Town still evoke fond memories for many Los Gatans. On the list are Mimi's Rooftop Café, Walden Pond Bookstore, B.J. Bull's, Morrow's Nut House, Mud in Your Eye Pottery, Tharp Did It, El Gordo's Mexican Restaurant, and Sandalmakers, where owner Peter James Rundberg (pictured) played great rock 'n' roll while handmade leather shoes and handbags were made and sold. (LGWT.)

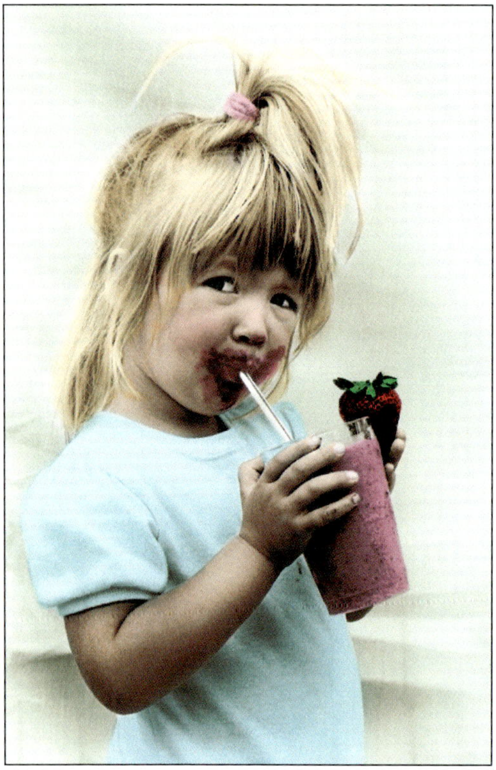

STRAWBERRY FESTIVAL. A summertime tradition in Los Gatos for 36 years, the Strawberry Festival began as a backyard fundraiser in 1960. By 1996, it attracted 70,000 people and raised $65,000 annually for Eastfield Ming Quong mental health services. Nearly 1,000 local volunteers ran the event. When the Civic Center could no longer accommodate the crowds and traffic backed up for miles, the event was transferred to West Valley College. (LGWT.)

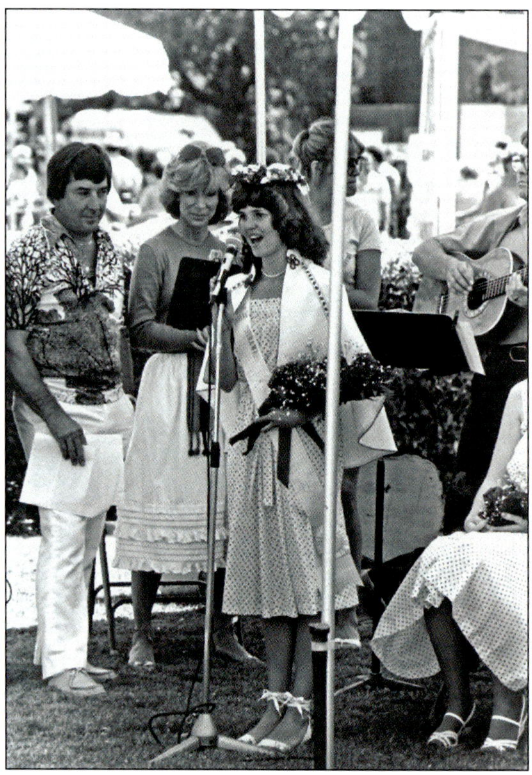

STRAWBERRY QUEEN. At the Strawberry Festival, crowning a Strawberry Queen, arts and crafts, live bands, a children's carnival, dancing, games, and an auction kept the crowds busy when they were not engaged in gorging on strawberry pancakes, nonalcoholic strawberry daiquiris, strawberry milkshakes, strawberry shortcake, and strawberries dipped in chocolate. Fresh strawberries were donated by local growers. Identified in this photograph are John Lochner (left) and Strawberry Queen Jennifer LaForce (standing at microphone). (LGWT.)

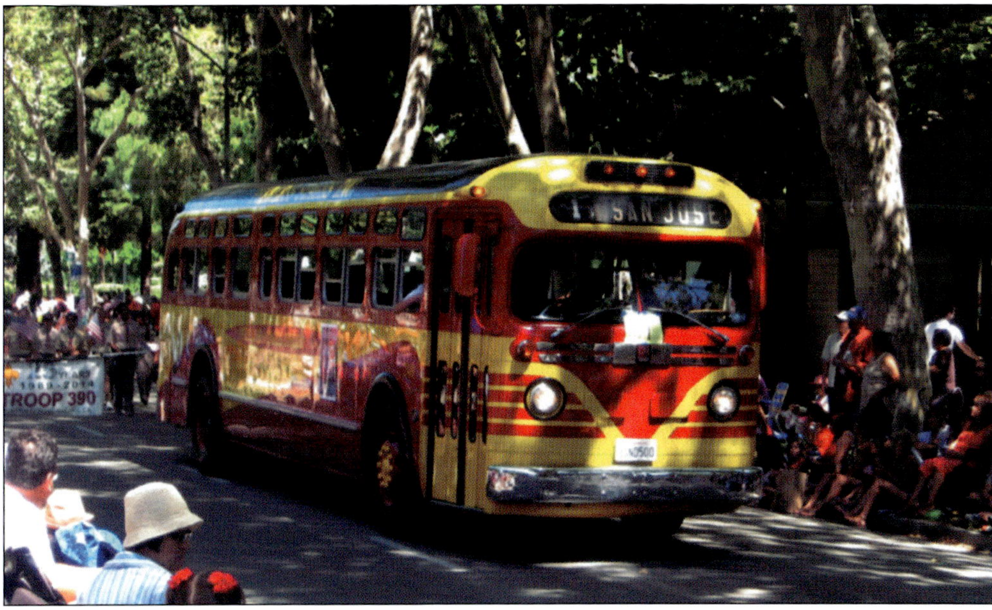

Peerless Stage. The green-tiled Art Deco building at 145 North Santa Cruz Avenue was home to Peerless buses in Los Gatos. Founded in 1916, Peerless provided Los Gatans with transportation to San Jose and Santa Cruz. A unique drive-through passageway for loading travelers lasted until the 1960s, and the adjacent tiny lunch counter, said to serve the worst burgers in town, lasted until the 1970s. (Harry Stewart.)

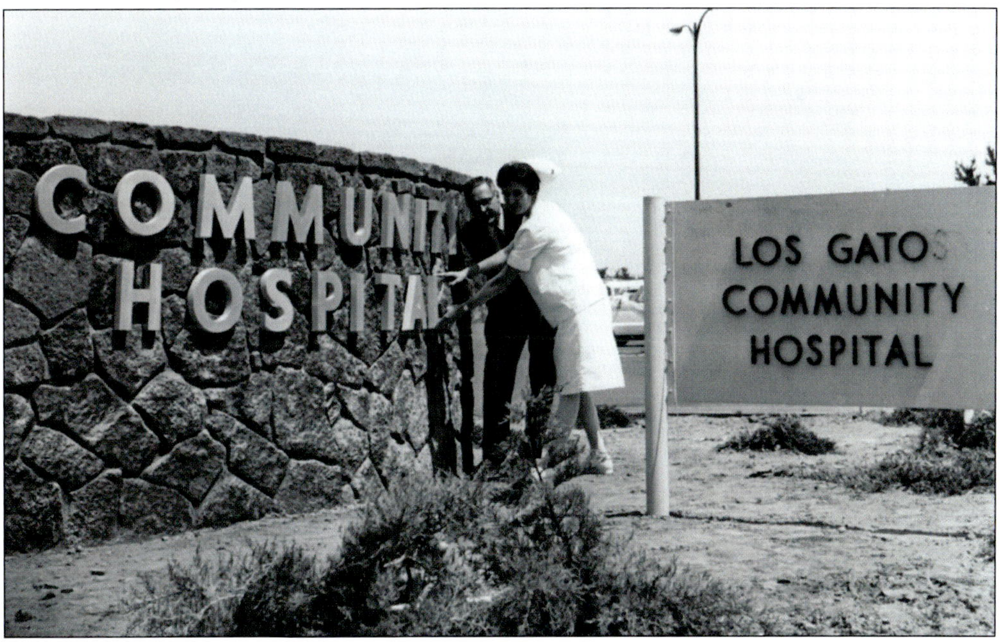

Los Gatos Community Hospital. In 1962, the 9,000 residents of Los Gatos welcomed Los Gatos Community Hospital to town. Before that time, doctors made house calls, and the critically ill were sent to hospitals in San Jose in an ambulance owned by a local mortuary. In 2009, at the height of the recession, Community Hospital's land and buildings were purchased by El Camino Hospital of Mountain View. (LGWT.)

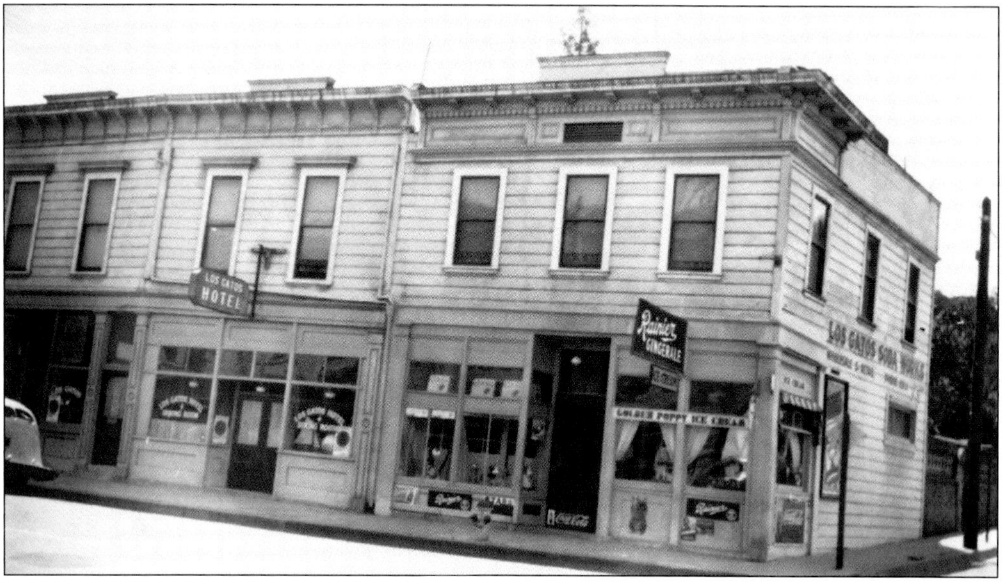

LOS GATOS HOTEL AND SALOON. The Mariotti and Puccinelli families, related by marriage, owned and operated various eating, sleeping, drinking, and dining establishments in this building at the southeast corner of East Main Street and College Avenue from 1904 until the end of the 1960s. The lot then stood vacant for 30 years until Soda Works Plaza was built on the site. (LGWT.)

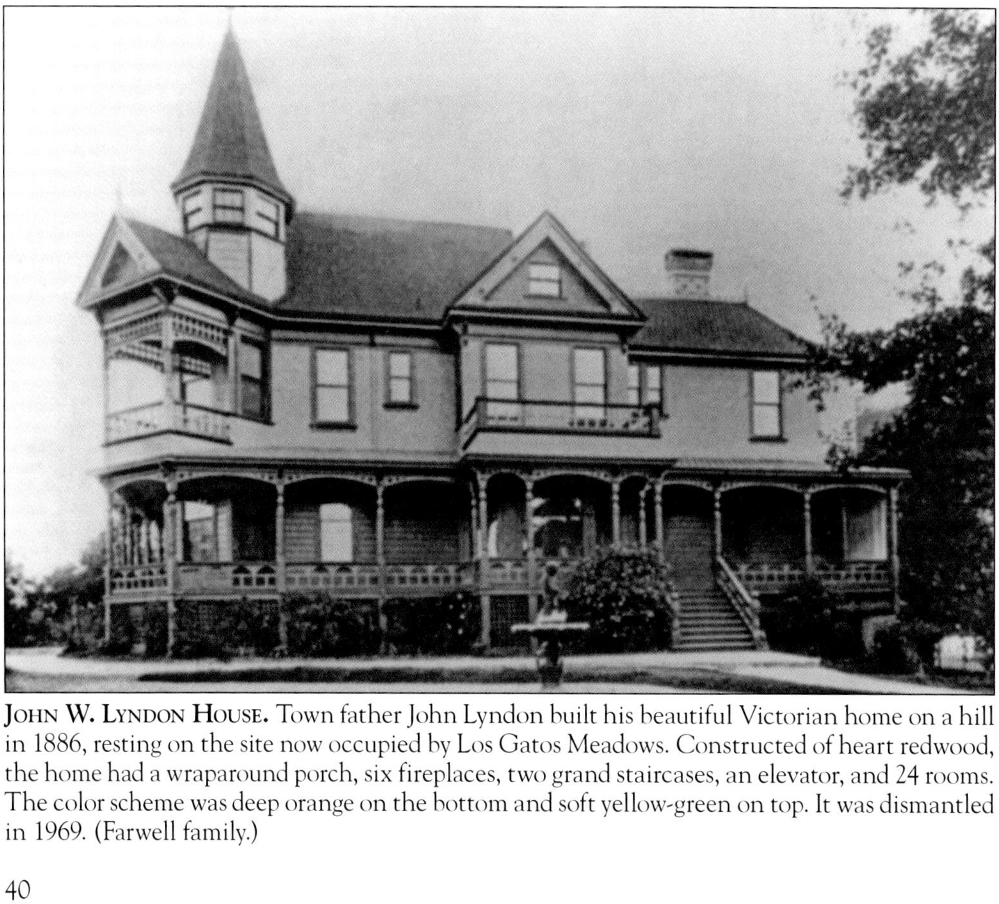

JOHN W. LYNDON HOUSE. Town father John Lyndon built his beautiful Victorian home on a hill in 1886, resting on the site now occupied by Los Gatos Meadows. Constructed of heart redwood, the home had a wraparound porch, six fireplaces, two grand staircases, an elevator, and 24 rooms. The color scheme was deep orange on the bottom and soft yellow-green on top. It was dismantled in 1969. (Farwell family.)

Three

A Town in Flux

The 1970s

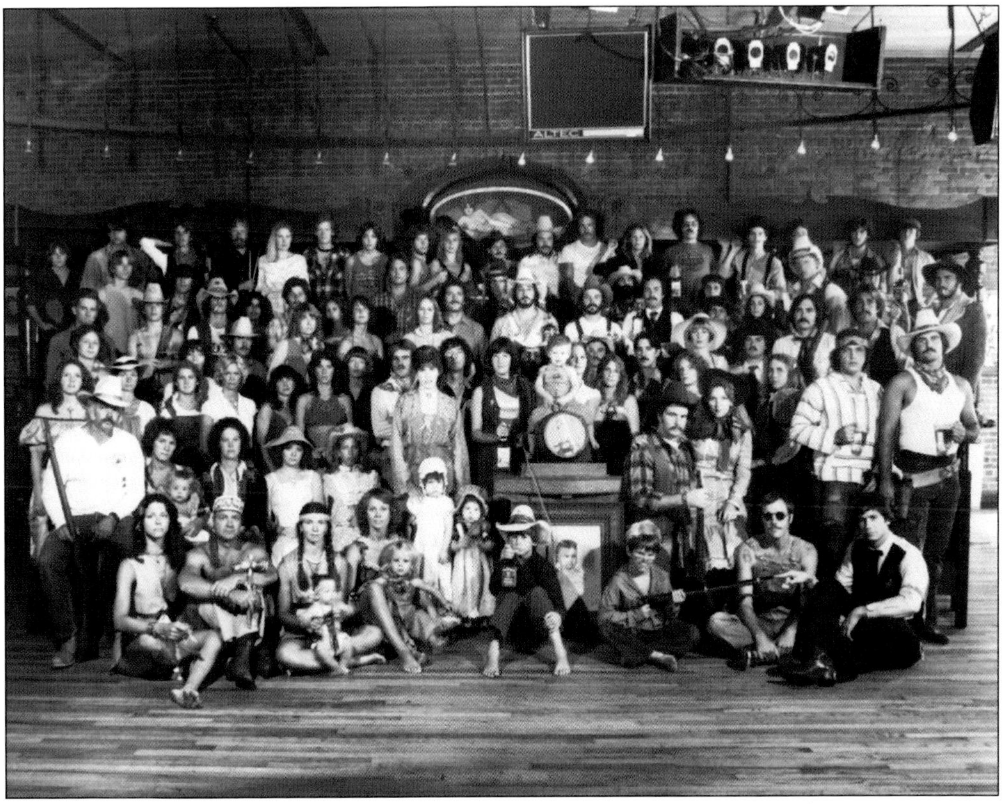

The Gang's All Here. Named for Charles Henry McKiernan (c. 1830–1892), a mountain man of local renown, Mt. Charley's Restaurant and Saloon was established in 1972 by Jim Farwell, a Vietnam War veteran and descendent of town founder John W. Lyndon. The staff were young and enthusiastic, as shown in this "class photo" from the 1970s. Farwell (first row, far right) died in 1992. (Sue Farwell.)

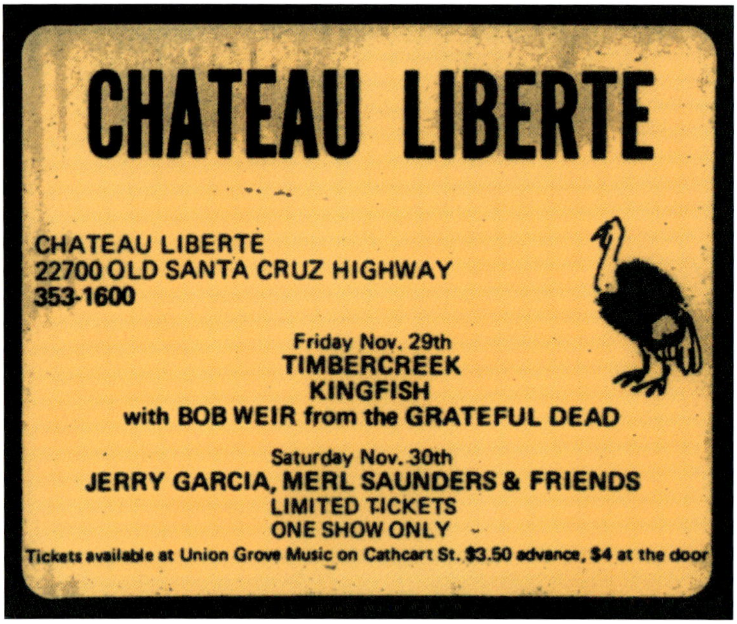
CHATEAU LIBERTE

CHATEAU LIBERTE
22700 OLD SANTA CRUZ HIGHWAY
353-1600

Friday Nov. 29th
TIMBERCREEK
KINGFISH
with BOB WEIR from the GRATEFUL DEAD

Saturday Nov. 30th
JERRY GARCIA, MERL SAUNDERS & FRIENDS
LIMITED TICKETS
ONE SHOW ONLY

Tickets available at Union Grove Music on Cathcart St. $3.50 advance, $4 at the door

LEGENDARY CHATEAU LIBERTE. Located on a muddy dirt road just off Old Santa Cruz Highway, this wild-and-wooly rock 'n' roll venue was set among stately redwoods. The Doobie Brothers played here, as did Jerry Garcia and Hot Tuna. When Tower of Power performed in 1972, 3,000 people showed up and parallel parked on Highway 17. From 1920 to 1945, this was Chateau Boussy, a rumored rendezvous for lovers. (AC.)

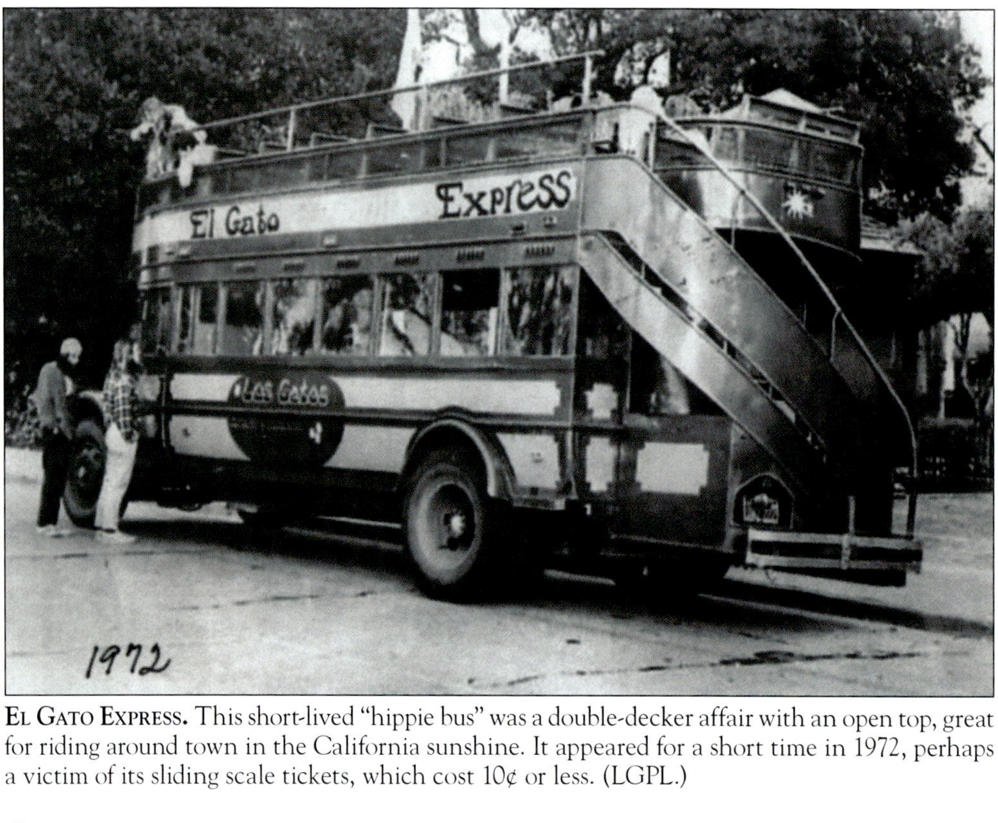

EL GATO EXPRESS. This short-lived "hippie bus" was a double-decker affair with an open top, great for riding around town in the California sunshine. It appeared for a short time in 1972, perhaps a victim of its sliding scale tickets, which cost 10¢ or less. (LGPL.)

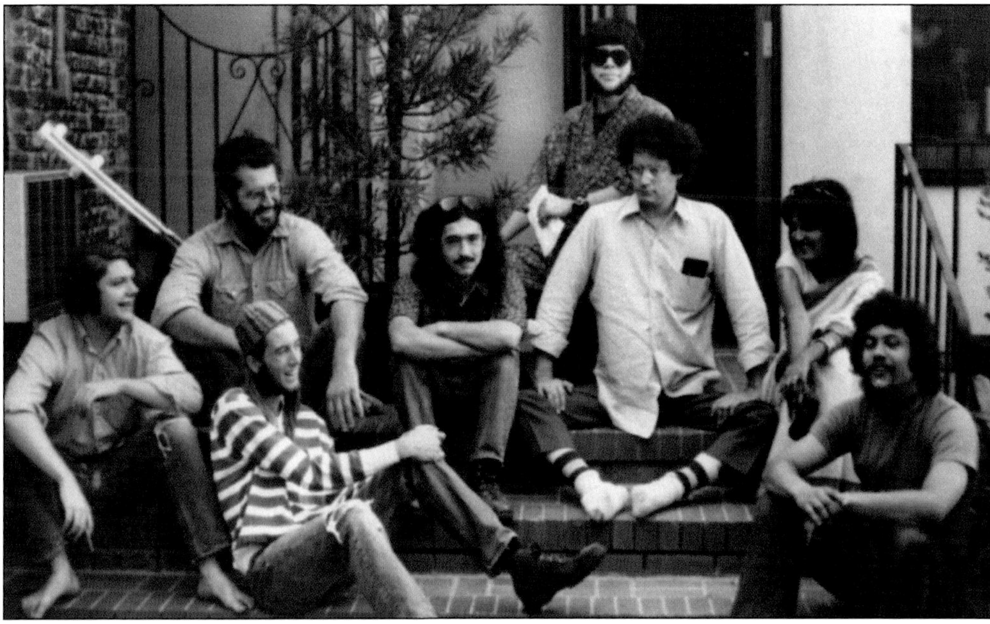

Counterculture on the Air. KTAO-FM Radio at 5 University Avenue in Los Gatos was described by its owner, Lorenzo W. Milam, as "commercial, cooperative, free-form, neo-listener, contributive, pseudo-quasi avant-garde, diversal, retinal, Taoist, concoursal, recto-linear, palsy, dyno, fabbish, mod." Nothing was politically correct, nor was it meant to be. Milam is sitting on the top step in stocking feet with his staff in 1971. (Geoff Alexander.)

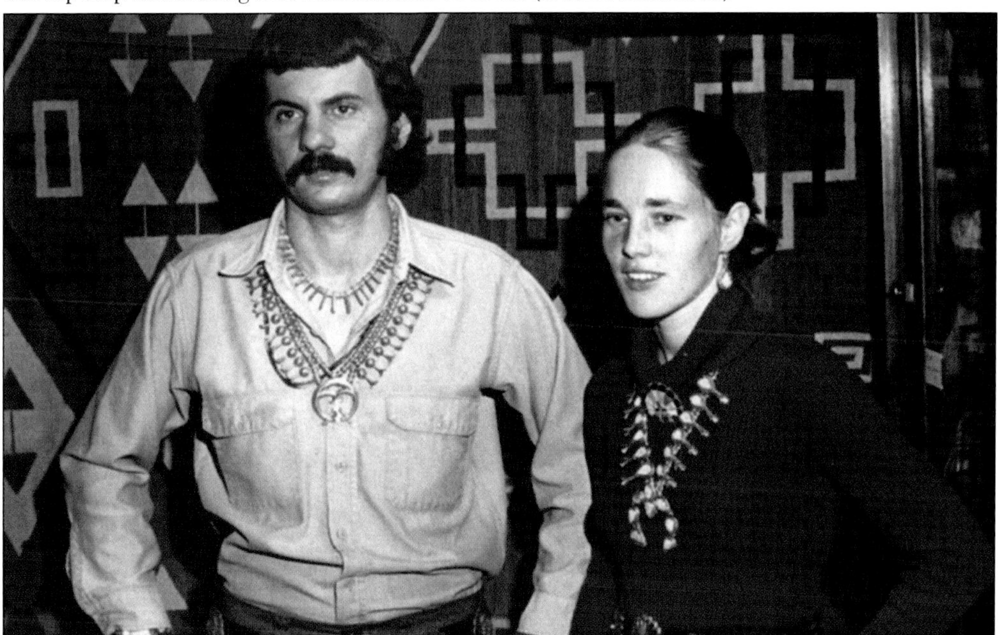

The Indian Store. Much of the charm and vitality that defined Old Town in the 1970s centered on the collection of unique businesses that set up shop there, right in the heart of town. The Indian Store, opened on the lower level in 1972 by Janice Benjamin and Larry Roviello, offered Native American art and jewelry handpicked by the proprietors. (Janice Benjamin.)

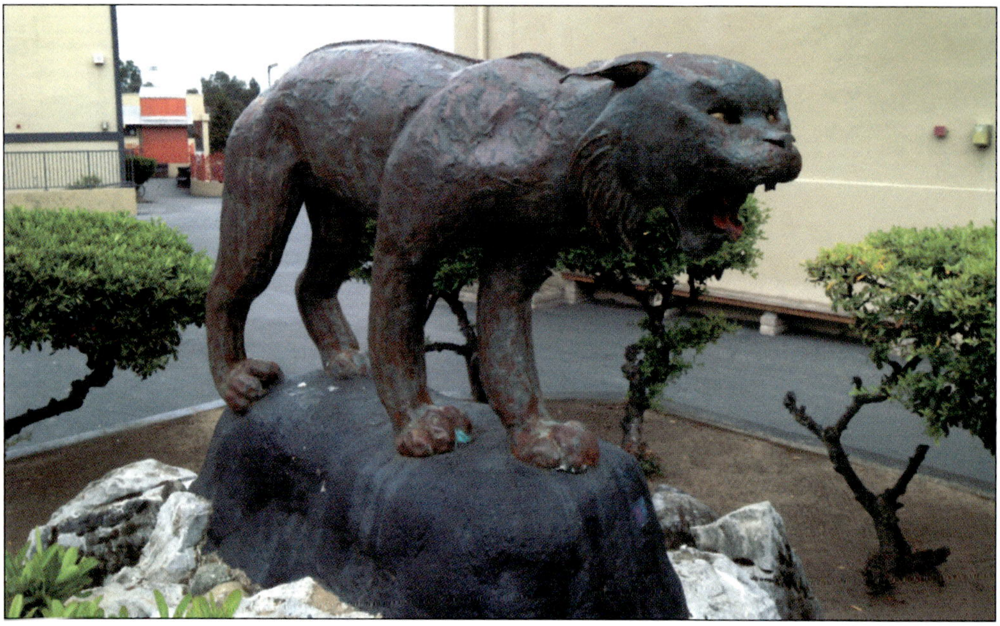

El Gato. Oliver Hurtley was the artist responsible for the ferocious, brazed steel wildcat that guards the inner quad of Los Gatos High School. The graduating class of 1967 provided funding for the sculpture, which took several years to complete. Before it was installed at the high school, it was displayed at Old Town. (BB.)

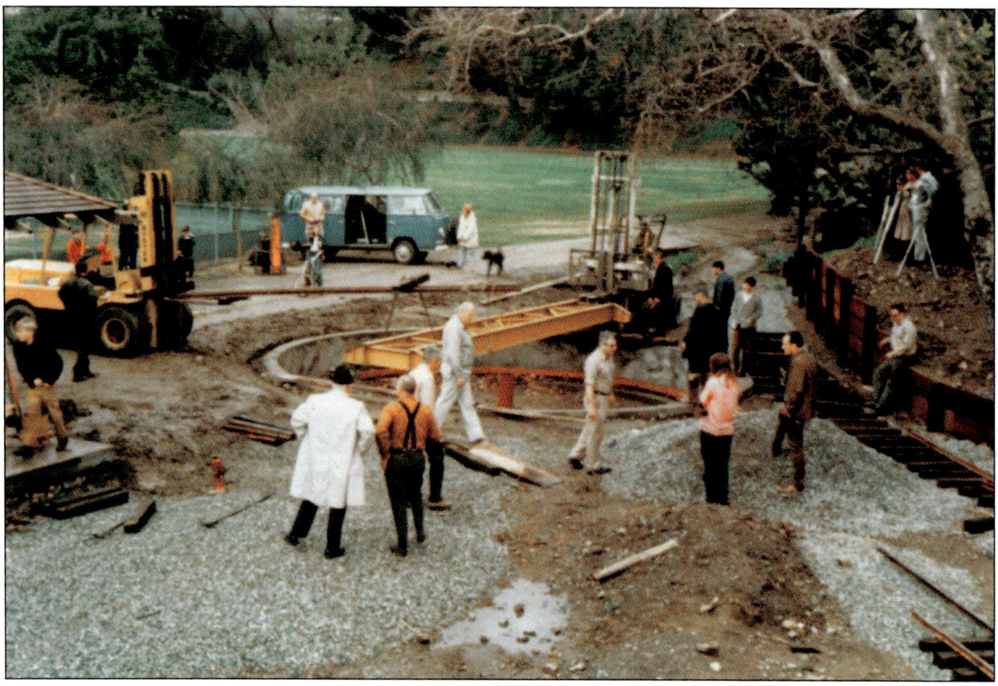

Back on Track. After the death of Los Gatos railroader Billy Jones in 1968, his Wildcat Railroad was moved from his Daves Avenue prune orchard to Oak Meadow Park and adjoining Vasona Park. In a corner of Oak Meadow Park, volunteers, including US Navy Seabees, constructed a 25-foot turntable in 1970. (Billy Jones family.)

MADAM MAYOR. Ruth Cannon, the first female mayor of Los Gatos, served in 1972 and 1973, when issues symptomatic of the uneasy 1970s began to surface. One hot August weekend, 25,000 people showed up for the annual Wine Festival, including motorcycle gangs who "guzzled cheap wine from half-gallon jugs." Two policemen were injured controlling the crowd. "It's the worst trouble we've ever had here," she said, and was quoted in newspapers nationwide. (LGPL.)

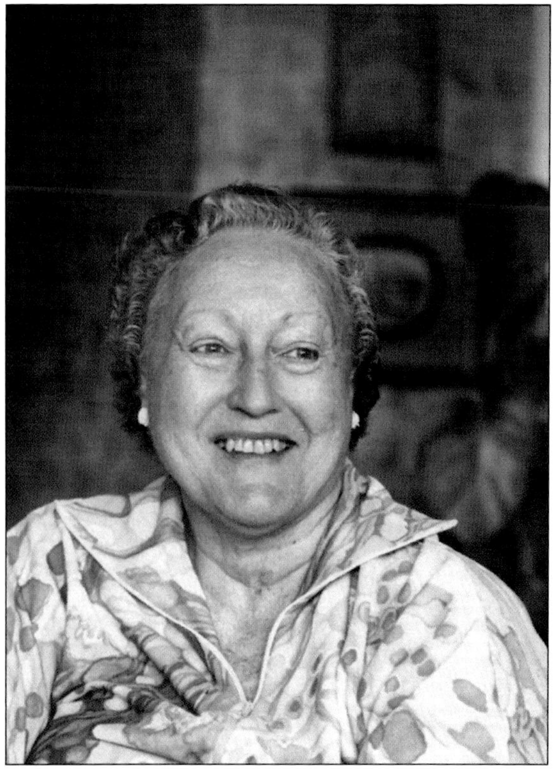

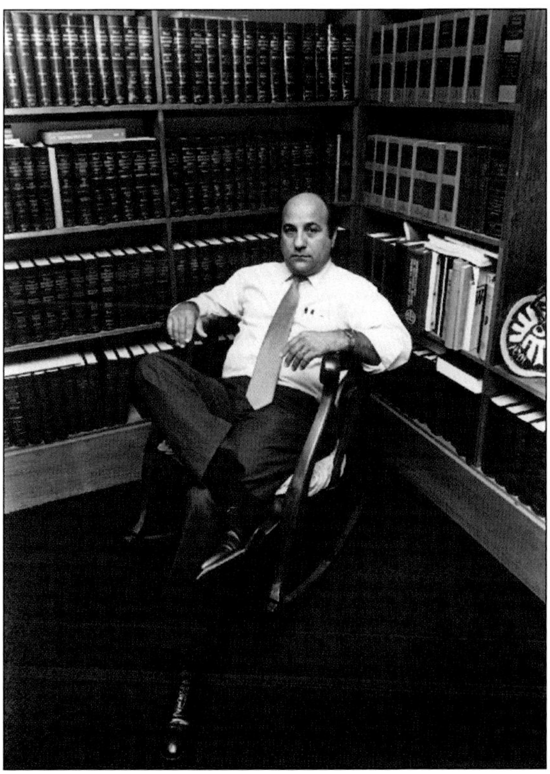

GROWING PAINS. Concerned with the direction the town was taking, local attorney Tom Ferrito won a seat on the town council in 1978 and served for 12 years. He, along with a second councilman, Pete Siemens, favored tougher development standards, controlled growth, and fewer bars and restaurants. "Enough is enough," they said. The Wine Festival soon went on the wagon. (LGWT.)

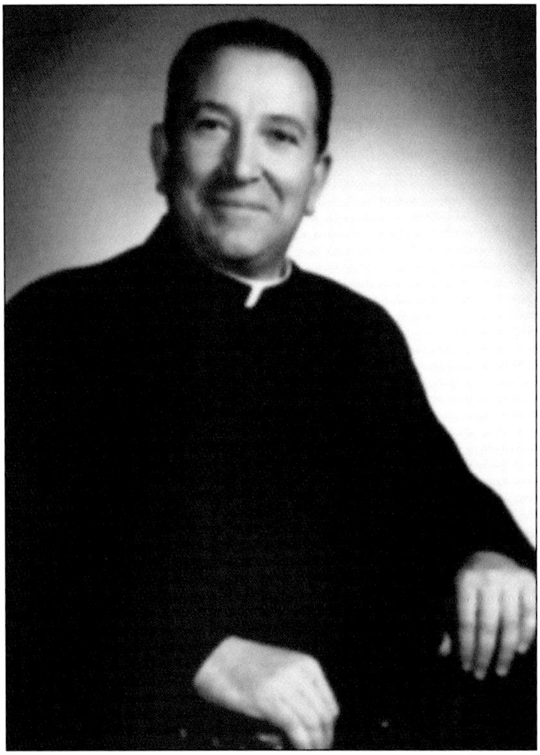

Tragedy at St. Mary's Catholic Church. On November 2, 1972, Los Gatos was shaken by the vicious murder of Fr. Henri Antonio Tomei. A native of Marseilles, France, Father Tomei was a gifted musician noted for his kind and gentle manner. His assailant, responsible for multiple murders, first requested that Father Tomei hear his confession and then stabbed the priest to death. (Sr. Nicki Thomas, SNJM.)

Marketing Phenoms. In 1975, the alchemy of turning rocks into gold worked out well for Los Gatans Gary Dahl (right) and George Coakley. The Pet Rock, a bizarre concept and marketing masterpiece, is now part of business history. The instruction manual that accompanied each "pet" was humorous, and for six months, everyone in the country wanted one. Dahl (1936–2015) was the inventor. Coakley helped finance and promote the product. (LGWT.)

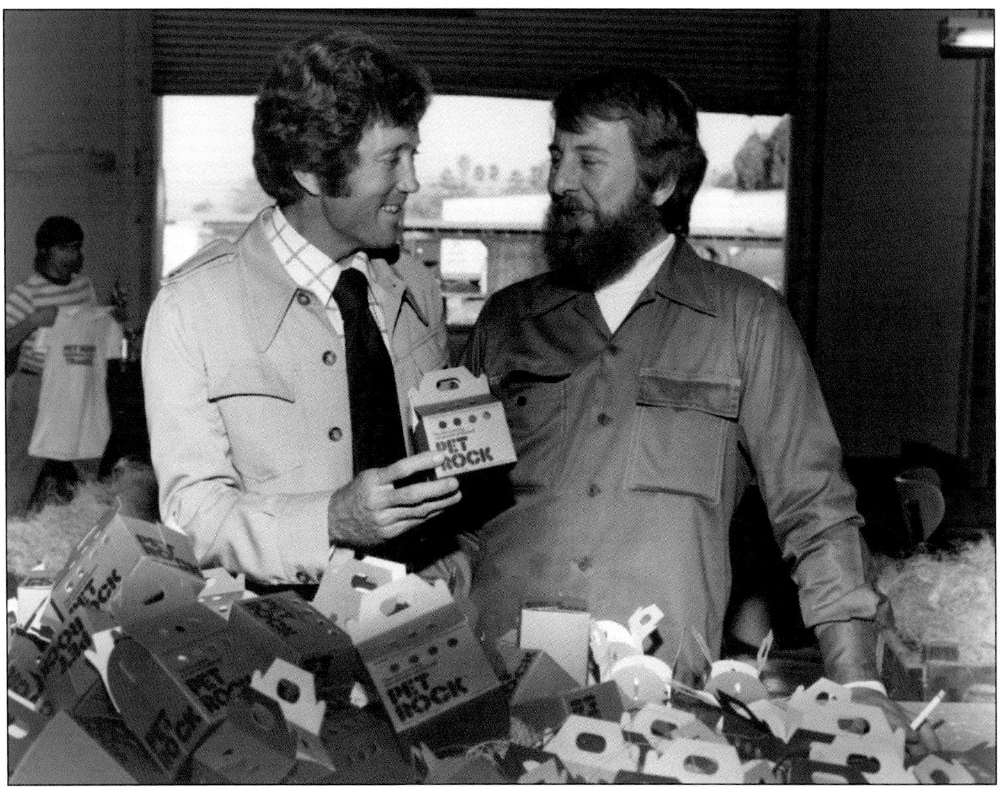

Dances on the Green. Before the California Actors Theater presented Shakespeare's *Hamlet* at Old Town from September 30–October 3, 1976, festivities included ballerinas dancing on Old Town Green, adjacent to the theater. A procession and madrigals were also staged, all a part of "CAT Week," proclaimed by Mayor Ruth Cannon in honor of the regional professional company. (LGWT.)

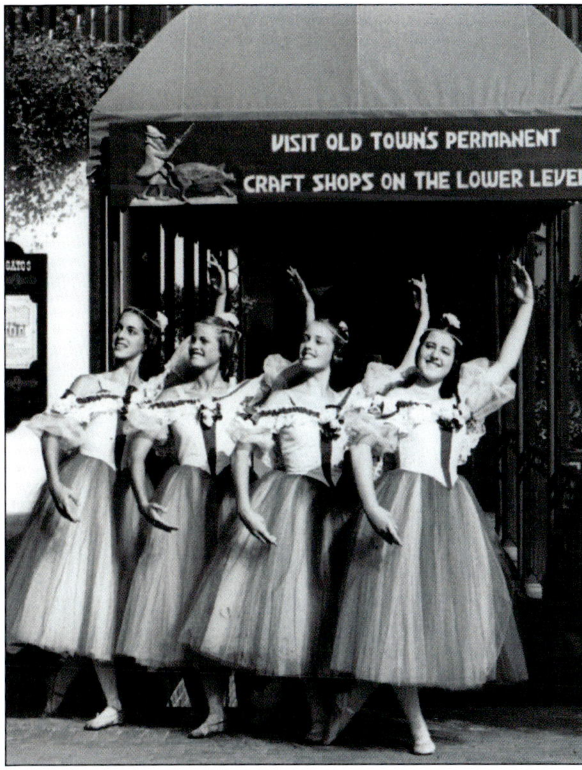

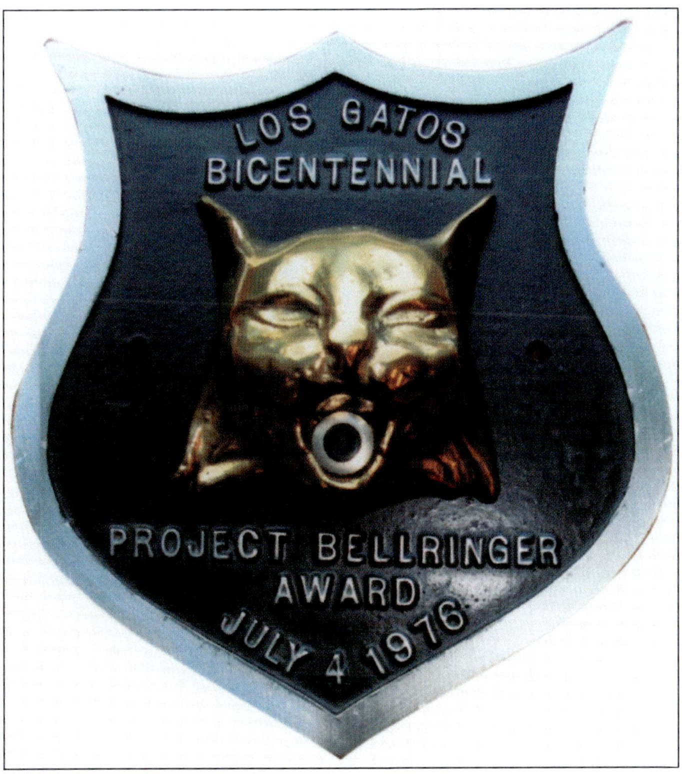

Project Bellringer Awards. An innovative program to rehabilitate pre-1900 homes helped Los Gatos commemorate the United States bicentennial in 1976. Some of the town's Victorian homes needed repair and restoration. Under the leadership of Mayor Mardi Gualtieri, both federal aid and private donations were secured to help homeowners in their preservation efforts. Eventually, 100 homes received the brass plaque pictured here, designed to house a doorbell. (AC.)

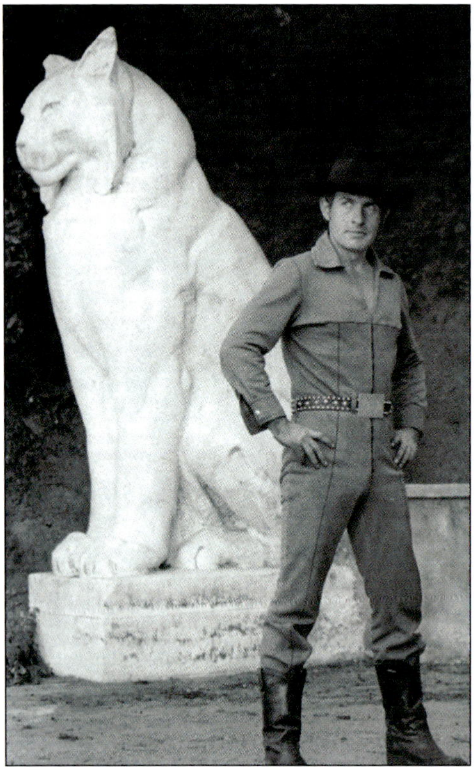

The Road Ranger. From 1979 to 1983, Alan Norman Little, known as the "Road Ranger," roamed Highway 17 on the lookout for motorists in trouble. Mechanical problems, empty gas tanks, overheated engines, and flat tires were all in his purview. He became a local folk hero for his efforts and attracted national attention. Little (1948–2004) was a native of Watsonville and served two tours of duty in Vietnam. (LGWT.)

The Cradle of Los Gatos. Forbes Mill Annex was constructed in 1880 to store wheat and flour. By the late 1970s, it had fallen into serious disrepair. Councilwoman Mardi Gualtieri and Eureka Federal Savings were instrumental in the restoration of the building, which then served as the History Museum of Los Gatos from 1982 to 2014. This local history treasure is State Historical Landmark No. 458. (BB.)

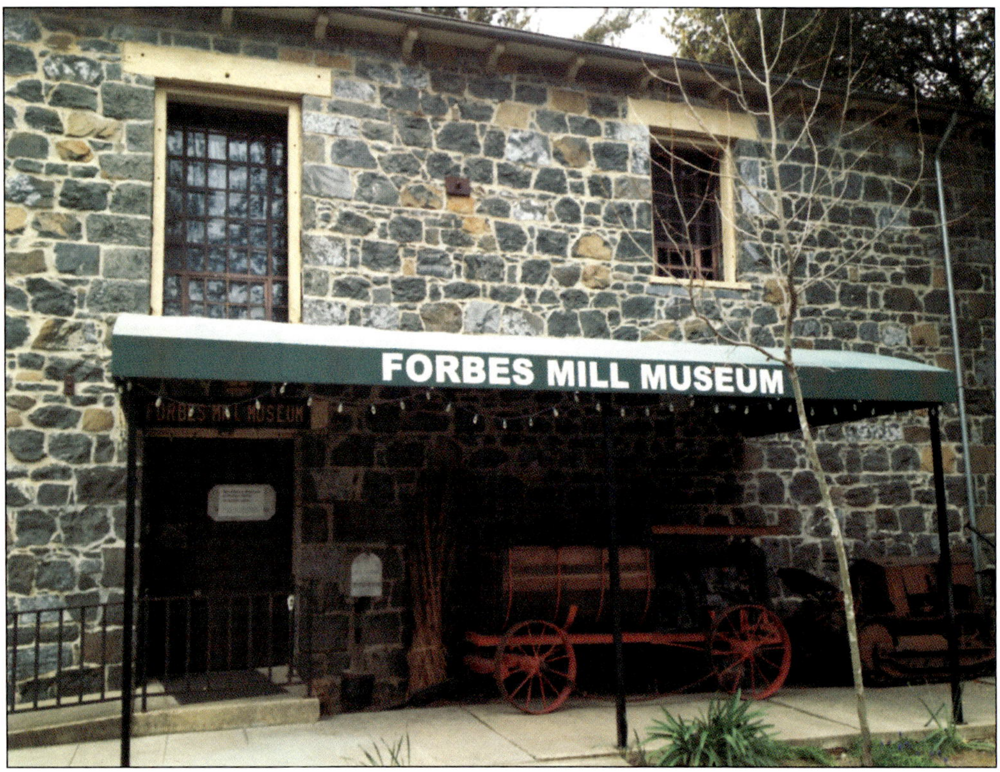

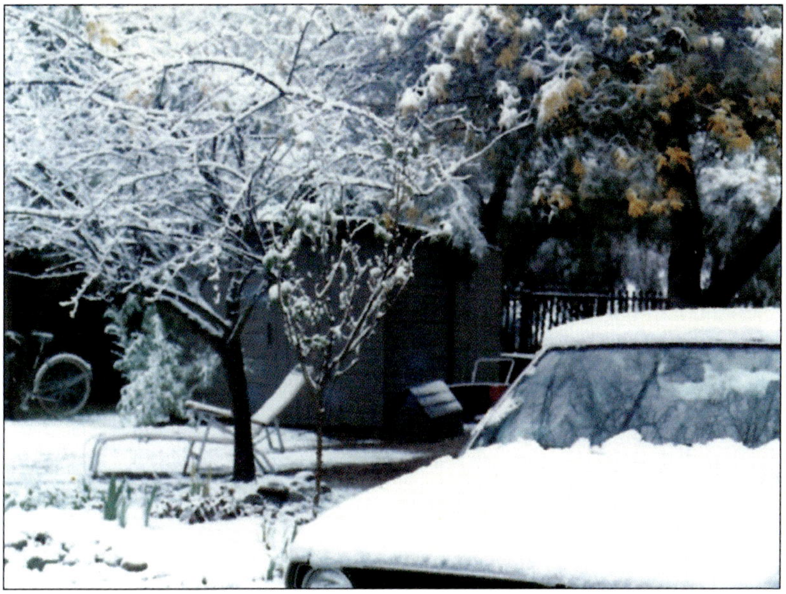

Snow Globe World. Snow occasionally falls in the Santa Cruz Mountains, but it is very rare in Los Gatos. The two inches that fell on February 5, 1976, remain the most snow on record since 1900. The snowflakes, pictured here on Pleasant Street, were greeted with glee. (Maralyn Miller.)

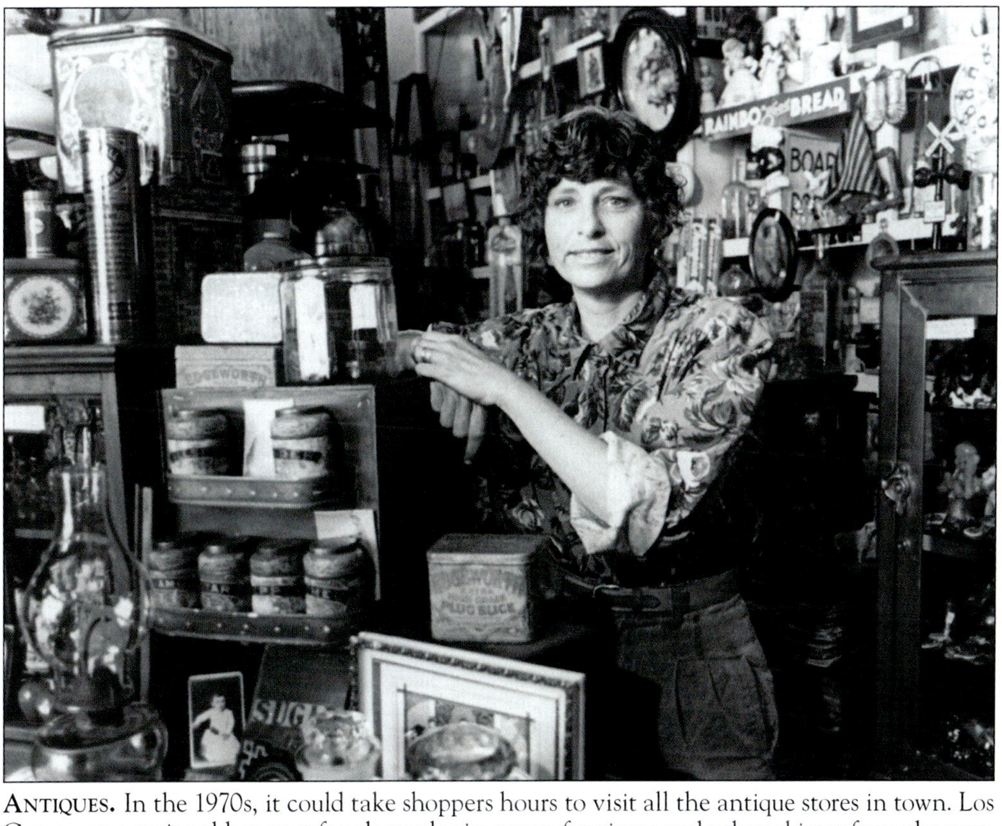

Antiques. In the 1970s, it could take shoppers hours to visit all the antique stores in town. Los Gatos was a regional hot spot for elegantly timeworn furniture and other objects from the past. Old-timey items could be found in cozy little shops such as The Antiquarium; proprietress Denise Harr is pictured here. (LGWT.)

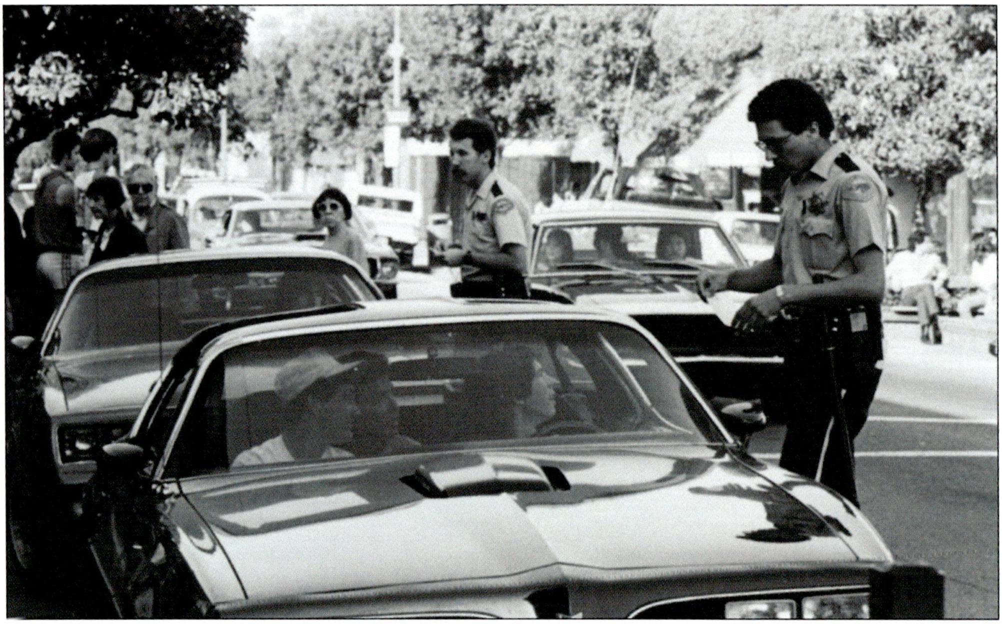

CRUZIN'. It was the summer of 1978, and the cruising was easy, at least for the teens driving their Camaros, Trans Ams, and other assorted vehicles up and down North Santa Cruz Avenue. Business owners complained about severe congestion, noise, and the loss of customers. Police cited motorists for vehicle and municipal code infractions, including the local 10:00 p.m. curfew for persons under 18. Officer Tim Burns is at left. (LGWT.)

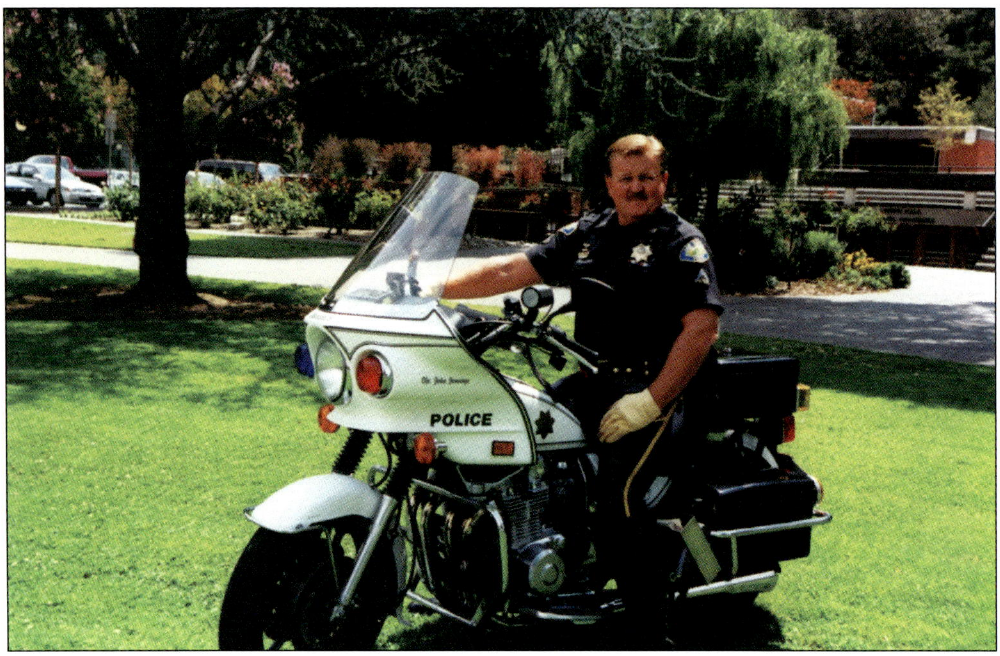

A TOWN FAVORITE. John Jennings served as a Los Gatos police officer from 1972 to 2001. He was the first officer selected to patrol on motorcycle, and during that time he handed out many tickets. But his determination to be fair and show respect was noticed. He loved his job, and Los Gatos loved him. He retired with the rank of sergeant. (John Jennings.)

Four

The Earth Moved Under Our Feet

The 1980s

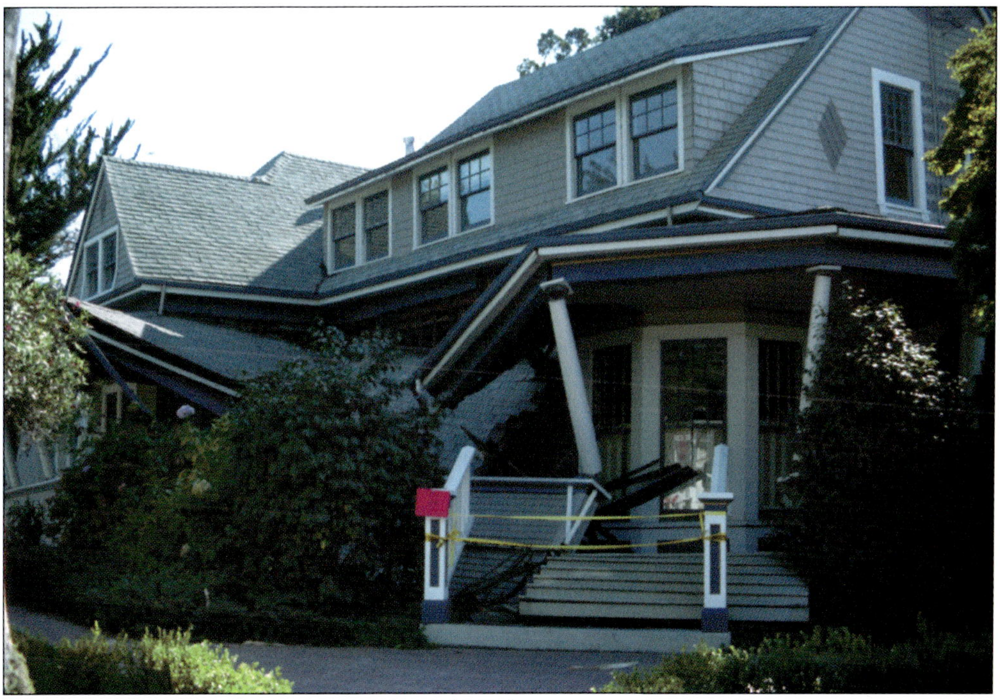

On Shaky Ground. Everyone remembers where they were on October 17, 1989, at 5:04 p.m., when the Loma Prieta earthquake snarled down from the Santa Cruz Mountains, wreaking havoc on Los Gatos and the entire Bay Area. Los Gatos suffered mightily, as did many other communities. This turn-of-the-20th-century home at 54 Los Gatos Boulevard had been completely renovated just before the earthquake struck. (USGS.)

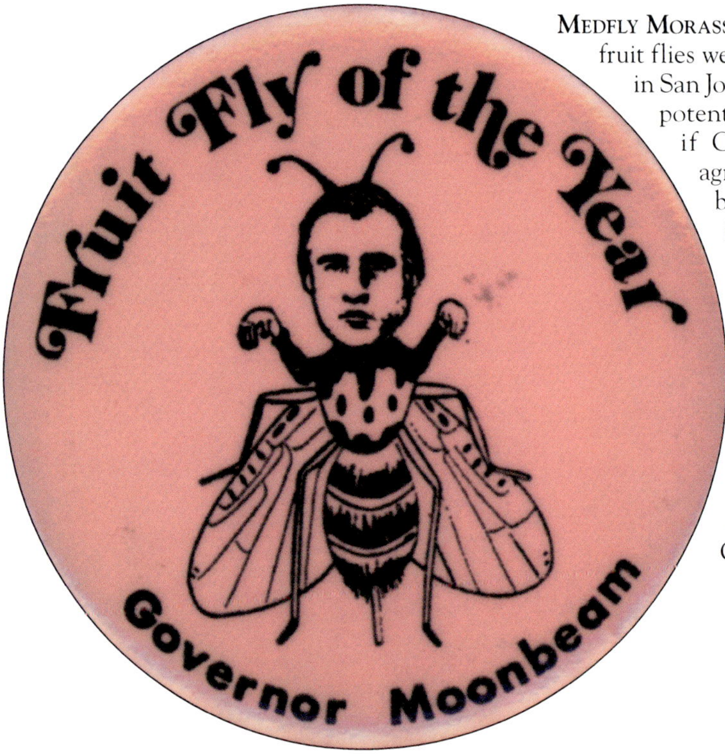

Medfly Morass. In 1980, Mediterranean fruit flies were trapped in a citrus tree in San Jose. Officials recognized the potential for economic disaster if California's $14 billion agricultural industry were to be shut down by the highly invasive pest. Experts recommended aerial spraying of an insecticide, Malathion. Residents complained en masse, and Gov. Jerry Brown was reluctant to comply. Spraying commenced after the federal government threatened a quarantine on all California produce. (AC.)

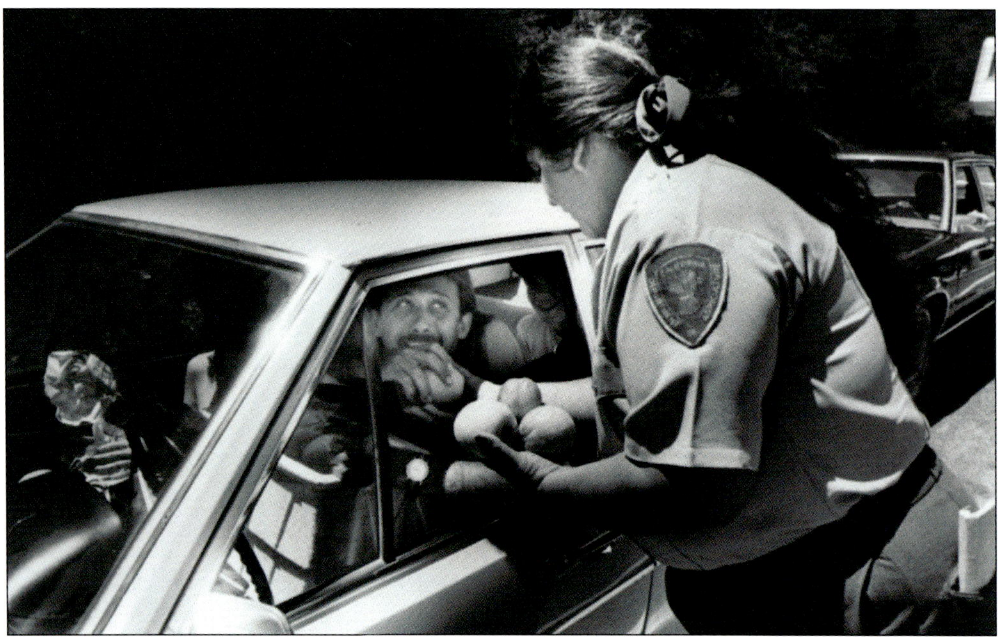

"I Stripped for Medfly." Thousands of residents in Santa Clara, San Mateo, and Alameda Counties stripped the fruit from their trees, and the National Guard picked up and buried tons of produce. Helicopters swooped in over homes, spraying a sticky mix of insecticide and bait. It sounded like a war zone, and it was. Here, an inspector confiscates apples from a family heading from Los Gatos to Santa Cruz. (AC.)

IMAGIC. Formed in June 1981 by executives who defected from Mattel and Atari, Imagic was a video game developer and publisher headquartered on University Avenue in Los Gatos. With sales of $75 million in its first fiscal year, Imagic employed up to 230 people. Unfortunately, the success was fleeting, due to an oversaturated market and developing competition from home computers. Imagic president Bruce L. Davis is pictured here in 1983. (AC.)

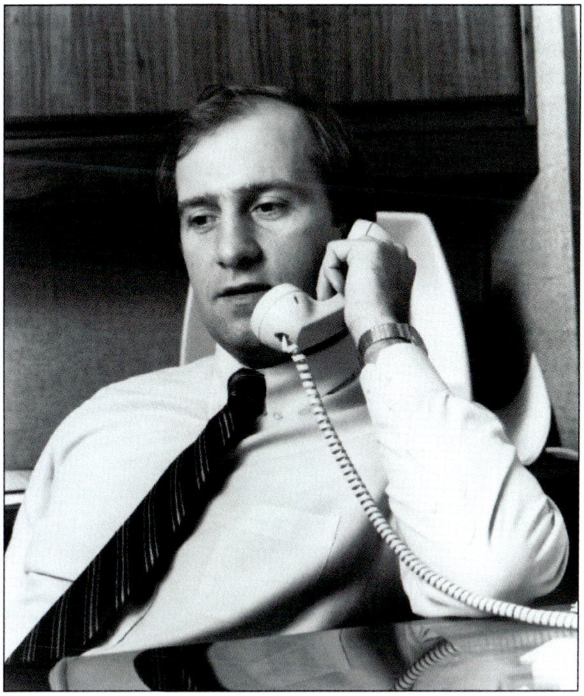

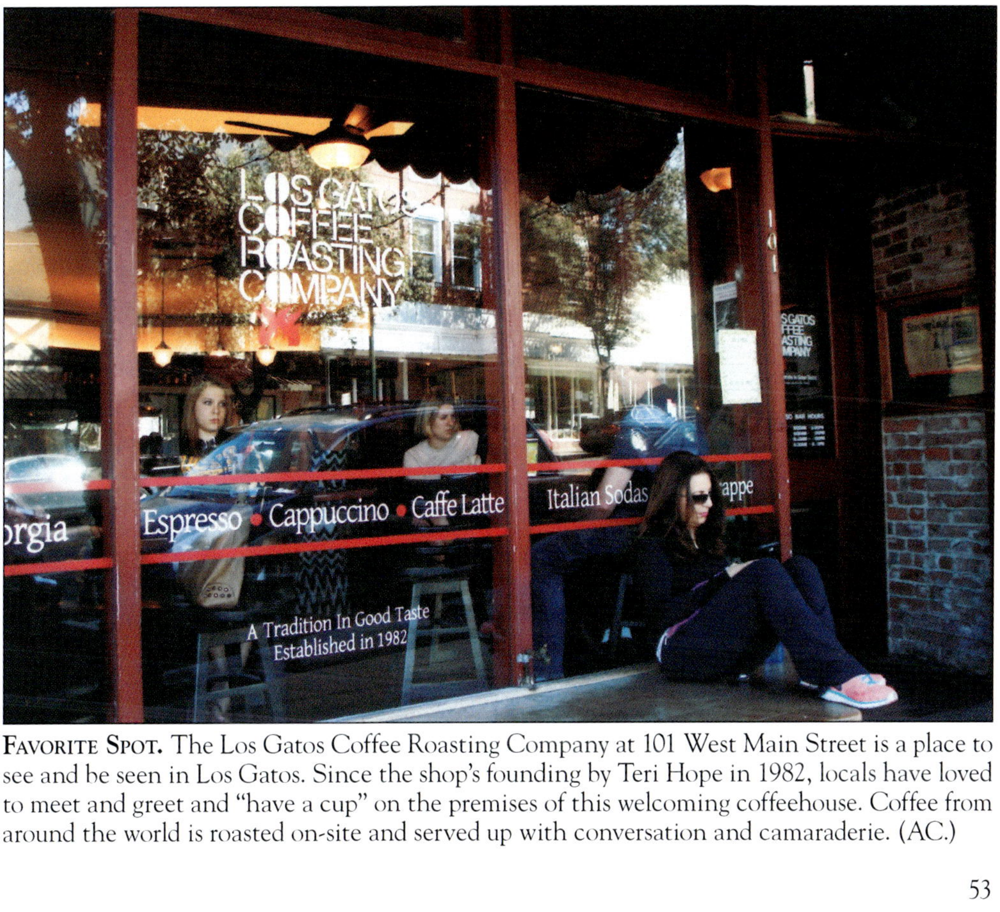

FAVORITE SPOT. The Los Gatos Coffee Roasting Company at 101 West Main Street is a place to see and be seen in Los Gatos. Since the shop's founding by Teri Hope in 1982, locals have loved to meet and greet and "have a cup" on the premises of this welcoming coffeehouse. Coffee from around the world is roasted on-site and served up with conversation and camaraderie. (AC.)

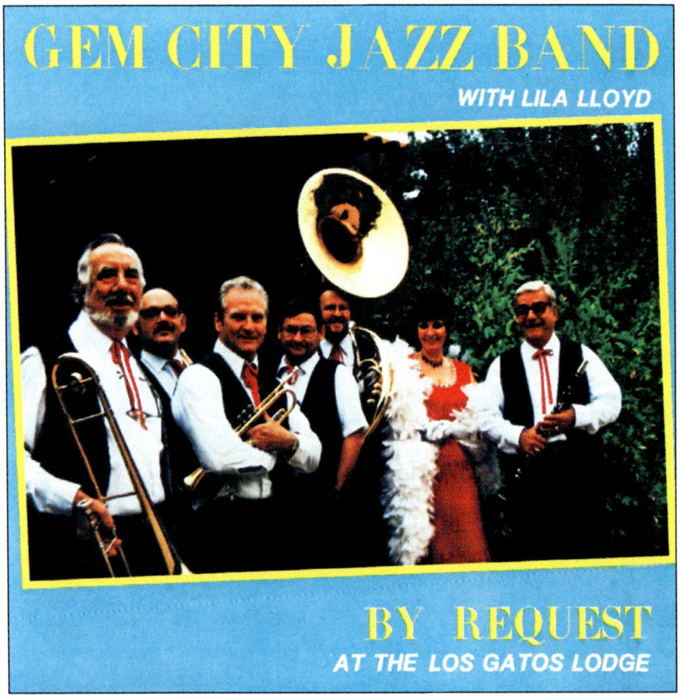

GEM CITY JAZZ BAND. Orrin "Fess" Blattner (1917–2006), pictured here at far left, taught music at Los Gatos High School from 1944 to 1977. He played 20 instruments, performed with the San Jose Symphony, and was captivated by jazz. He organized the Gem City Jazz Band in 1977 and entertained at Los Gatos Lodge. The band's musicians included drummer Sammy Cohen (second from left) and Lila Lloyd (second from right), "the girl with a thousand voices." (CB.)

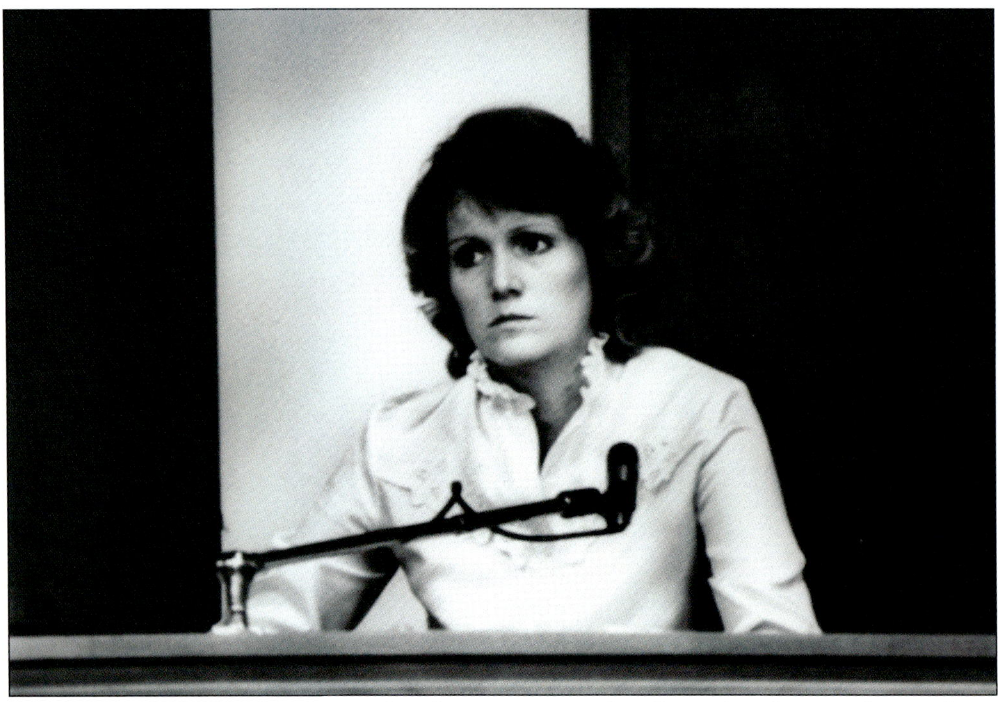

FELLMAN MURDER. Serious crime and violence are rare in Los Gatos, but the town has not been immune from grisly criminal acts over the years. In early 1985, a Main Street hair stylist was convicted of shooting her husband, dismembering and burning his body, and then reportedly biting into his charred arm. Dianne Fellman, pictured at her trial, was sentenced to serve 27 years to life in prison. (LGWT.)

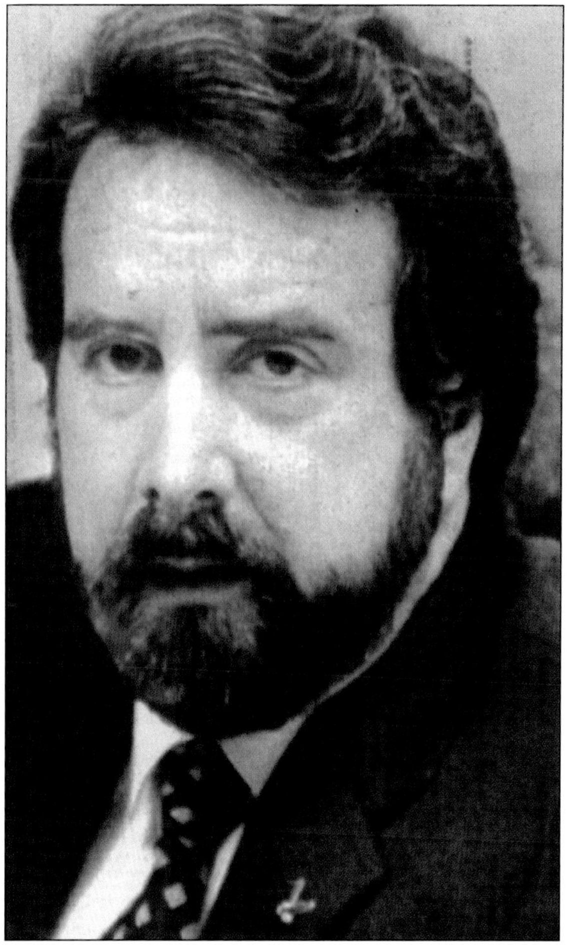

Death in a Ferrari. Dennis Barnhart, the 40-year-old president of Eagle Computer, was killed on June 8, 1983, hours after his company went public and he had become a multimillionaire. The former Navy aviator left his University Avenue office in his red Ferrari, lost control of the car, and plunged down an embankment near the base of Vasona Dam. He was dead on arrival at Los Gatos Community Hospital. (AC.)

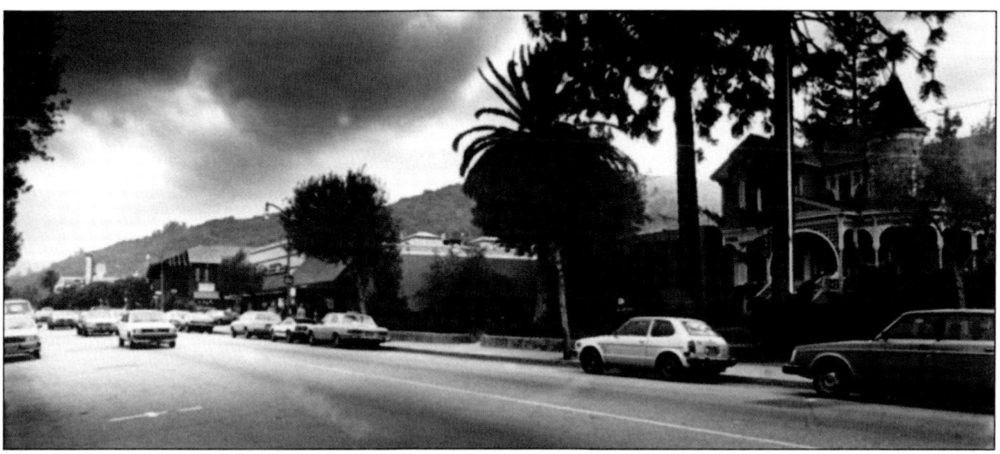

Lexington Reservoir Fire. In July 1985, a wildfire burned 14,000 acres of chaparral-covered hills near Lexington Reservoir. The fire, driven by hot, capricious winds, raged for one long week. About 4,500 people were forced to evacuate their mountain homes, with some taking shelter in the Los Gatos High School gym. The fire, caused by arson, destroyed 24 homes. This was the scene on North Santa Cruz Avenue. (LGWT.)

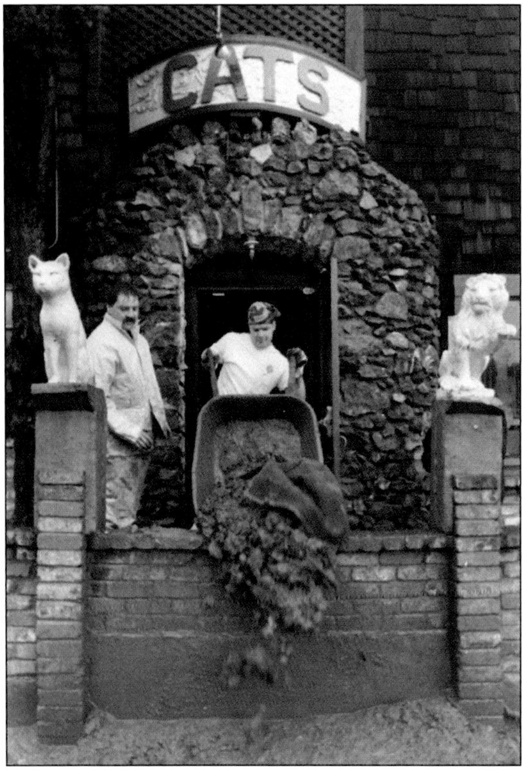

First Fire, Then Flood. A series of subtropical storms produced 25.5 inches of rain at Lexington Reservoir during February 12–19, 1986. The rain fell on unprotected, sodden, fire-devastated hillsides. The resulting runoff quickly filled the reservoir, and debris flowed downhill. A clogged drain behind the Cats Restaurant & Tavern resulted in a mudslide. Two feet of mud forced its way into the building and was shoveled out by hand. (LGWT.)

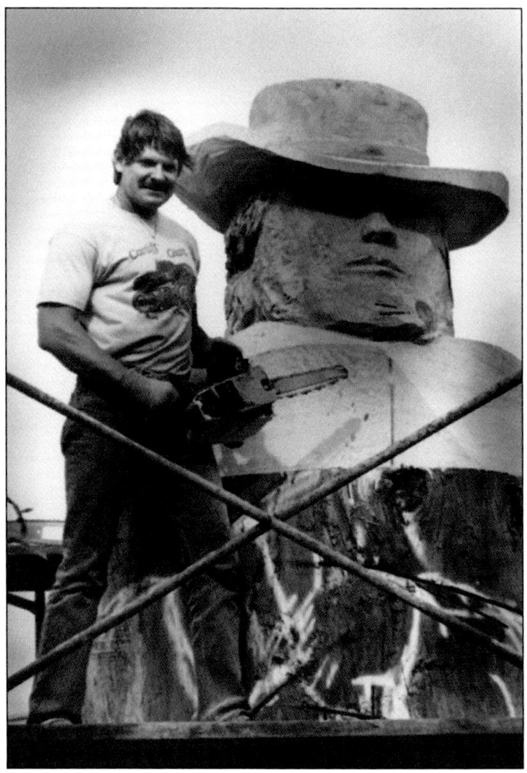

Chainsaw Artistry. The carved wooden statue of Mountain Charley near the entrance to Mountain Mike's Pizza on Santa Cruz Avenue was over 17 feet tall and weighed 12,000 pounds. Miles Tucker created the giant icon around 1986 with his chainsaw. In 1994, Brazilian media noted that Mountain Charley was dressed in a T-shirt welcoming soccer fans to Los Gatos. Mountain Charley was removed in 2007, riddled with termites. (LGWT.)

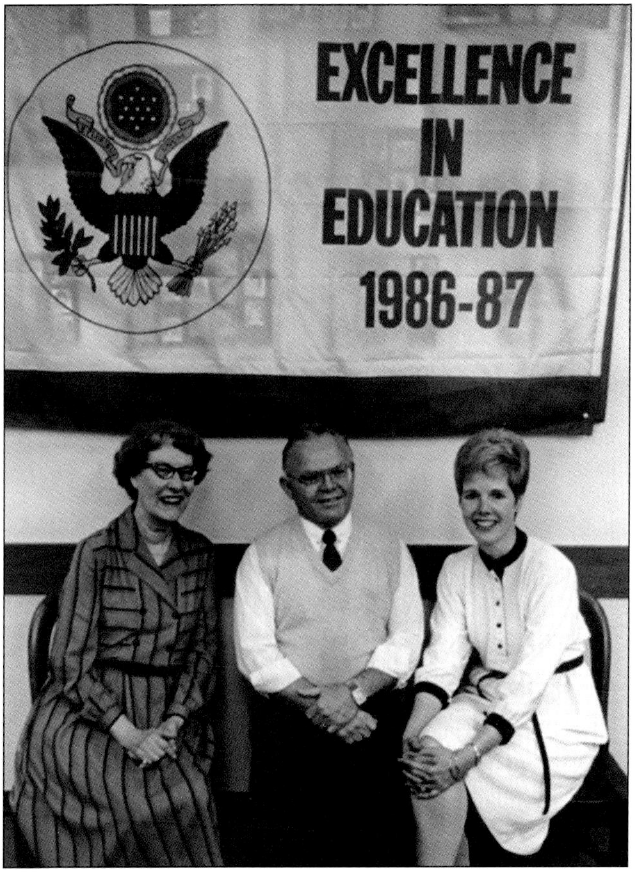

ACCOLADES. In 1987, Los Gatos High School (LGHS) was designated an outstanding school by the US Department of Education. Schools were judged on high expectations for students, clear academic goals, and development of character and values, among other attributes. From left to right are Atha Jane Haywood (1927–2013), who taught at LGHS for 38 years; Ted Simonson (1925–2012), principal; and Patti Hughes, vice-principal. (LGWT.)

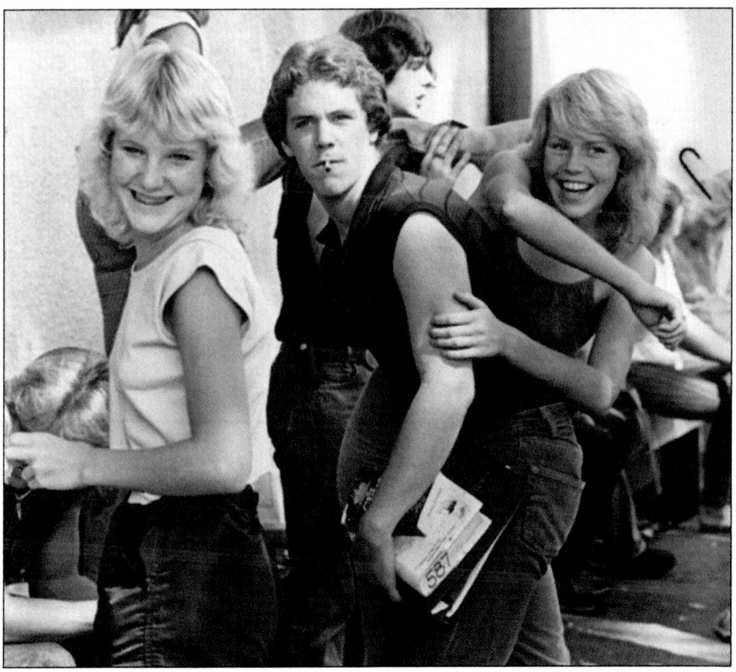

DOWN BY THE SCHOOLYARD. In the 1980s, many California high schools set up smoking areas in an attempt to move smokers out of the lavatories and away from other students. At Los Gatos High School, painted lines defined small areas on campus where the students could smoke, as shown here in 1985. However, since existing laws outlawed minors from smoking, such areas were banned in 1986. (LGWT.)

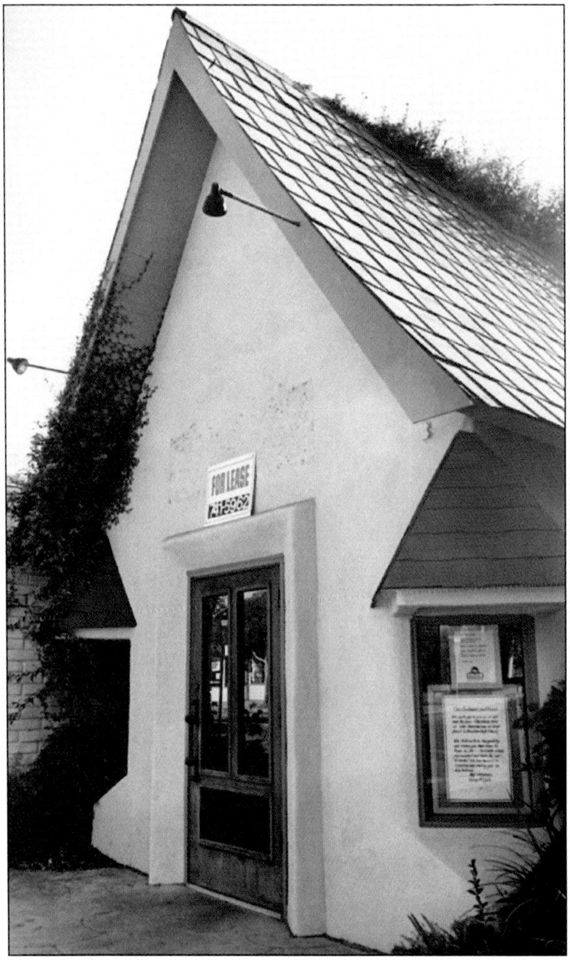

"The Egg." Realtor Effie Walton was enamored with the whimsical and the inventive, as evidenced by the storybook architecture of her shopping center, Little Village. In this 1986 photograph, a favorite breakfast place, the Broken Egg, has lost its lease after 15 years in business at 340 North Santa Cruz Avenue. This location now houses the Los Gatos Café. (LGWT.)

Los Gatos Academy of Dance. For more than 30 years, Paul E. Curtis Jr. trained local dancers, some of whom went on to professional careers. He is remembered for spectacular productions of *The Nutcracker* each December, dazzling audiences with expert dancing, exquisite costumes, and a "growing" Christmas tree. The 1987 *Nutcracker* auditions were held at his dance studio, which was built in 1927 as the Los Gatos Armory. (LGWT.)

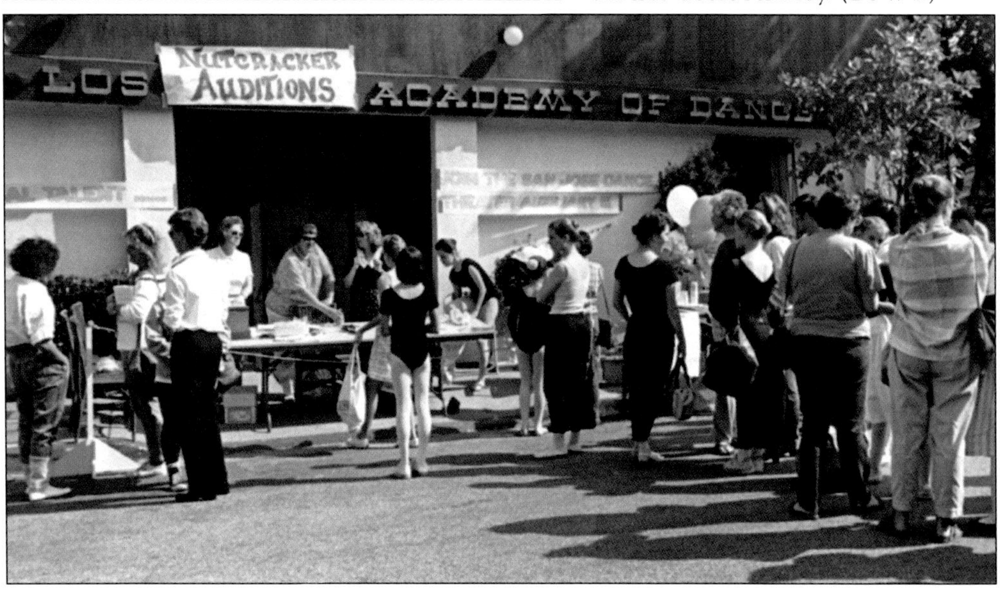

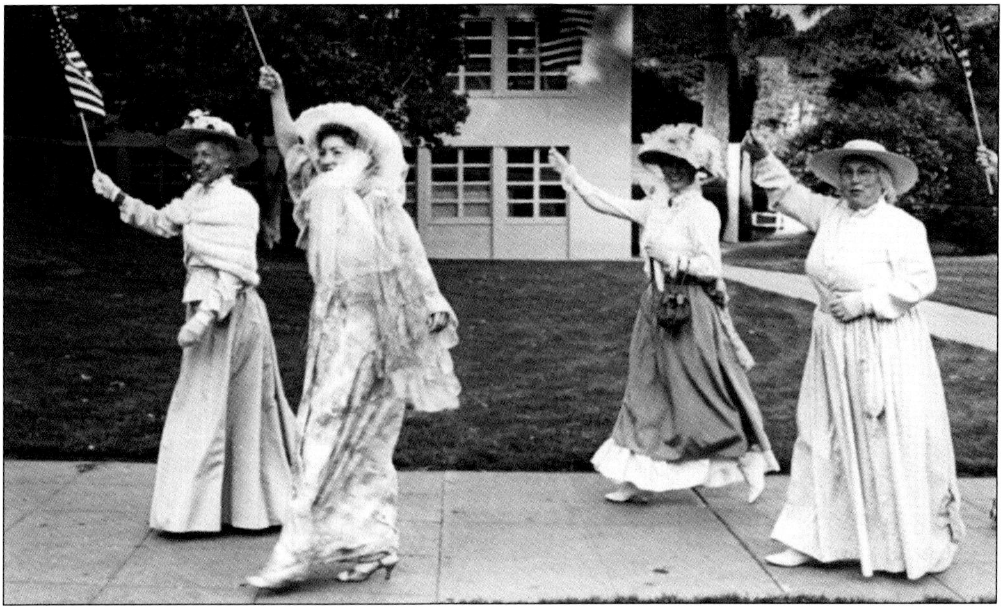

HURRAH FOR 100 YEARS! Old-fashioned costumes, a parade, lots of American flags for waving, and a historical pageant were all part of the 100th birthday celebration commemorating the August 1887 incorporation of Los Gatos. The pageant recalled the great outdoor spectacles presented in town most years between 1919 and 1947. The centennial pageant was written and directed by Kathryn Morgan. Barbara Baggerly appears at far right. (LGWT.)

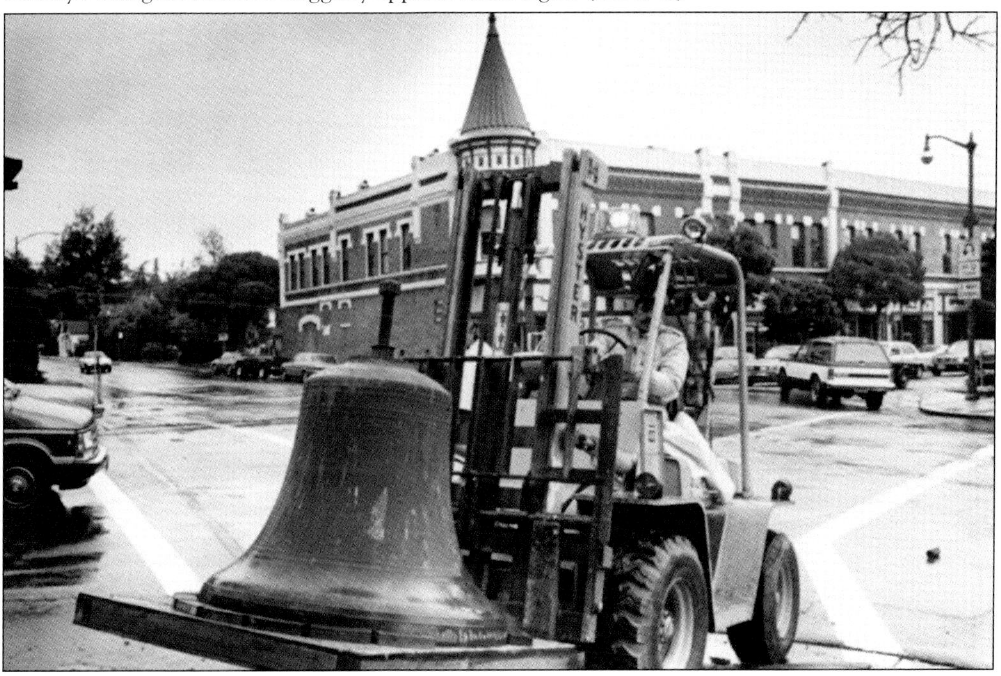

COMING HOME. In honor of the Los Gatos Centennial, native Los Gatan Andy Kinyon rescued the town's 1899 fire bell from a barnyard display in front of a chicken restaurant in Lodi, where it had resided for 40 years. The Lions Club paid to transport the bell back home. It was installed in a tower at Town Plaza Park on December 2, 1987, where it stayed for a dozen years. (LGWT.)

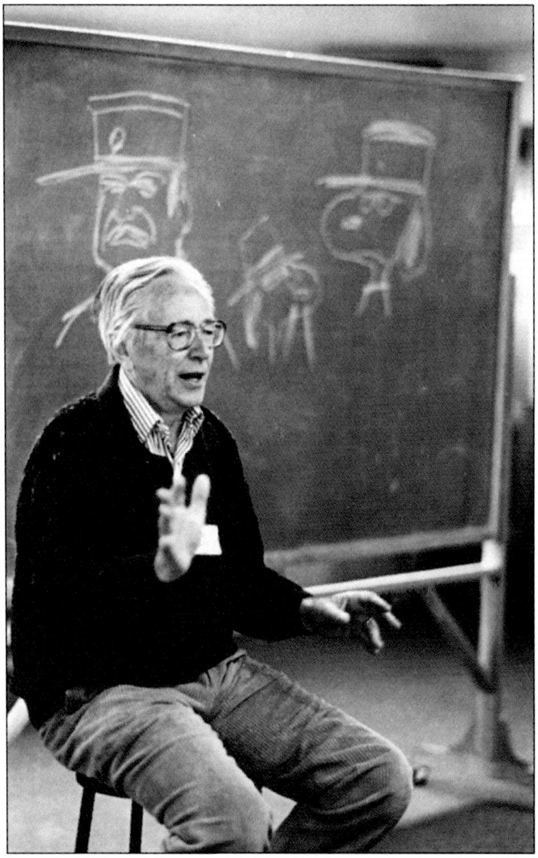

Charles Schulz Visits Hillbrook School. On March 9, 1988, *Peanuts* creator Charles Schulz visited Hillbrook School to participate in "Celebrity Reading Day." He was invited by Peggy Fleming Jenkins, a Hillbrook parent. Schulz sits in front of his sketch of Sergeant Lejaune, a malevolent character from the great adventure novel, *Beau Geste*. He drew Snoopy as an ever-imaginative member of the French Foreign Legion. (LGWT.)

Trouble in Garlic Gulch. John and Carol Steinbeck built a house on Greenwood Lane and lived there from 1936 to 1938. Steinbeck wrote *The Grapes of Wrath* in the 800-square-foot cottage, and he named his little estate "Garlic Gulch" (Arroyo Del Ajo). All was well until neighbors moved in. "Voice culture on one side, linemen shrieking on another," he complained. His hand-carved sign was still in place in the 1980s. (LGWT.)

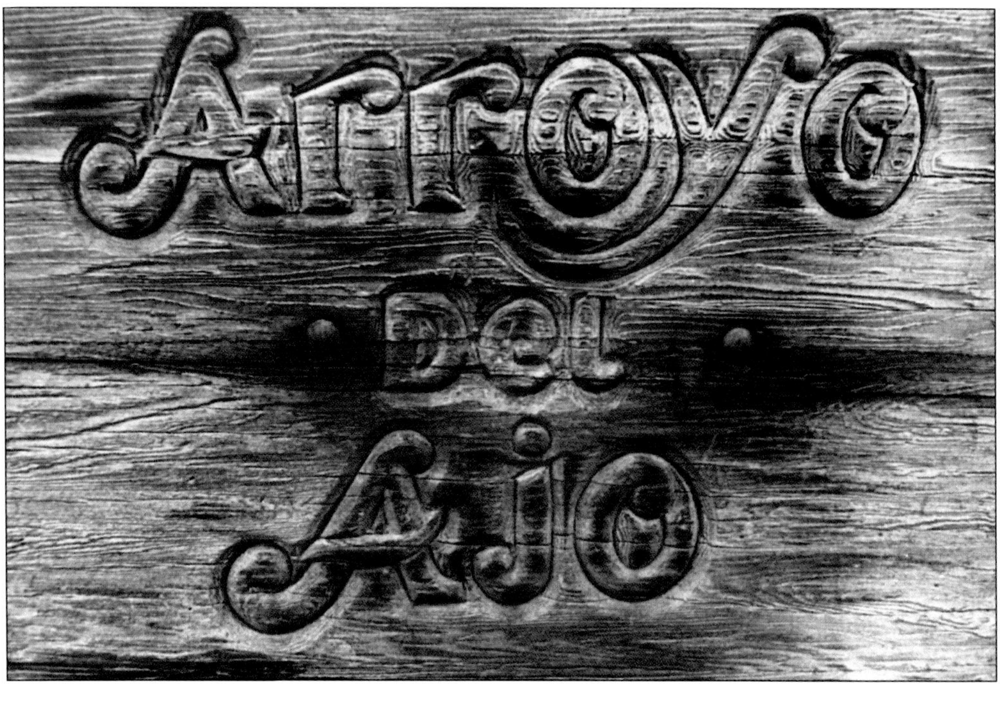

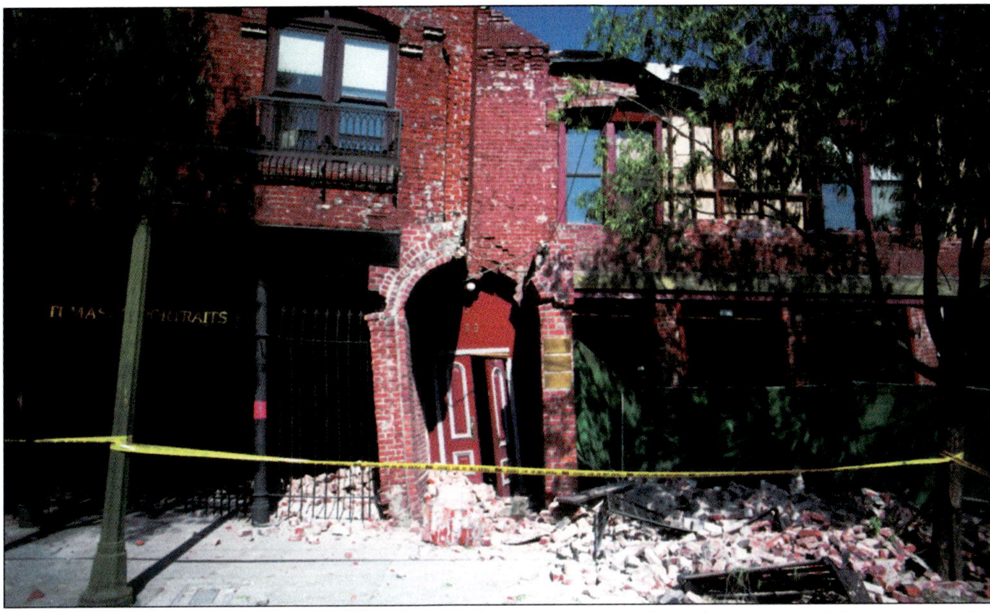

Wow! 6.9! The Loma Prieta earthquake was the strongest earthquake to hit California since the San Francisco disaster in April 1906. Parts of Los Gatos were shattered, including the buildings at 37–45 East Main Street. The majority of the damage downtown resulted from unreinforced masonry, common in older construction. In residential neighborhoods, houses detached from their foundations. (USGS.)

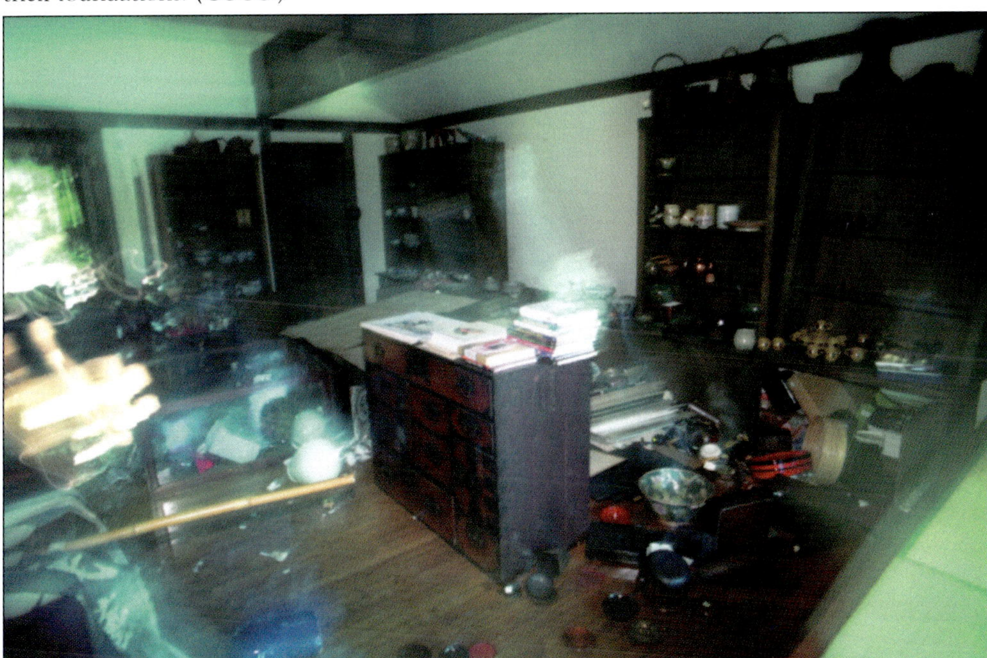

Aftershock! Photographer J.K. Nakata from the US Geological Survey took this photograph in a ceramics shop during one of dozens of aftershocks of magnitude 3.0 or larger that occurred during the first 24 hours after the main quake. The frequent aftershocks caused confusion and fear. People slept on their front lawns or in their cars for fear their homes would collapse. (USGS.)

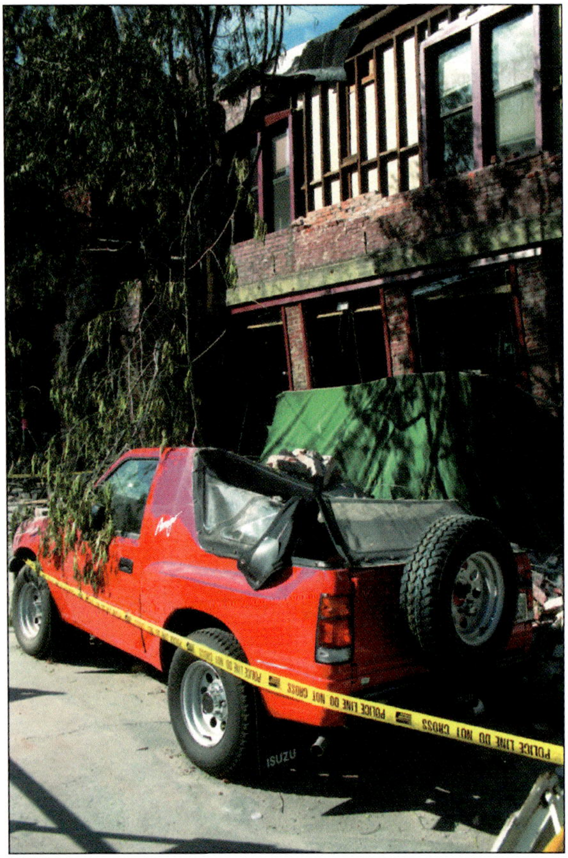

Danger Zone. Los Gatos was located in the epicentral area of the cataclysm and suffered significant property damage. Falling bricks and masonry were especially dangerous. In the greater Bay Area, damage was estimated at $6 billion, and 63 people lost their lives. While there were no deaths Los Gatos, local hospitals treated many residents for cuts, bruises, concussions, and broken bones. (USGS.)

Communication. Following the quake, electricity was out in Los Gatos for four days, and phone lines were down or overloaded. A few shortwave radio operators brought their equipment to the emergency operations center at town hall, but for many people, messages taped on the side of this van had to suffice. (USGS.)

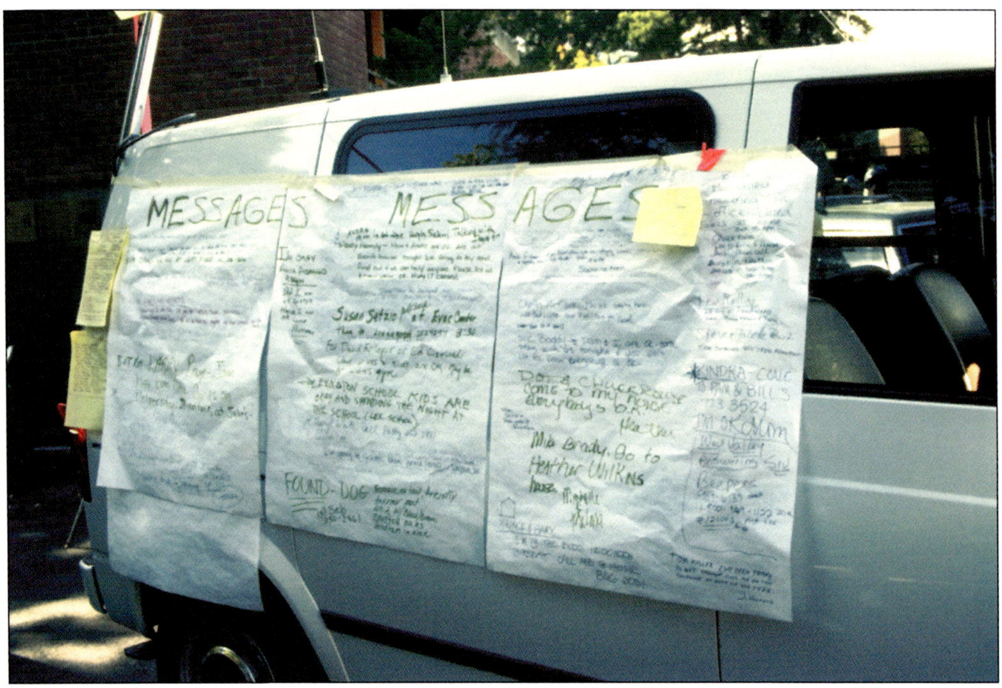

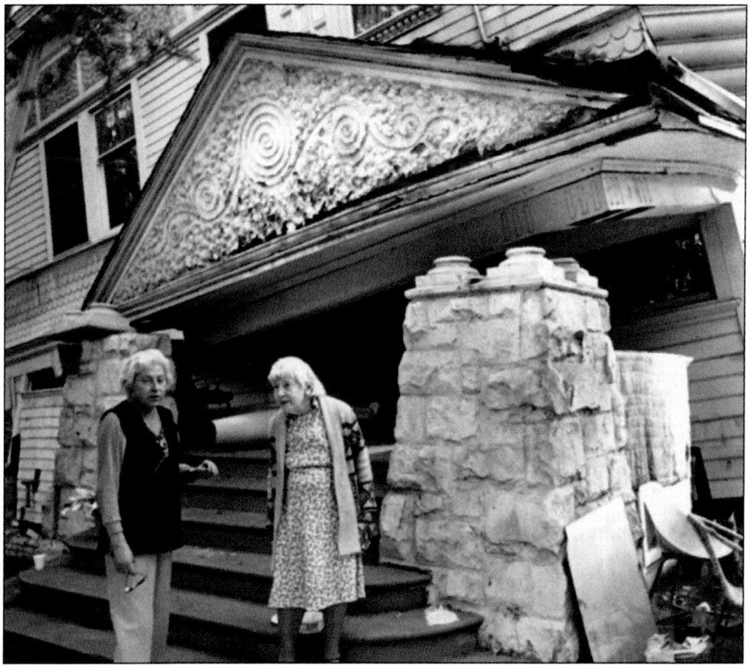

A Plucky Lady. The 1887 Malpas House at 55 Hernandez Avenue was purchased by Rev. Lawrence Taylor (1902–1986) and his wife, Katherine McCurdy (right), in 1947. The home was nearly destroyed during the earthquake when the second floor crashed into the floor below. Katherine had the house restored, but did not live to enjoy it. Her daughter, Lysbet Taylor (left), died in 1997. (LGWT.)

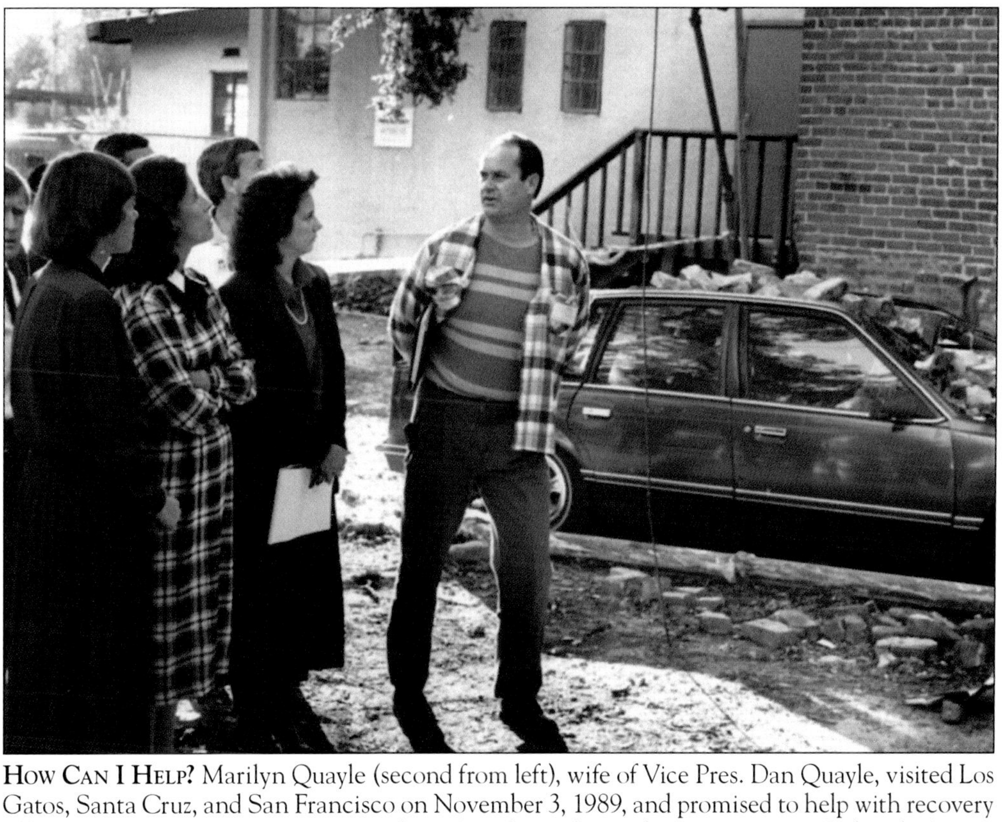

How Can I Help? Marilyn Quayle (second from left), wife of Vice Pres. Dan Quayle, visited Los Gatos, Santa Cruz, and San Francisco on November 3, 1989, and promised to help with recovery efforts. Mayor Joanne Benjamin stands to Quayle's right, and Town Manager Deborah Acosta stands to her left. At center is Scott Baker, the town's Director of Building Services. (LGWT.)

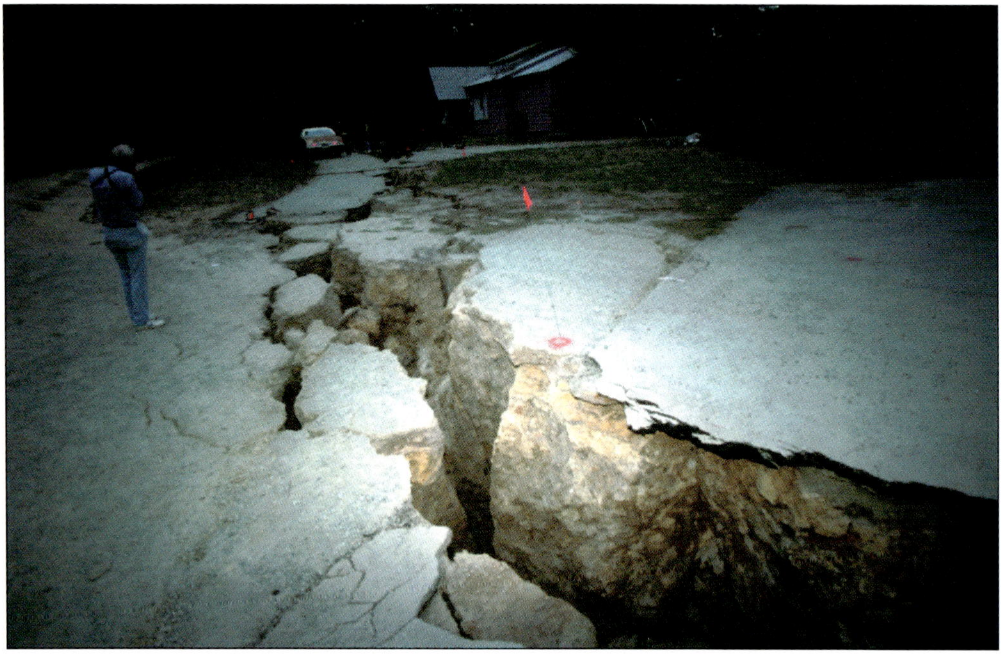

It's Our Fault. Although the earthquake struck about 11 miles below ground, the frightful fissures it produced looked like the stuff of nightmares. John and Freda Tranbarger's house, adjacent to Summit Road and near the epicenter, sat dangerously close to a 70-foot-long crack in the earth that was five feet across and seven feet deep. "It sounded like the end of the world," said John Tranbarger. (USGS.)

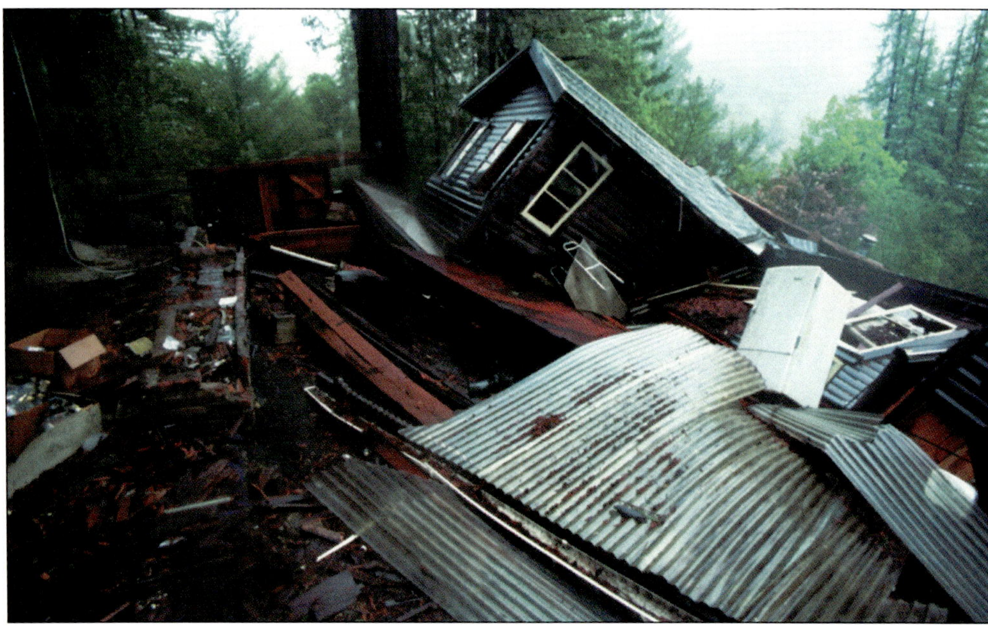

Topsy-Turvy. According to a report from the US Geological Survey, this house in Redwood Grove in the Santa Cruz Mountains was pushed laterally off its cement foundation. The fury of the quake precipitated more than 1,000 landslides and rock falls in the mountains south of town. One slide on Highway 17 disrupted traffic for a month. (USGS.)

Five

Los Gatos Takes the Fast Track

The 1990s

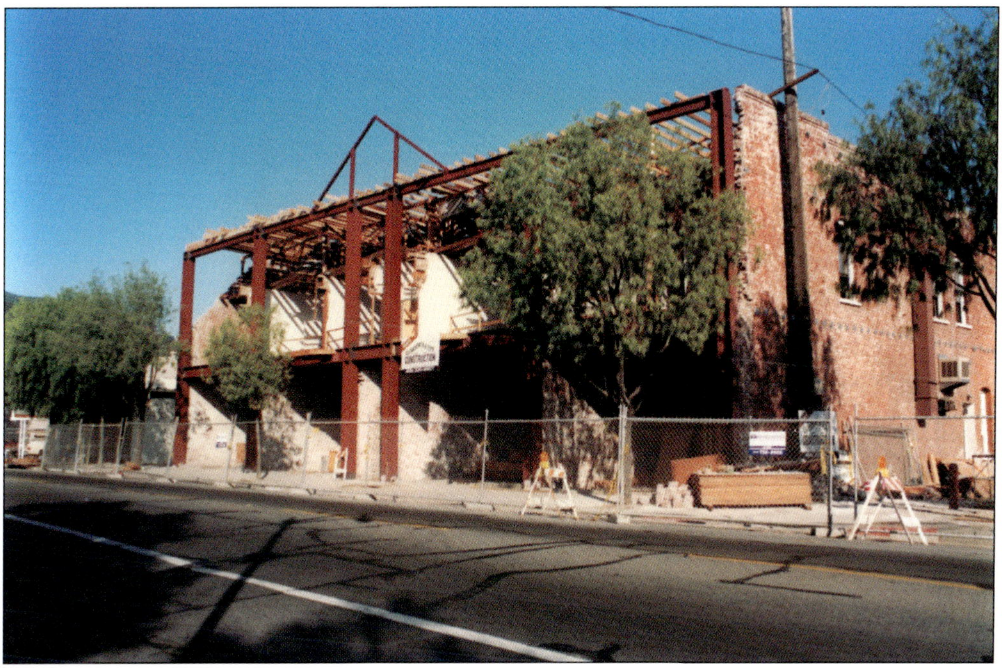

Road to Recovery. Los Gatos was severely shaken by the Loma Prieta earthquake, and hundreds of buildings were badly damaged. Within days of the disaster, the town council met and established policies designed to expedite rebuilding. A fast-track, no-fee process was established for buildings replaced in kind. Great emphasis was placed on restoring rather than demolishing historic buildings, such as the Beckwith Block, pictured here. (Ed Lucey.)

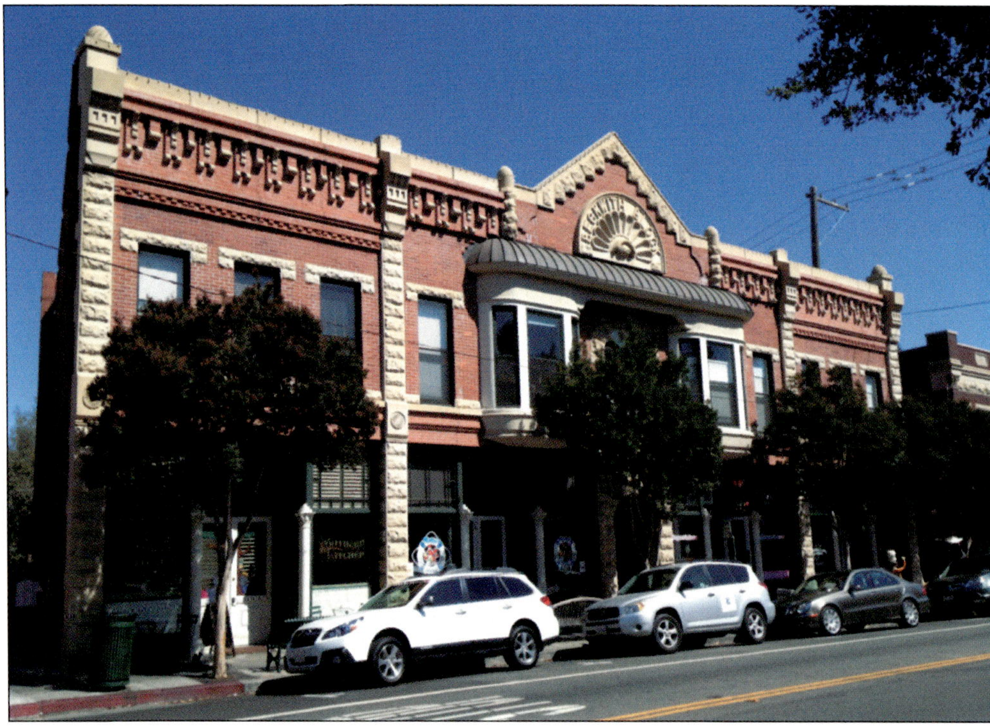

BECKWITH REBUILT. For much of its existence, the formidable Beckwith Block served as the Rex Hotel. When the 1989 earthquake caused the face of the 1893 building to pull away from the rest of the structure, the owner removed the facade, giving passersby a look into what had been bedrooms. After extensive repairs, the building reopened, looking very much as it had when it was first constructed. (BB.)

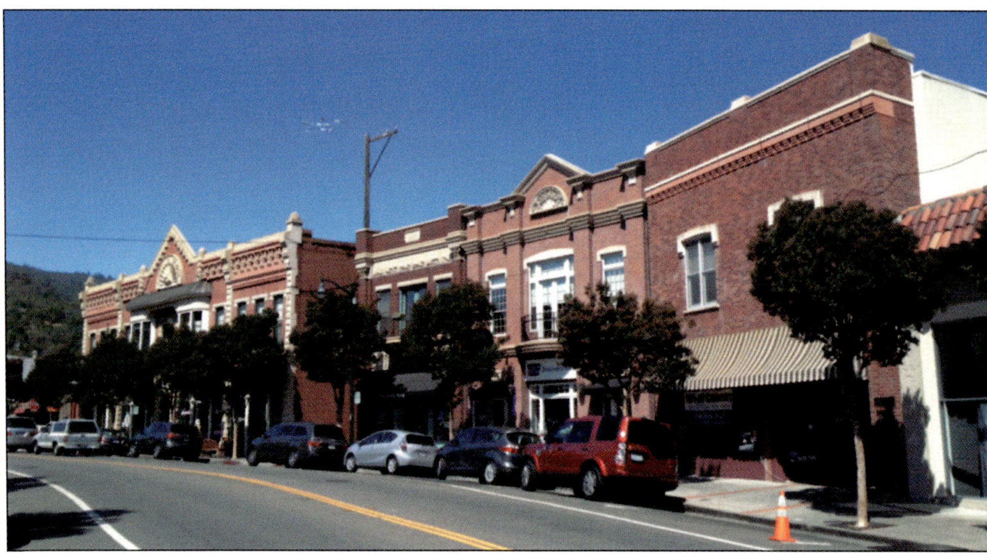

FULL COMPLEMENT. The buildings that had occupied 37–45 East Main Street before the earthquake could not be saved. In their place, three different owners and their architects created the trio of buildings at right. They were constructed over a period of several years in a manner that both echoes the design of the adjacent Beckwith Block and complements the historic downtown area. (BB.)

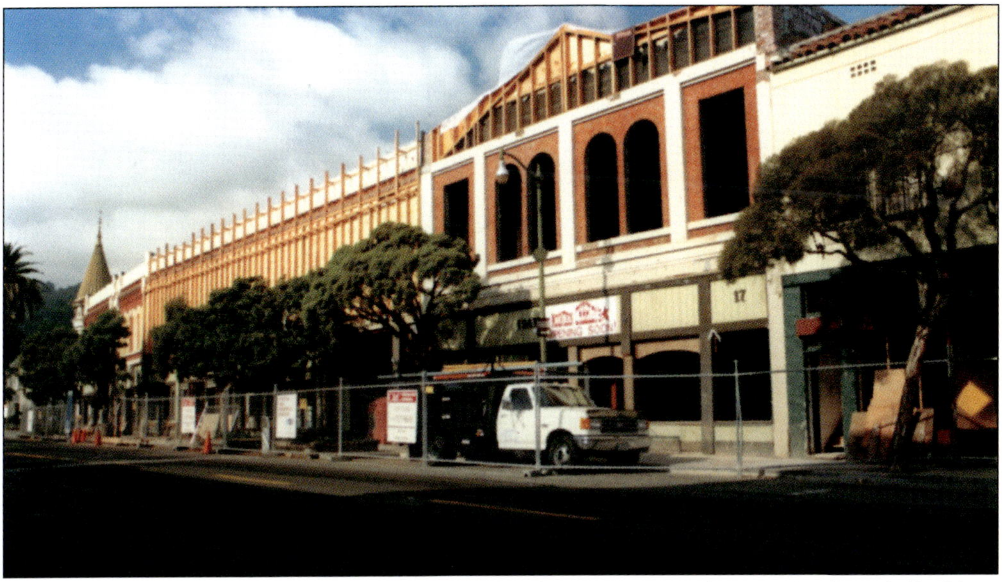

SAVING LA CAÑADA. During the 1906 earthquake, the entrance to the 1894 La Cañada Building was fractured and displaced. In 1989, the venerable building fared even worse. The town's historic centerpiece had to be repaired brick by brick, and it took more than a year to begin to bring the building back to life. The biggest challenge was bringing the structure up to modern building and seismic codes. (Ed Lucey.)

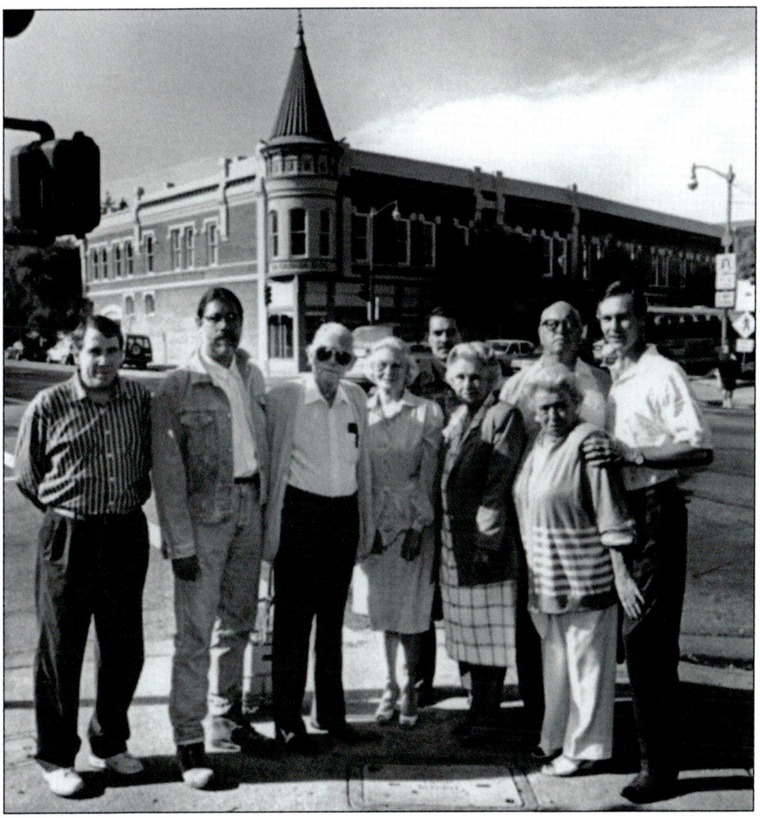

FAMILY HERITAGE. Members of the extended family that owns the La Cañada Building stood in front of the completed project for this 1991 photograph. From left to right are Ed Brady, James A. Bacigalupi Jr., James A. Bacigalupi, Mary Anne Van Dalsem, Jim Brady, Louise Farwell, Jeanne Brady, Dr. Volney Van Dalsem, and Jim Farwell. One of the businesses in the building is the popular Mt. Charley's saloon. (LGWT.)

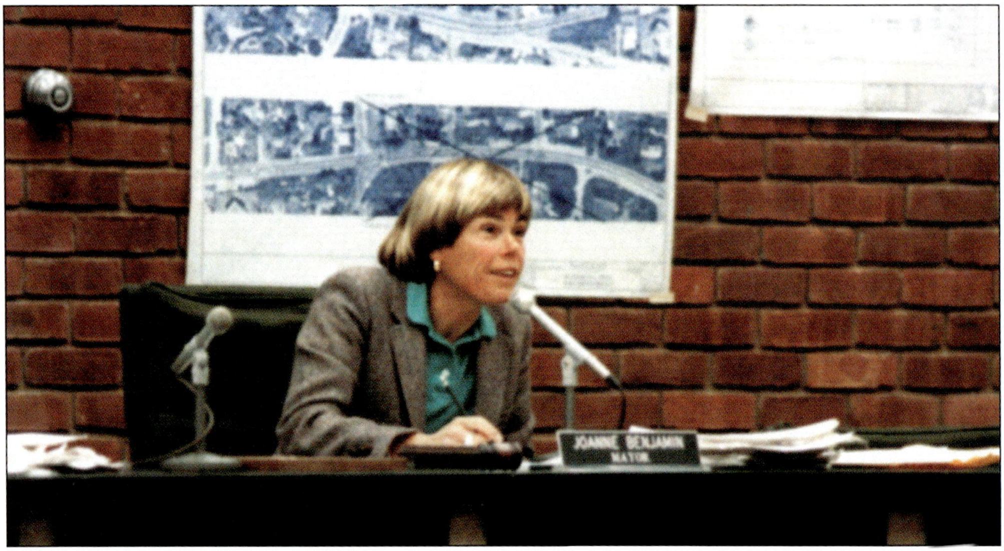

MAYOR JOANNE BENJAMIN. Benjamin served four terms on town council, including four years as mayor. When the earthquake struck, Benjamin worked with staff to set up an emergency center at town hall. Under her leadership, the town council quickly established a road map to dig out from under the devastation and destruction of the earthquake, providing a helpful structure for many people who had suffered losses. (Joanne Benjamin.)

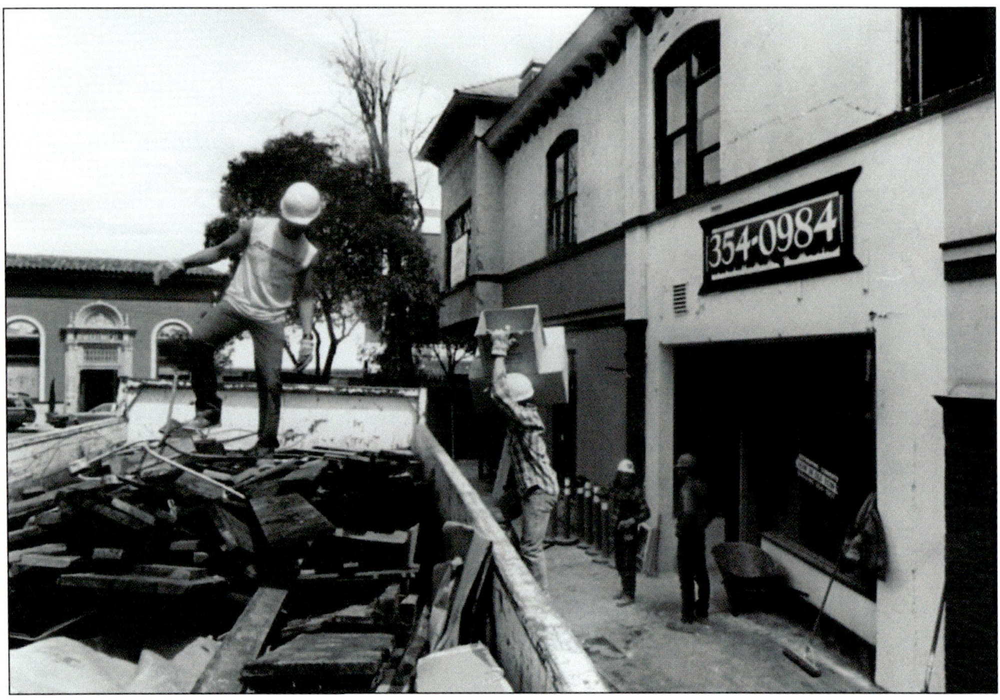

THE RANKIN BLOCK. One of the most challenging decisions in post-earthquake days involved the fate of the severely damaged Rankin Block (right). The building's owner thought it would be most cost-effective to replace it with a new structure, one that replicated its 1904 appearance, but town council members did not want to lose one of the town's historic buildings. A consortium purchased the building and it was repaired. (LGWT.)

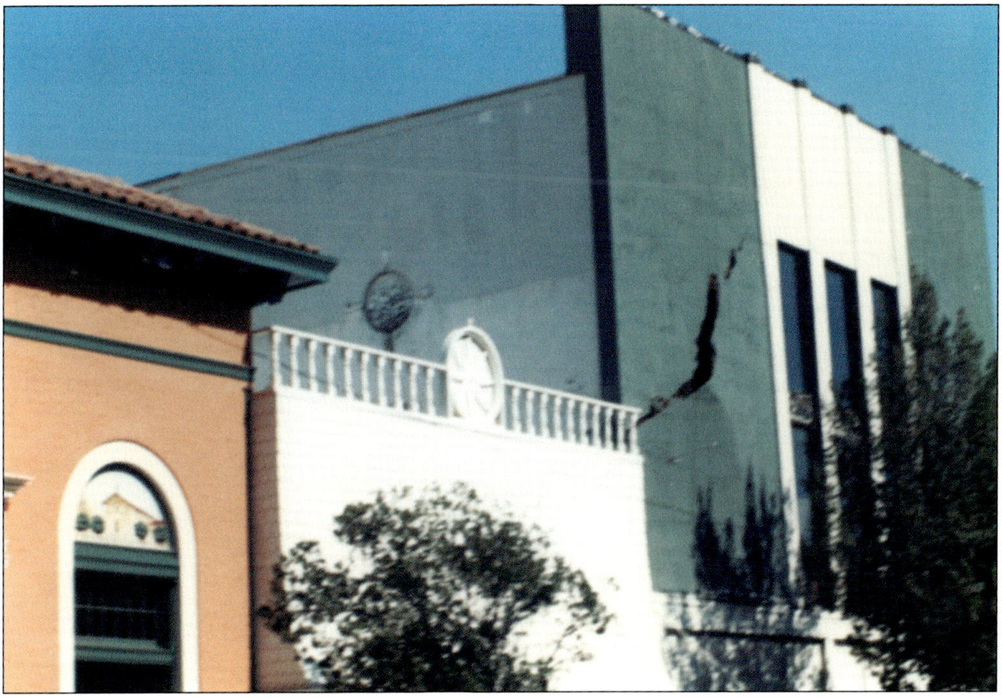

Ford's Opera House. Ford's Opera House was constructed in 1904 with a triangular pediment and decorative balustrade. The elegant building featured pressed metal panels on its high ceilings and upper walls. The structure suffered an unattractive modernization in 1940, when rectangular panels were affixed to its neoclassical facade. Major structural damage in the 1989 earthquake is evidenced by the large crack visible here. (Greg Stepovich.)

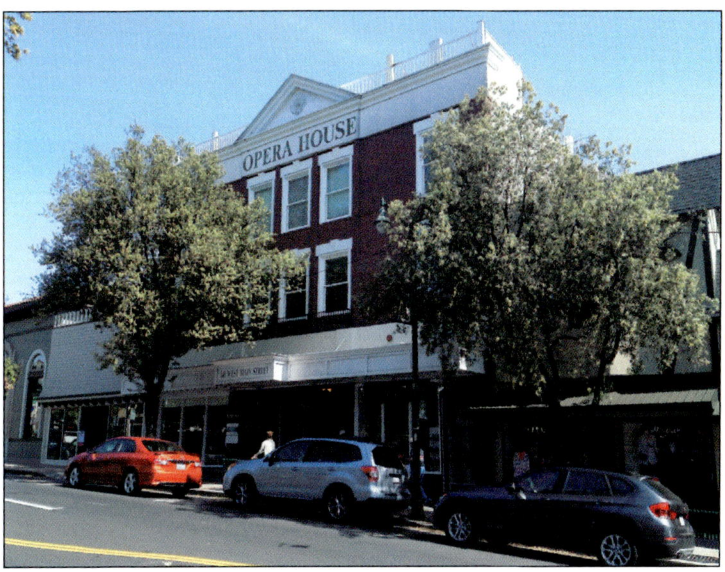

Restoration. In the years following the earthquake, many Los Gatans came to believe that the disaster they had experienced helped bring the town together. Another result was greatly improved viability of many Los Gatos buildings. Today, all of the buildings in downtown have been reinforced with steel rods. Ford's Opera House (pictured) was restored to its original appearance. (BB.)

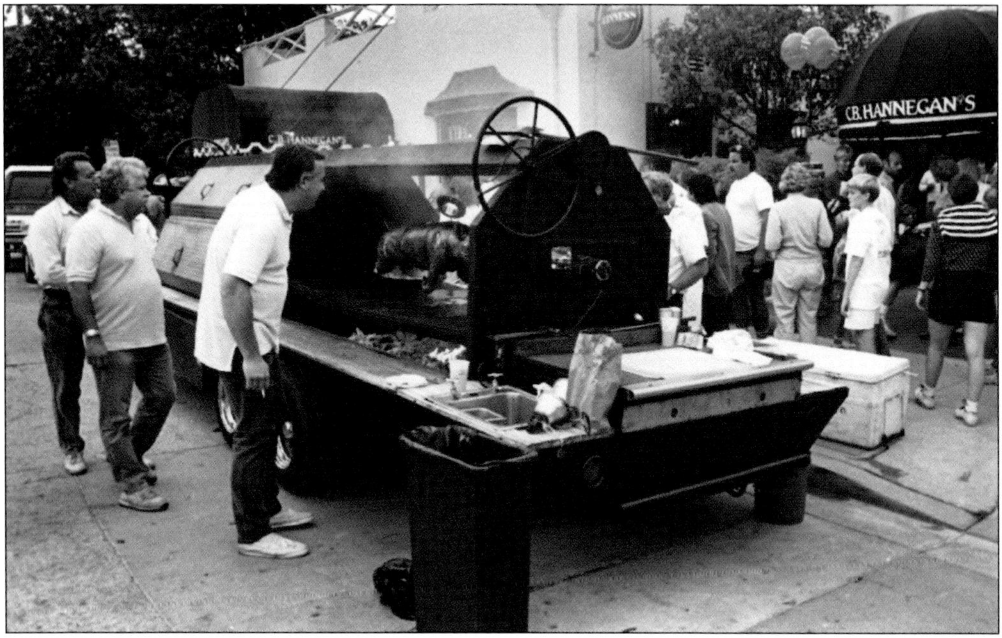

PITCHING IN, HELPING OUT. C.B. Hannegan's Irish pub forever earned the gratitude of Los Gatans by staying open after the Loma Prieta earthquake hit. As one of the few businesses that had power, Hannegan's generously supplied coffee, soft drinks, and sandwiches for many stunned residents. On October 17, 1991, the second anniversary of the temblor, the pub staged an "Earthquake Survival Revival" celebration, pictured here. (LGWT.)

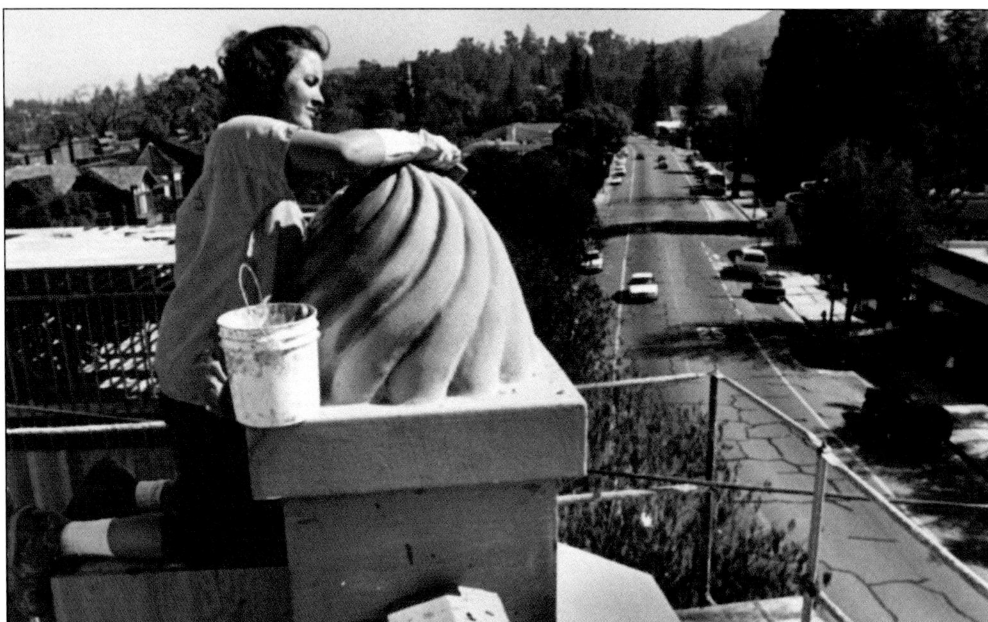

FINISHING TOUCHES. Photographer George Sakkestad climbed to the top of the newly restored Beckwith Block in order to record this image of Catherine Trzybinski working on an architectural element on the roof. Earthquake restoration continued for an extended period of time. (LGWT.)

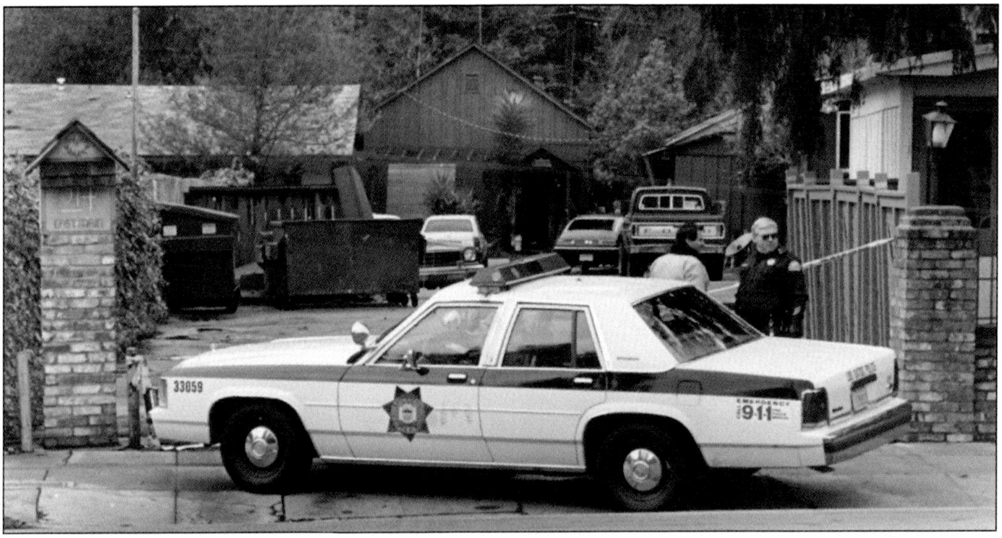

TOBY'S MOTOR INN. Twelve people were arrested on March 15, 1991, in a drug sweep at a dilapidated 25-unit complex, built as a vacation motel in the 1930s, at 214 East Main Street. Charges ranged from possession of drugs and drug paraphernalia to being under the influence of a controlled substance. Diane Ogilvie, who owned the property, opened her Hotel Los Gatos on this site in 2002. (LGWT.)

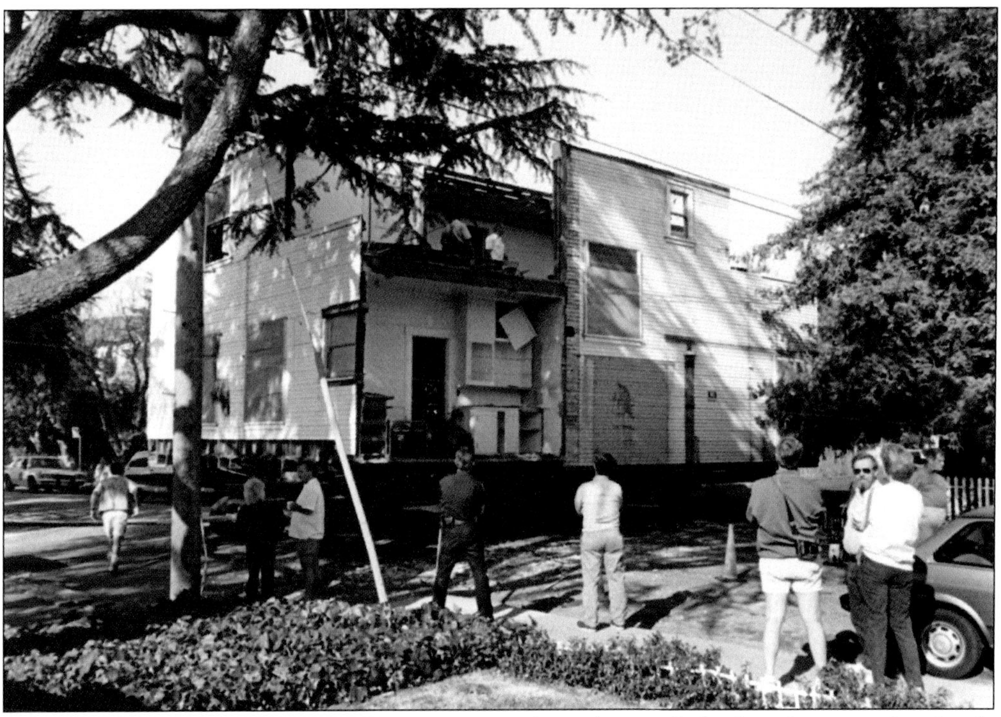

MARIA'S BERRY FARMHOUSE. Maria Kern encouraged people to pick the fruit that grew abundantly on her property. In 1987, ill health forced her to sell her land to the California Department of Transportation. Before Highway 85 was built through the center of her farm, the town rescued her buildings by declaring them historic landmarks. In 1992, the old farmhouse was moved to Miles Avenue to house the Parks and Public Works Department. (LGWT.)

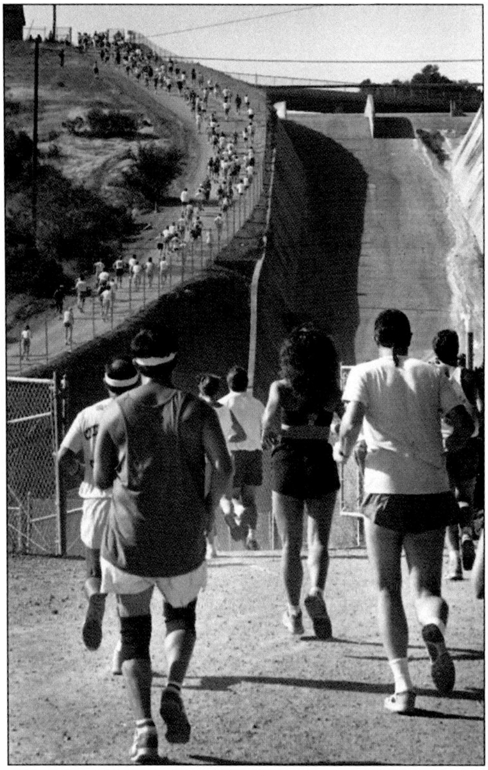

The Dammit Run. For 40 years, runners have gathered at Los Gatos High School, taken a lap around the track, and then started on a rugged and challenging course up to Lexington Dam and back. In this August 1992 photograph, they are shown running up to the reservoir. The Lexington Dam spillway (at right) is dry. (LGWT.)

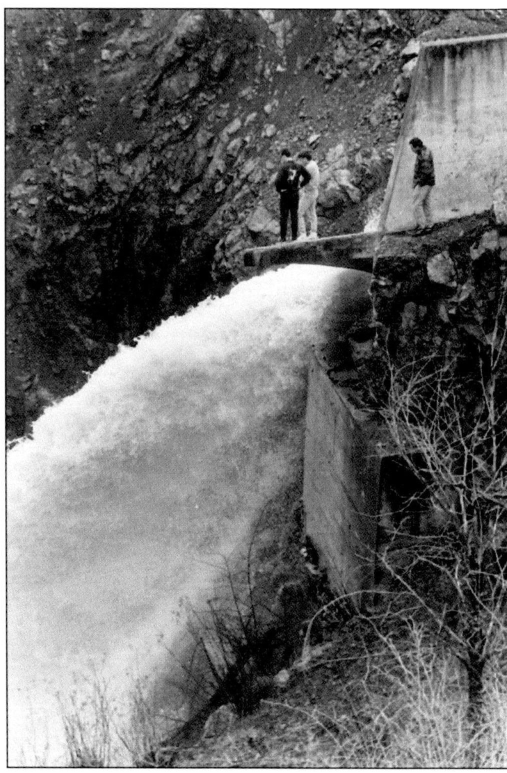

Overflow! In 1993, Los Gatos experienced its wettest January in a quarter-century. Rain, sometimes torrential, fell for 14 days in a row, beginning to scuttle a seven-year drought. The rain continued in February, causing water to cascade over the Lexington Dam spillway for the first time since 1986. Thousands of people showed up to watch. Mandatory water rationing ended. (LGWT.)

VILLA TUSCULUM. Pat O'Laughlin and his wife, Maggie Kilkenny, are pictured with their children in front of their stately Queen Anne–style home at 54 Chestnut Street. The house was built of redwood in 1894 by C.M. Meriam. The tower, originally taller, toppled in the 1906 earthquake. The owners had completed two years of renovations and repairs after the 1989 earthquake when this photograph was taken in 1992. (LGWT.)

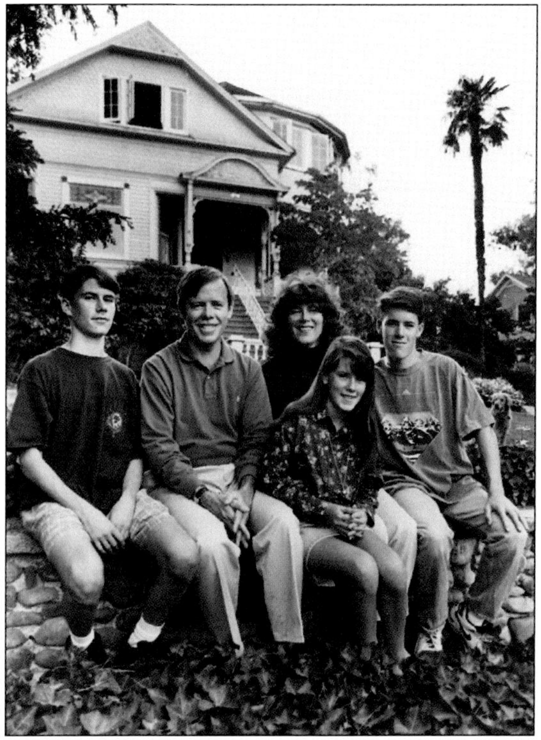

KENNY LOGGINS AT LGHS. Singer-songwriter Kenny Loggins stopped by Los Gatos High School on September 17, 1992, sat on the front steps, and taped a public service announcement on behalf of public education. Loggins was in town for a five-night run at the Paul Mason Mountain Winery. Loggins, a generous fundraiser for numerous charities, held a show the previous evening that benefitted the Crippled Children's Society. (LGWT.)

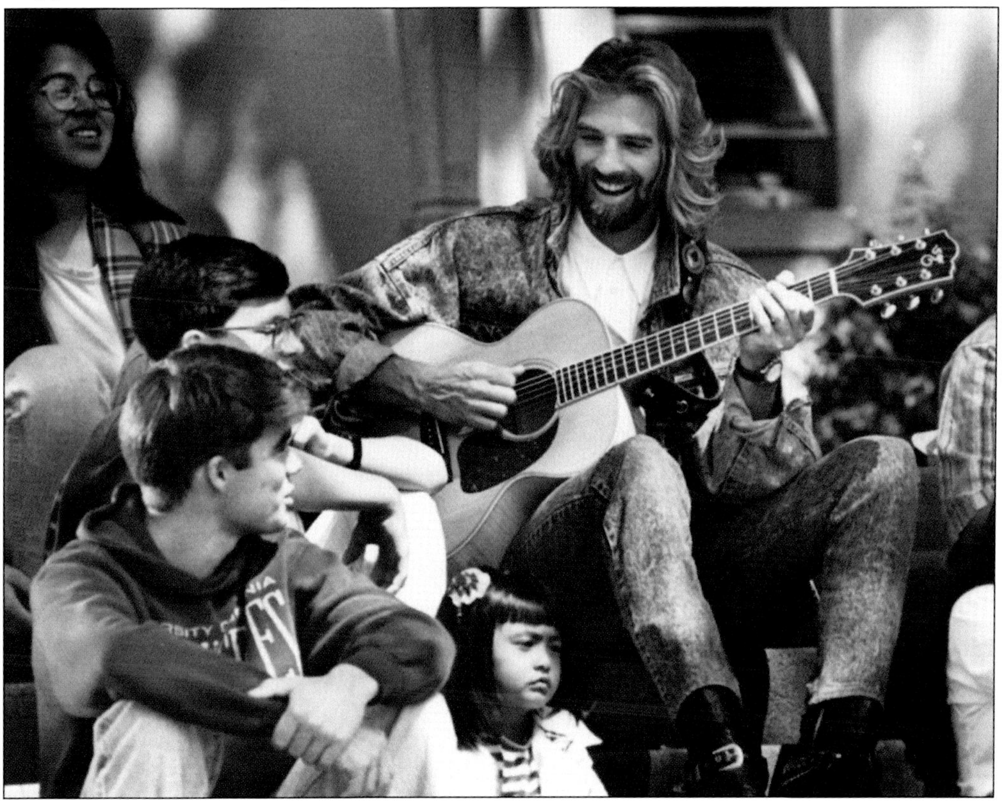

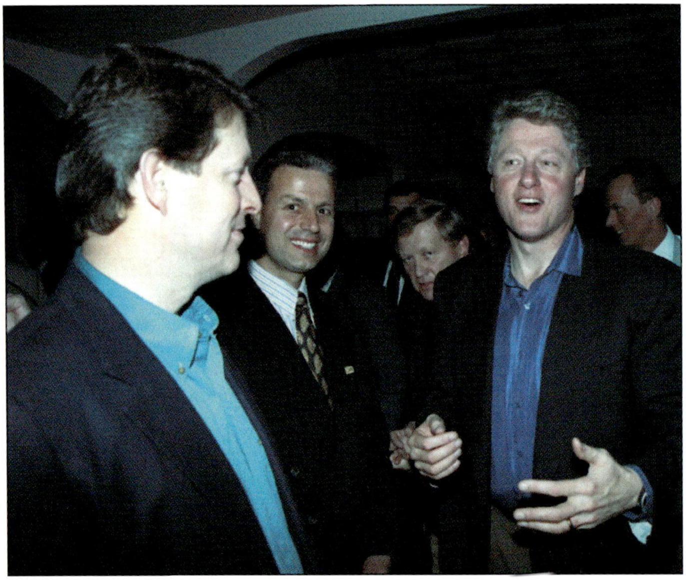

Dinner Guests. When Pres. Bill Clinton and Vice Pres. Al Gore (left) came to dinner at the California Café in Old Town on February 21, 1993, the *San Jose Mercury News* called it a "technology love-fest." The charismatic president and tech-savvy vice president came to commune with Silicon Valley leadership. Adoring fans waited in the chilly night air outside the restaurant to catch a glimpse of the president. (William J. Clinton Presidential Library.)

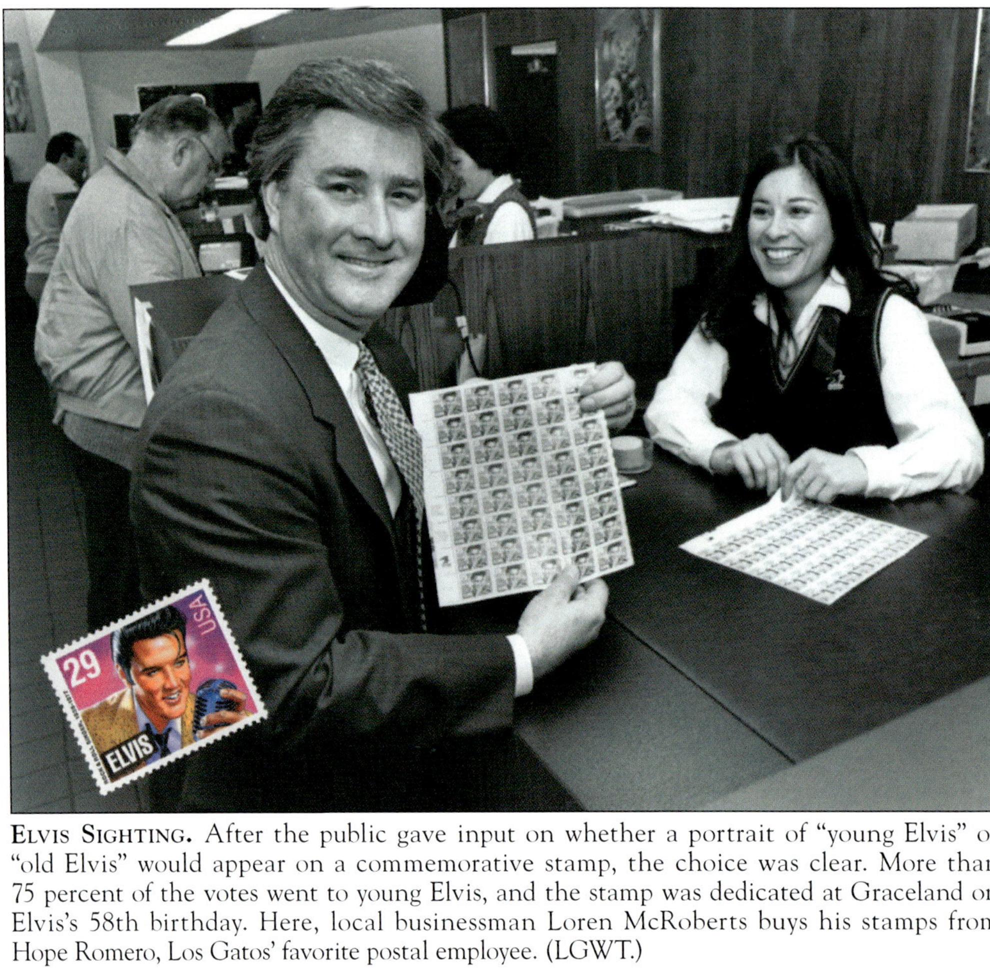

Elvis Sighting. After the public gave input on whether a portrait of "young Elvis" or "old Elvis" would appear on a commemorative stamp, the choice was clear. More than 75 percent of the votes went to young Elvis, and the stamp was dedicated at Graceland on Elvis's 58th birthday. Here, local businessman Loren McRoberts buys his stamps from Hope Romero, Los Gatos' favorite postal employee. (LGWT.)

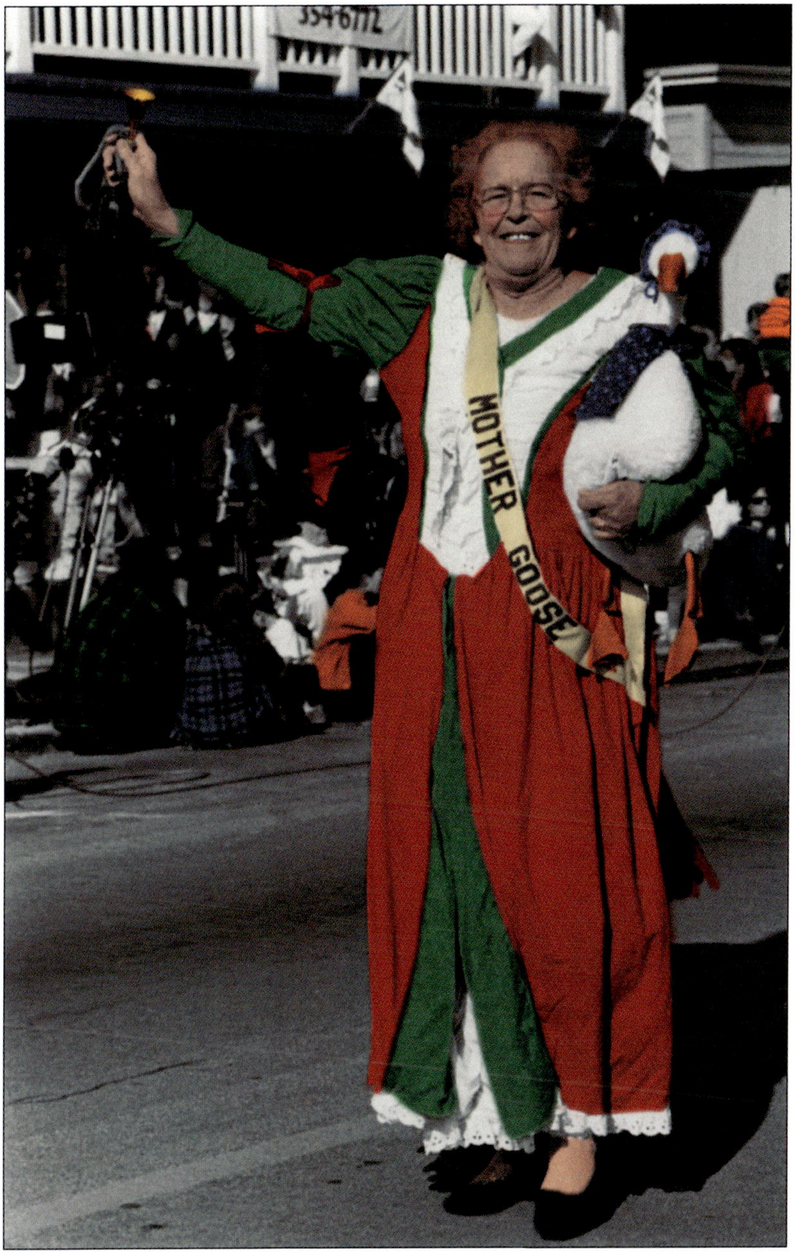

CHILDREN'S CHRISTMAS AND HOLIDAYS PARADE. Los Gatos traditionally celebrates the holidays with two memorable events. On the first Saturday in December, thousands of participants step off from the corner of Almendra and North Santa Cruz Avenues and march to the Civic Center. Thousands more line sidewalks along the way to enjoy the parade that was first organized in 1956. The Lions Club takes major responsibility for the event. The night before the parade, the town turns out to see the lighting of the 1923 Christmas tree. Mary Bryant Foster (1926–1998) is shown walking in the 1993 holiday parade. She is fondly remembered for her enthusiastic support of Los Gatos activities and more than 40 years of volunteerism. Her legacy includes videotaped interviews of 100 longtime Los Gatans, an archival treasure she produced for the History Museum of Los Gatos and KCAT television. (LGWT.)

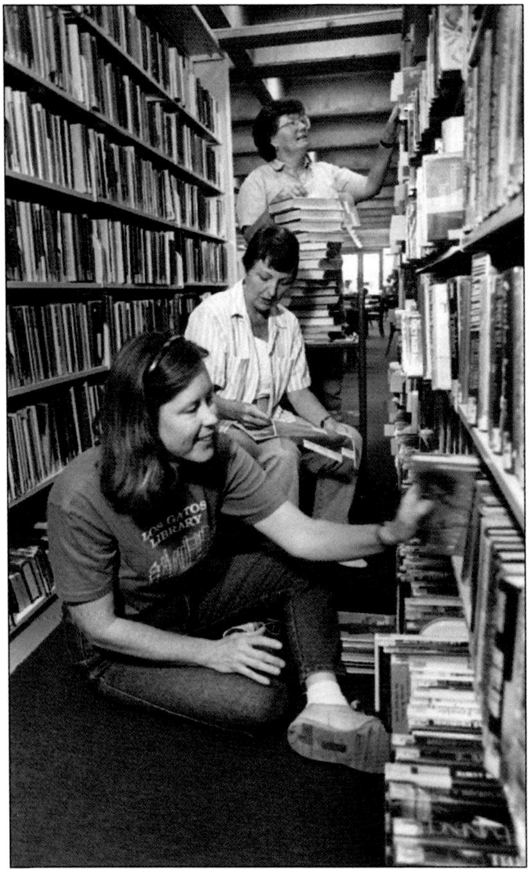

ONLINE PUBLIC ACCESS CATALOG. After almost 100 years of keeping its inventory in large ledger books or on small catalog cards, Los Gatos Public Library went digital in 1993. In order to make the transition, a bar code had to be affixed to each of thousands of volumes. Pictured here working on the task are staff members Judy Coughlin (left) and Jan Robinson (center) and volunteer Cheryl Huddleston. (LGWT.)

THE NEW OLD TOLL HOUSE. When the historic 1867 Toll House disappeared on December 31, 1993, town officials received a flurry of calls from history-conscious citizens, who feared the structure had been bulldozed. The small, sagging house had, in fact, been disassembled and its pieces saved for reassembly after a new foundation was built in the summer of 1994. Brian Leonardis is shown putting it back together again. (LGWT.)

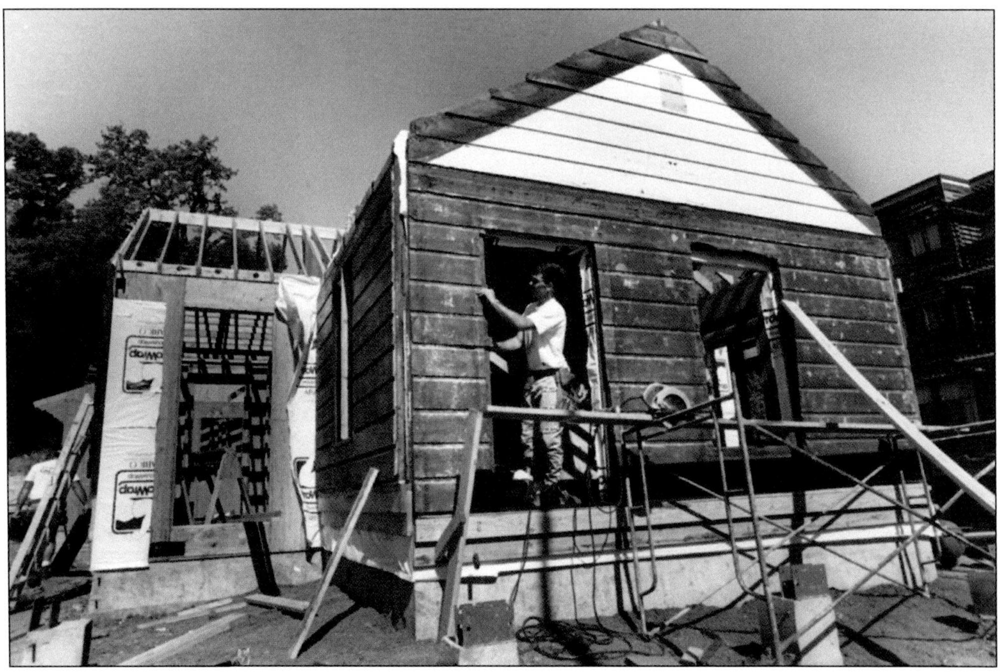

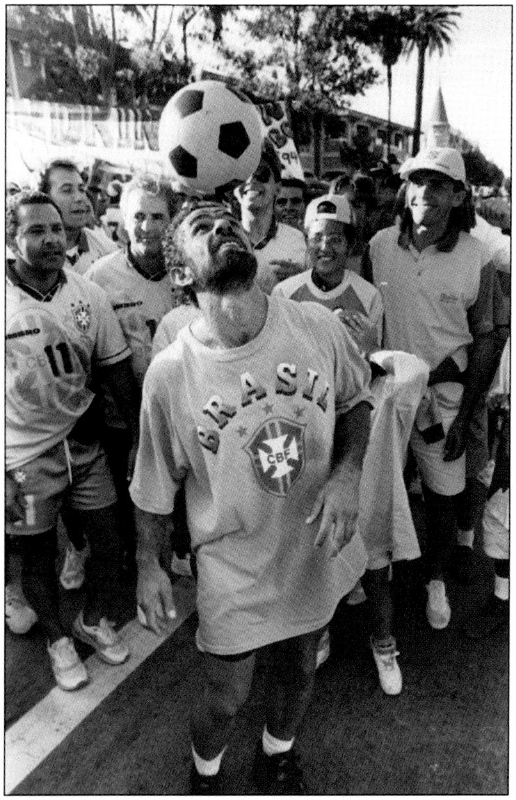

F*UTEBOL*. When Mayor Randy Attaway learned that the Brazilian National Soccer Team would be housed at Villa Felice Lodge on Winchester Boulevard in the summer of 1994 while competing for the Gold Cup, he decided to roll out the red carpet. Brazil beat the United States in a preliminary game on the Fourth of July, but Los Gatans turned out in droves to party with their guests on the streets of town. (LGWT.)

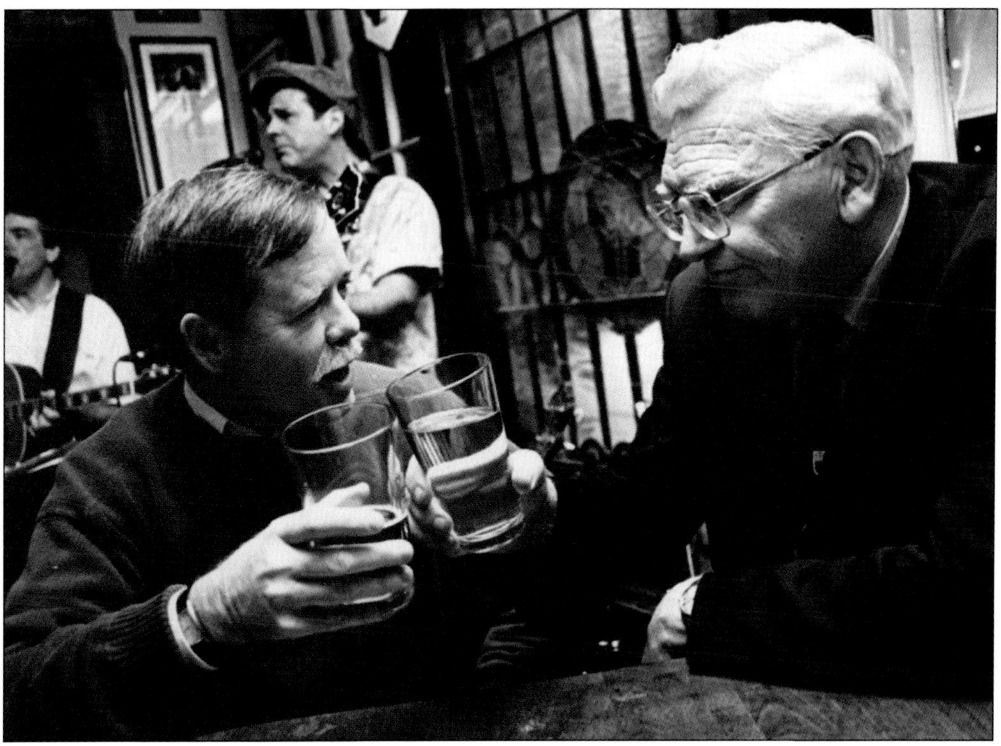

SLÁINTE! Pat O'Laughlin (left) was mayor of Los Gatos in March 1995, when he and Frank Feely, city manager of Dublin, Ireland, drank to mutual good health at C.B. Hannegan's. O'Laughlin was a popular local attorney and town council member who is largely credited with developing a sister-city relationship with Listowel, the "literary capital of Ireland." Sadly, O'Laughlin died in 2008 after a long illness. (LGWT.)

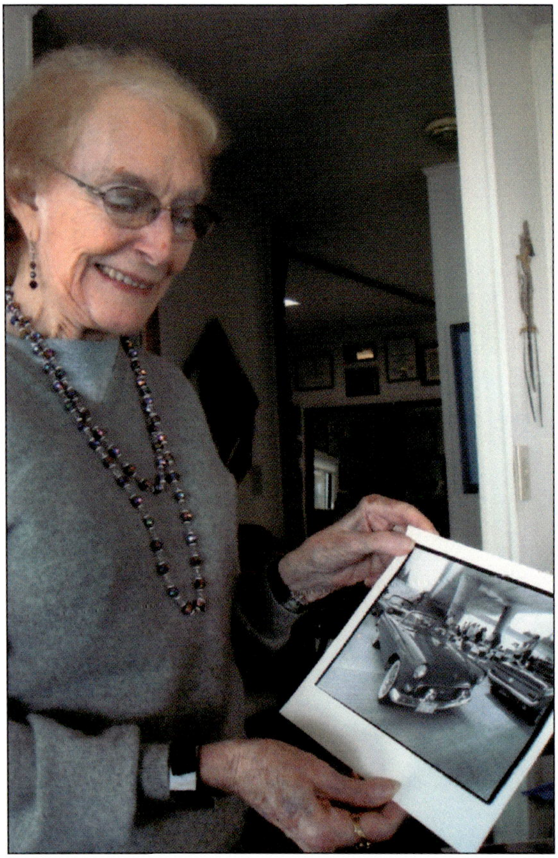

MOTHER OF HIGHWAY 85. Mardi Gualtieri Bennett Brick, Los Gatos town councilwoman from 1976 to 1980, served as mayor from 1978 to 1979. As chairwoman of the West Valley Mayors and Managers Committee, she founded the West Valley Multimodal Transportation Corridor Task Force to lobby for Highway 85, a badly needed east-west crosstown route for Santa Clara Valley. At left, she admires a photograph taken on October 19, 1994, when a new section of the highway from Almaden Expressway to Mountain View was about to open. Celebrations sprang up at every on-ramp along the way. The former mayor also founded the Los Gatos Preservation Society, established the Project Bell-Ringer Awards, preserved Forbes Mill, helped establish the History Museum of Los Gatos, wrote a newspaper column, published several books, founded her own consulting company, and served as president of the Santa Clara County Medical Auxiliary. (Left, AC; below, LGWT.)

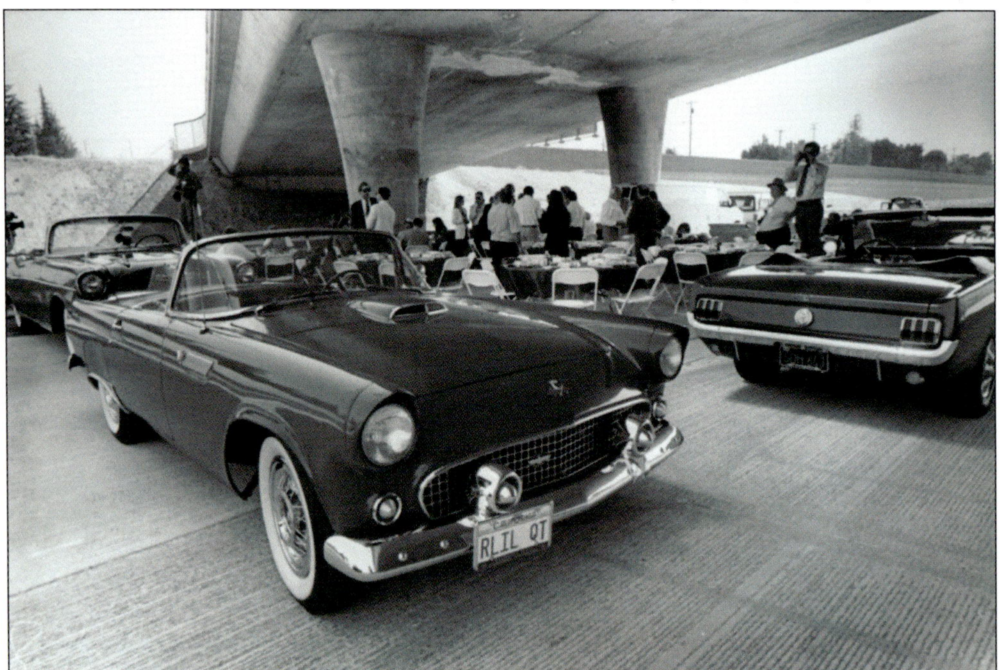

OMINOUS. On the sweltering afternoon of August 7, 1997, a plume of black smoke rose over town. "The Cats Fire" was witnessed by Janice Corbo and Larry Heard, who were sitting curbside on Santa Cruz Avenue. Hundreds of others filled the town plaza and lined the Highway 17 overpass to view the drama in the hillsides above. Fifty fire engines and 200 firefighters were deployed, and a fleet of water-toting airplanes and helicopters roared overhead. The fire was controlled by evening, but six homes were gutted. (LGWT.)

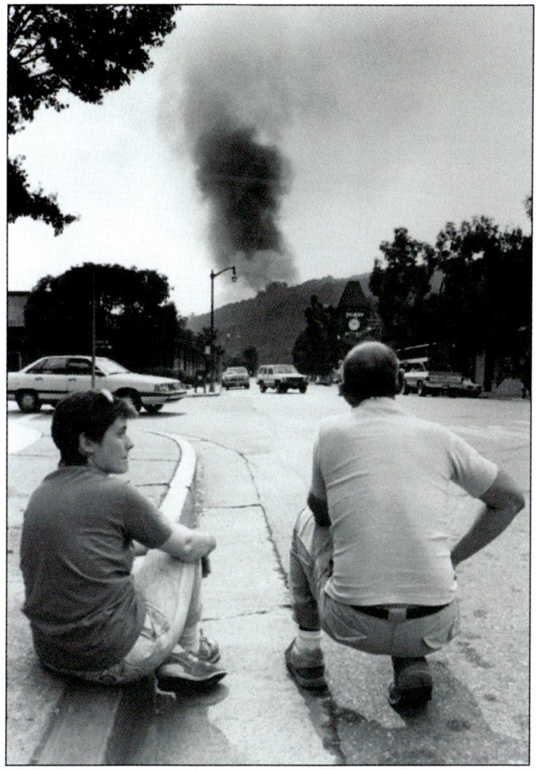

A TOUCH OF OLD LOS GATOS. Author Ruth Comfort Mitchell built a house, completed in 1917, high on Cypress Way with Chinese-inspired motifs. She and her husband, Sanborn Young, named it "Yung See San Fong," or "Young's House in the Heart of the Hills." The view from the home, purchased by Scotty Amende McEwen in 1975, stretches from San Jose to San Francisco. (BB.)

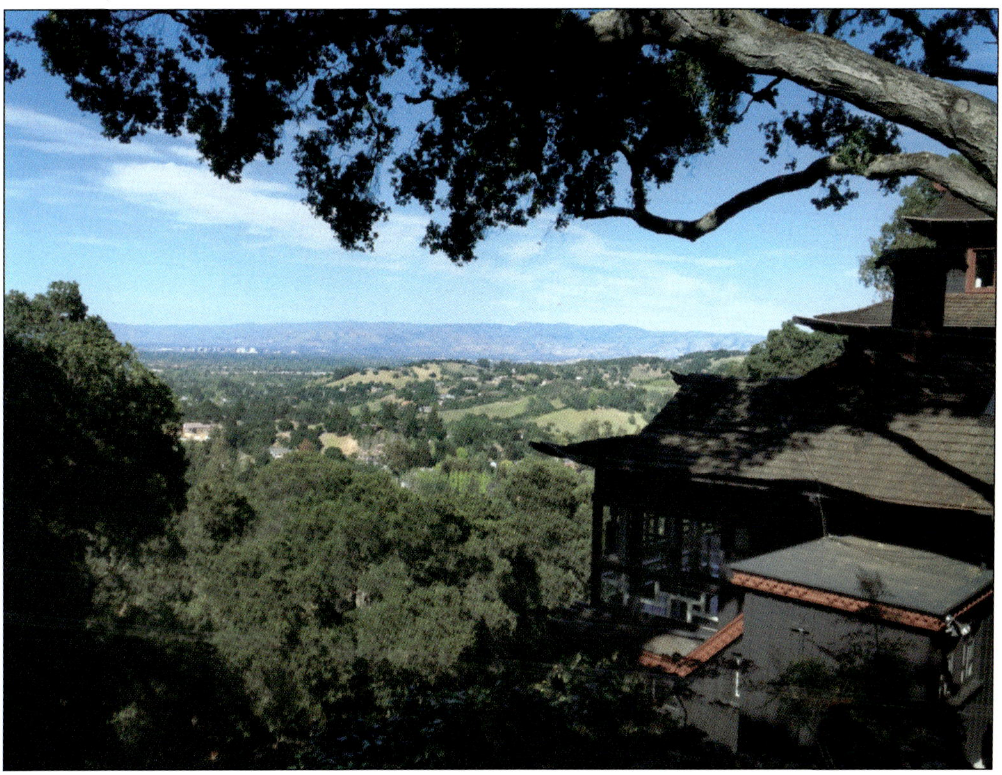

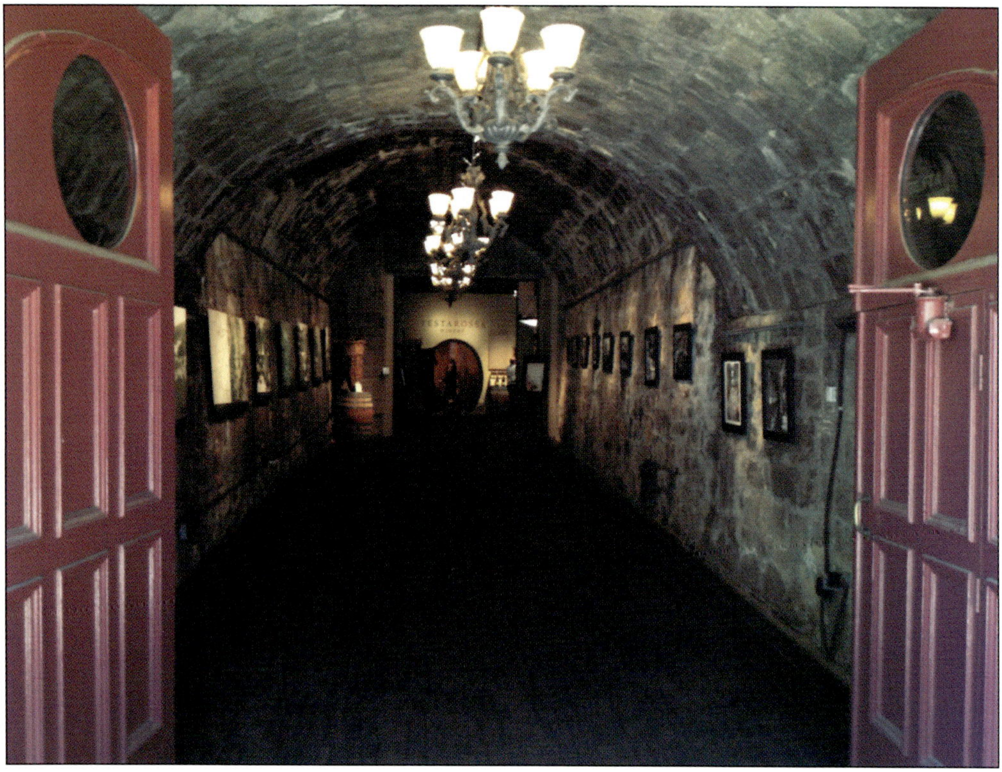

Testarossa Winery. While it is not unusual in Silicon Valley for two electrical engineers to invent something great in their garage, Rob and Diana Jensen are unique. Their weekend garage project in 1993 was so successful that it evolved into a state-of-the art winery, housed at the historic Novitiate in the hills above Los Gatos. The cave pictured here is the entrance to the tasting room. (BB.)

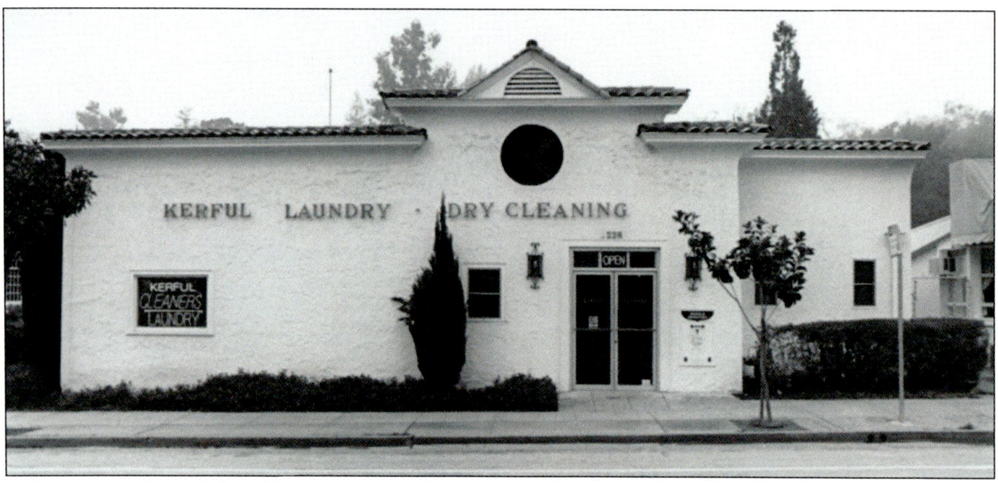

Kerful Laundry. This building at 226 East Main Street was constructed around 1900 as the Dashaway Stables, a good place to trade a horse or have its teeth attended to. From 1946 to 1990, James Stoops operated his Kerful Laundry here. Stoops, the town treasurer, managed the town's finances out of the laundry, using one telephone. This building was razed in 2000 to make way for Hotel Los Gatos. (LGWT.)

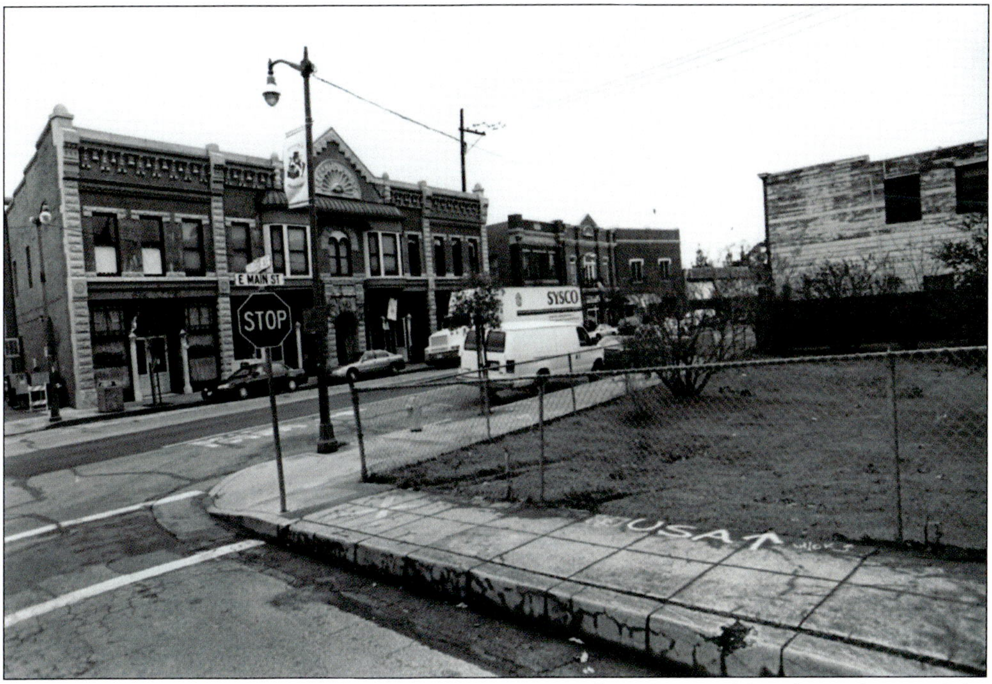

Prime Real Estate. This vacant lot on Main Street at College Avenue (above) was the site of the Los Gatos Hotel & Saloon until it suffered fire damage in 1968. The land, owned by the Puccinelli family, sat empty for 30 years. The family home and the hotel's old carriage house, later the Los Gatos Soda Works bottling plant in the 1920s, sat on the uphill portion of the parcel. Developer Dave Flick saved as much original material as possible from both buildings, including the original "Soda Works" sign, before the structures were bulldozed in 1997 to make way for the Soda Works Plaza, completed by Flick in 1998 (below). Both the house and the Soda Works building were replicated for retail use. At right in the above photograph, the 1881 wooden building, formally the Buffalo Trading Post, was also demolished in 1997. (Above, LGWT; below, BB.)

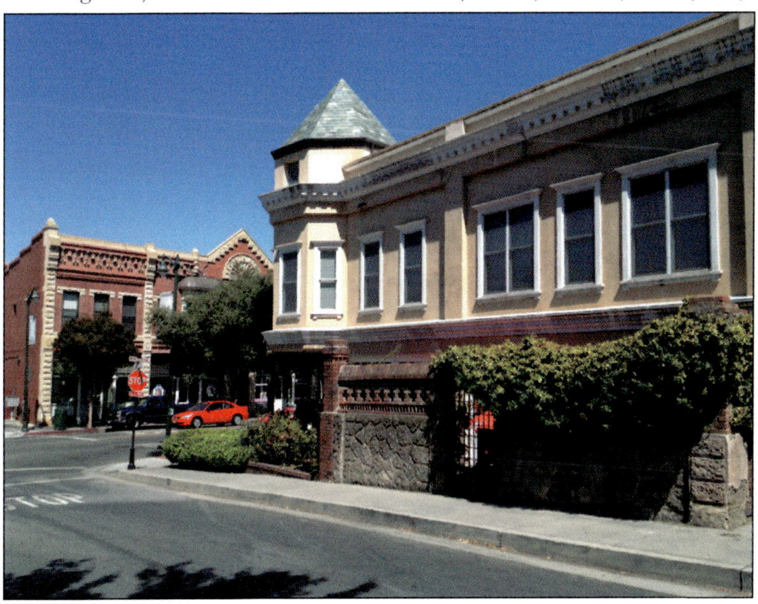

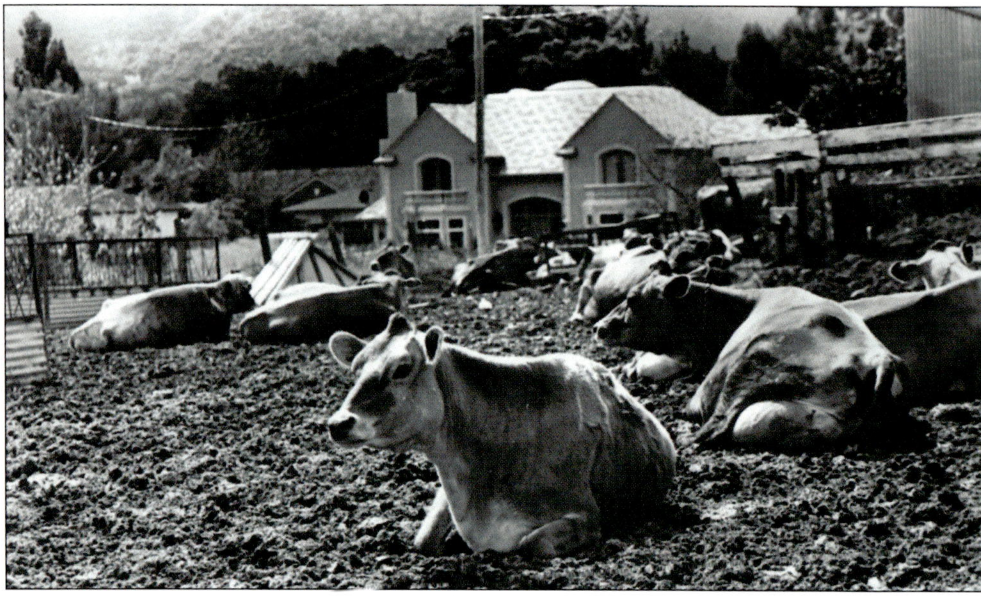

Moo-ve Over! Claravale Dairy's contented cows seem oblivious to encroaching housing in this 1998 photograph, but the times were quickly changing. Kenneth Peake provided unpasteurized milk to area families for 67 years, starting when he moved to his property on Bicknell Avenue in unincorporated Los Gatos in 1931. He sold his farm about a year before he died in 1999 at age 91. (LGWT.)

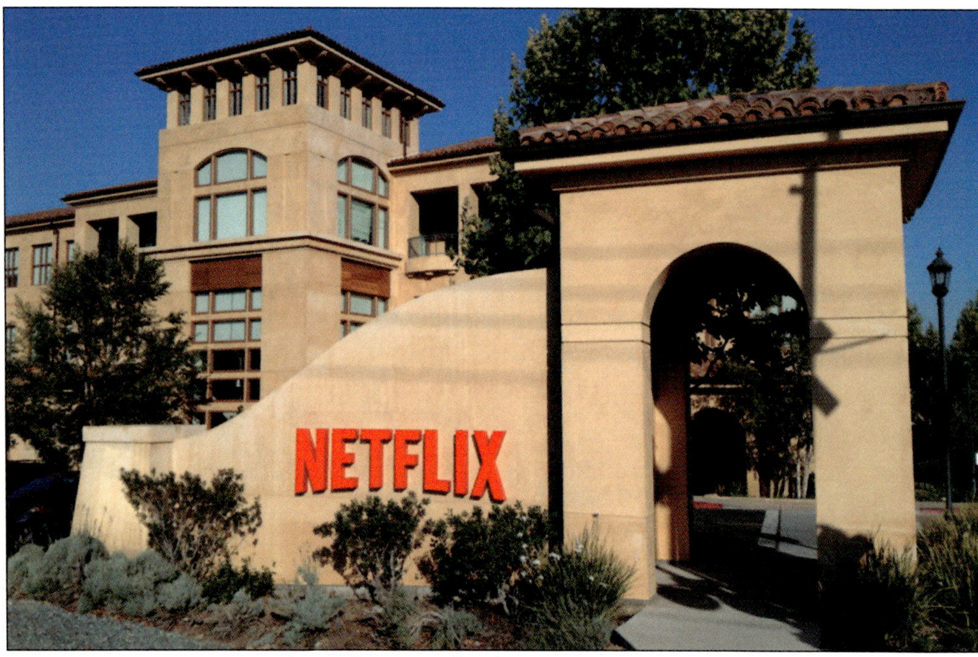

Successful Venture. Math teacher-turned-software tycoon Reed Hastings conceived the idea of Netflix after he rented a VHS tape, misplaced it, and owed a $40 late fee. He decided to offer a new technology, DVDs, delivered by mail. Netflix was established in 1997 and is headquartered in Los Gatos. Now, with about 50 million global subscribers and the addition of streaming video-on-demand, Netflix is a real dot.com success story. (BB.)

Six

The New Millennium
The 2000s and Beyond

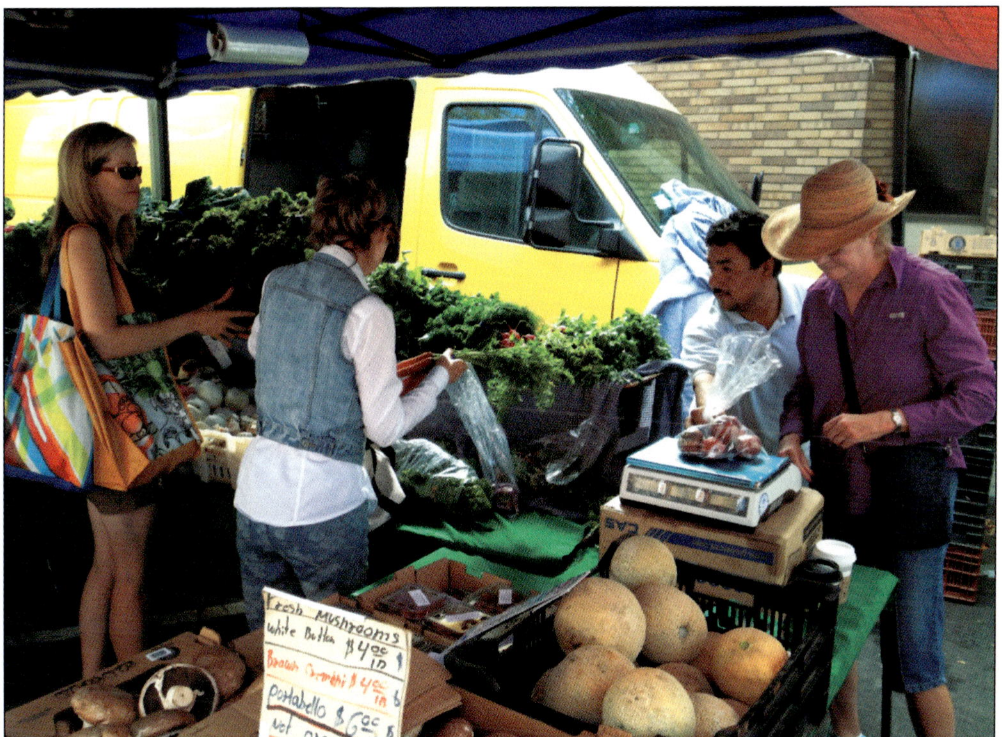

Farmers' Market. Fruit-raising was the prime industry in the Los Gatos area from about 1870 until 1950. The marvelously fertile soil and absence of extreme temperatures resulted in abundant crops. The produce that was grown in the Valley of Heart's Delight is represented every Sunday at the Farmers' Market on Montebello Way. (BB.)

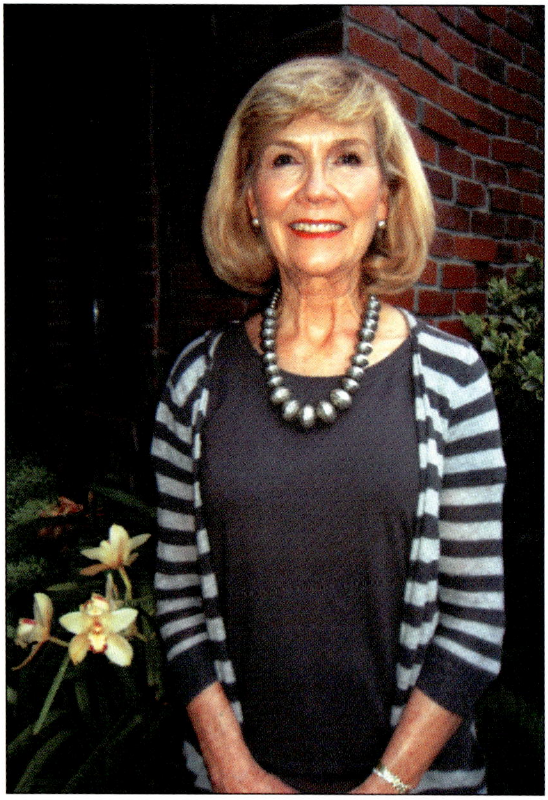

Making a Difference. Joanne Rodgers is a visionary leader who is wholly committed to the safety and success of young people. She is the cofounder of both CASA (Community Against Substance Abuse), established in 1984, and the New Millennium Foundation, which has raised millions of dollars to enhance the education of every student at Los Gatos High School. In addition she has facilitated parenting classes for thirty years. (Joanne Rodgers.)

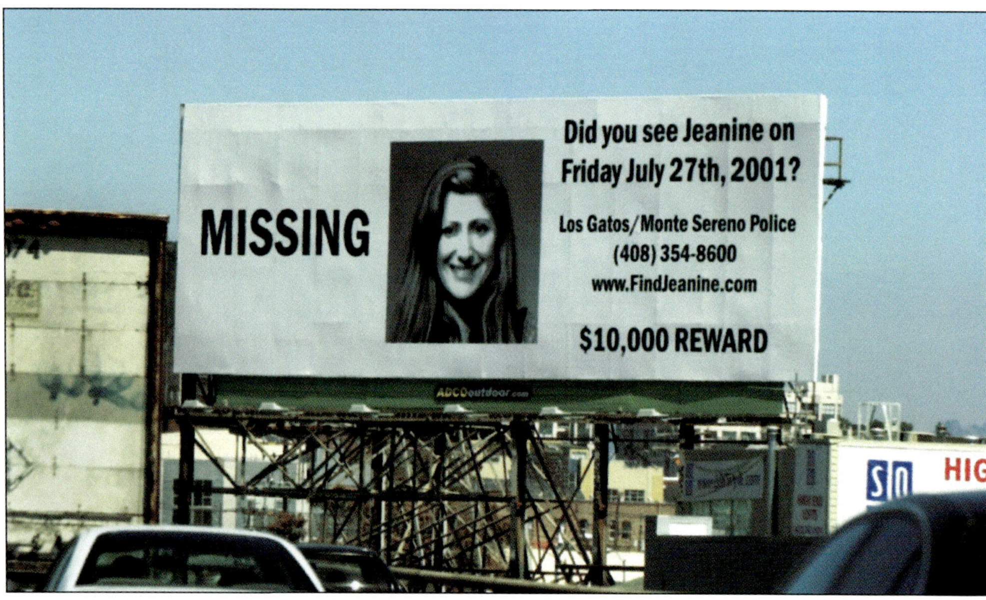

Touched by Tragedy. Several murders have jarred the town in recent years. Jeanine Harms of Los Gatos, 42, vanished July 27, 2001. Harms' suspected murderer was later shot and killed by her brother, who then killed himself. Another high profile homicide involved local businessman Mark Achilli, 53, shot to death on March 14, 2008, outside his condominium in a love-triangle, murder-for-hire case. (Darryl Bush/*San Francisco Chronicle*/Polaris.)

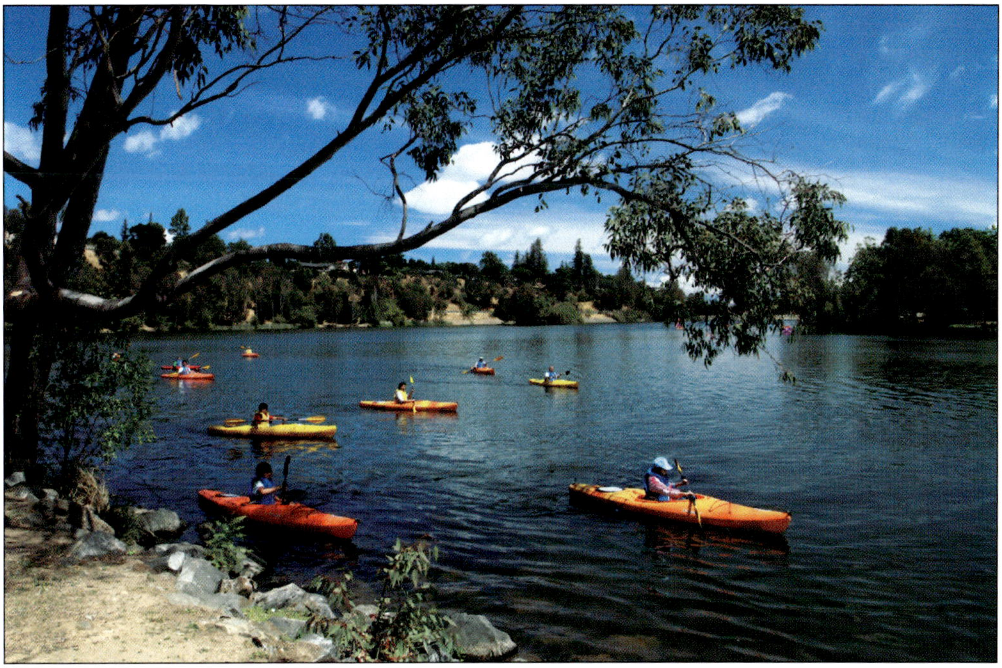

Parks and Recreation. Los Gatos is fortunate to have beautiful neighborhood parks as well as two larger adjacent parks, Oak Meadow and Vasona. People come from around the area to rent kayaks and sailboats and to hike, bike, picnic, and stroll through nature. Kids can climb on a real Air Force jet, ride on a historic carousel, and experience a one-third-scale steam train. (Ron Horii.)

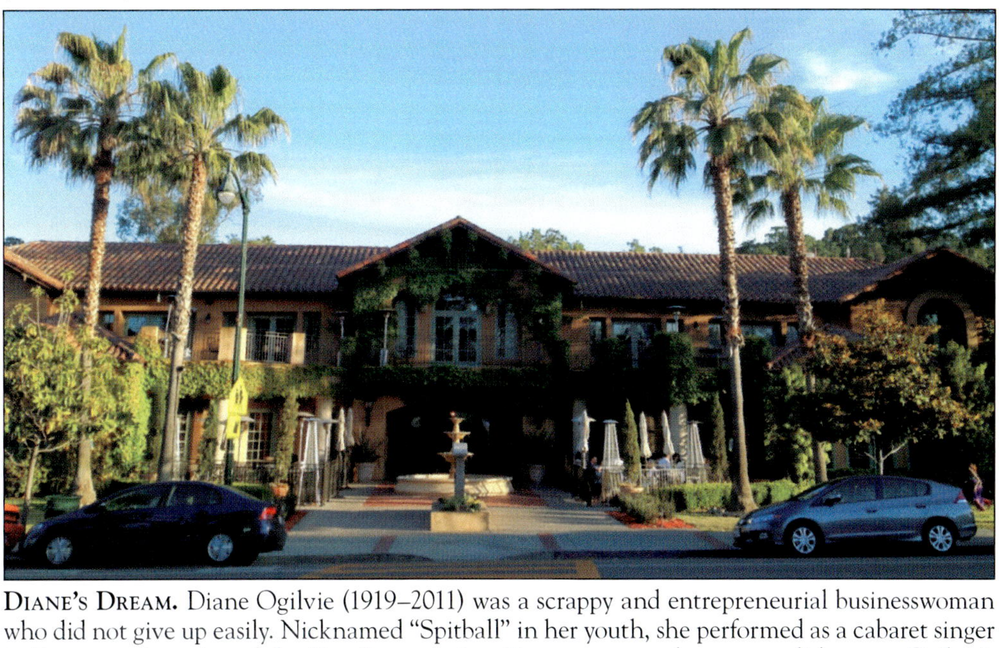

Diane's Dream. Diane Ogilvie (1919–2011) was a scrappy and entrepreneurial businesswoman who did not give up easily. Nicknamed "Spitball" in her youth, she performed as a cabaret singer in Europe and purchased the Cats Estate in Los Gatos, among other accomplishments. Ogilvie's dream was to build an elegant hotel on her East Main Street property. It took years to accomplish, but Hotel Los Gatos came to fruition in 2002. (BB.)

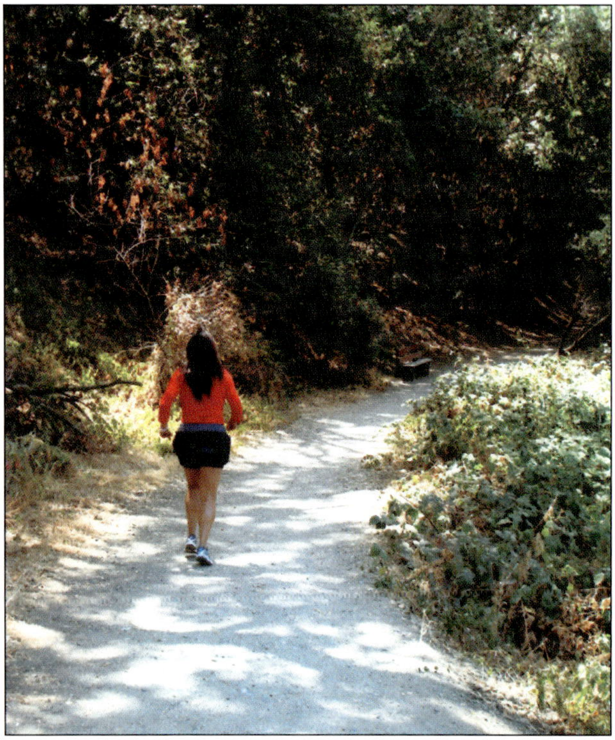

On the Run. A beautiful trail along Los Gatos Creek allows unrestricted access from Lexington Reservoir above Los Gatos to Meridian Avenue in San Jose, a distance of nearly 10 miles. Pedestrians, hikers, bicyclists, skaters, and nature lovers are all welcome. The trail passes through both Oak Meadow Park and Vasona County Park. (AC.)

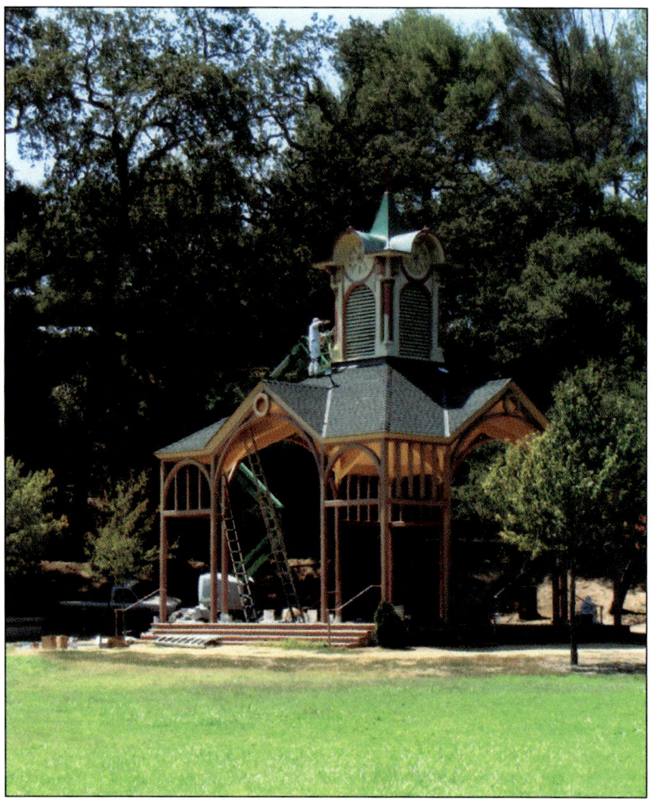

Lyndon Bandstand. The Los Gatos Community Foundation was incorporated in 1993 with the specific goal of building an old-fashioned bandstand in Oak Meadow Park. It took 10 years to raise the funds necessary to erect the structure and to crown it with the refurbished cupola from the carriage house at the John Lyndon estate. Much was accomplished under the direction of Paul Dubois, local businessman and volunteer. (AC.)

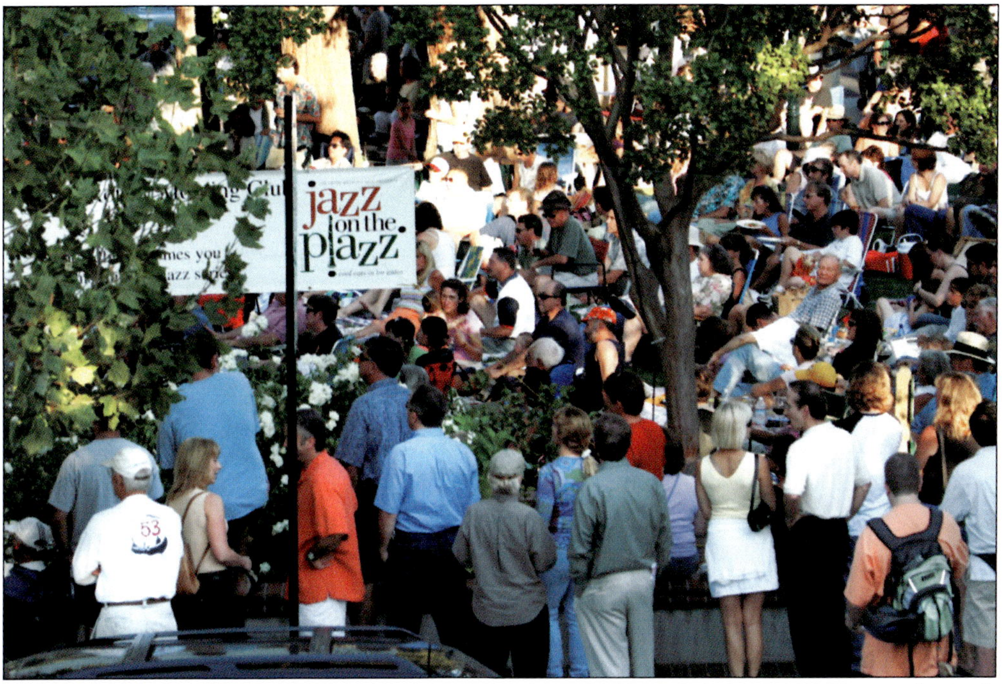

Summer Songs. Summertime in Los Gatos means music. Founded in 1988, Music in the Park happens on Sunday afternoons on the lawn of the Civic Center, featuring performances of folk, rock, country, bluegrass, Irish, and other world music. Founded in 2003, Jazz on the Plazz presents both local and legendary performers on Wednesday evenings, sometimes with a theme, such as "A Gershwin Summer" or "The Summer of Sinatra." (LGWT.)

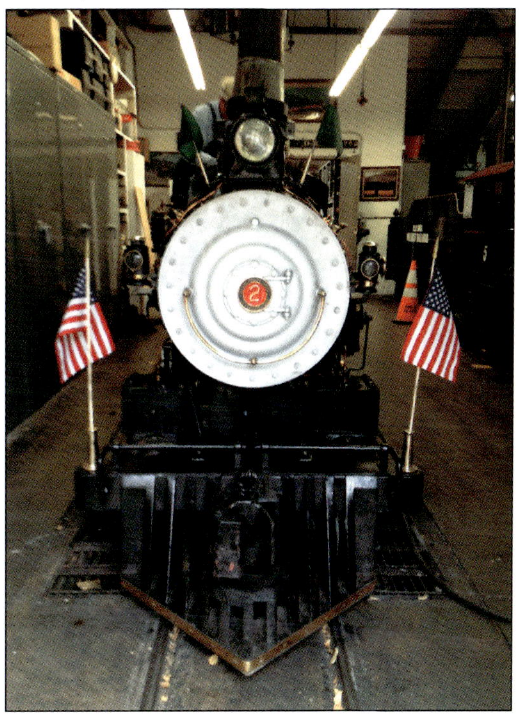

Little Engine That Could. In 1939, railroader Billy Jones purchased a 1905 miniature steam locomotive from a scrap heap on the docks of San Francisco. In July, 2005, the little "2-Spot" celebrated its 100th birthday by steaming along the rails at Oak Meadow and Vasona Parks. The intervening years included extensive restoration work and thousands of miles pulling delighted children along for the ride. (BB.)

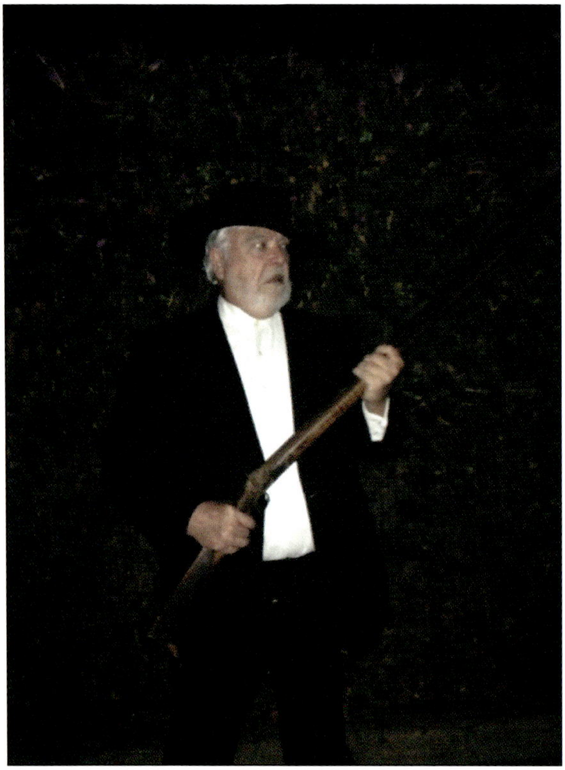

History Alive. D. Michael Kane is a consummate Los Gatos businessman and professional financial manager who has served his community for years on boards and commissions. Also a talented actor, he is known in Los Gatos for his uncanny portrayal of Mountain Charley McKiernan. That role provides him the opportunity to use his polished Irish brogue, the result of 30 years' experience with The Mostly Irish Theatre Company. (Andrea Skov.)

Built To Last. The Fretwell Block at West Main and University Avenue celebrated its 100th birthday in 2007. It was built by Phoebe Stanfield Fretwell, daughter of a prosperous Almaden farmer. After he was killed in a runaway horse accident in 1895, it was probably Phoebe's inheritance that enabled her to finance this historic, reinforced concrete gem, which suffered only a broken window pane in the 1989 earthquake. (BB.)

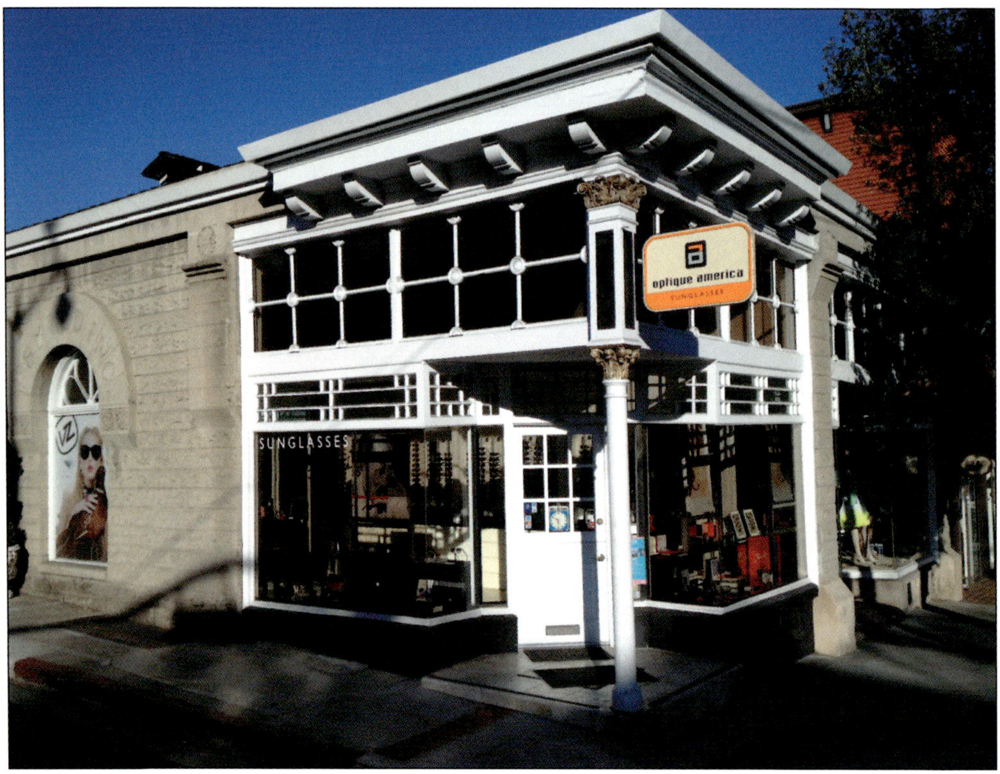

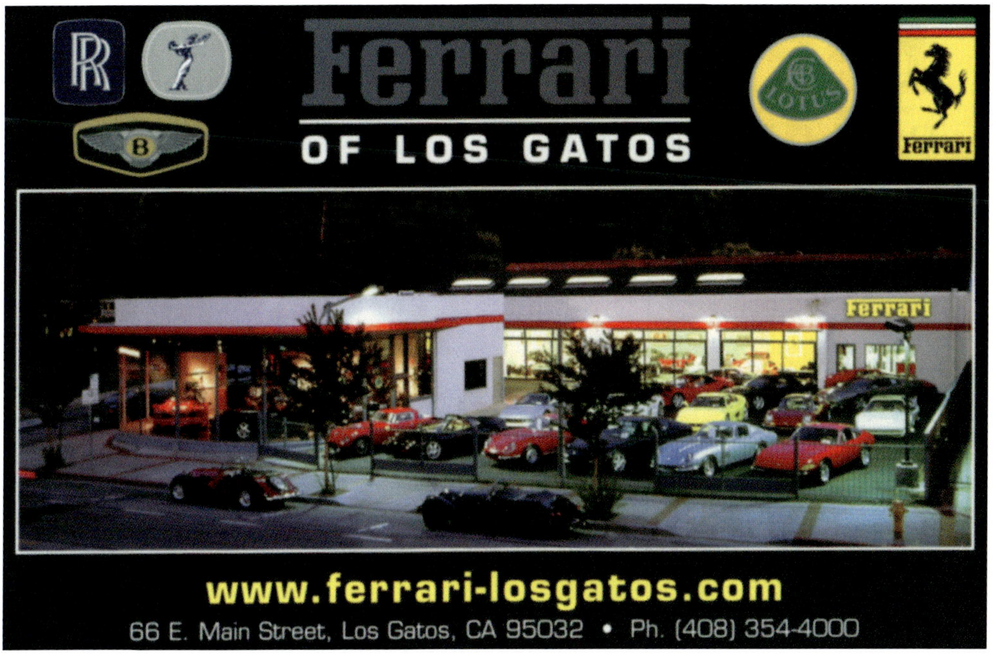

EXOTIC AUTOMOBILES. When Ferrari came to town in 1976, the corner of East Main and Pageant Way became a showcase for foreign automobiles and a magnet for car lovers. In 2003, the business's name was changed to Bentley of Los Gatos. Later known as Silicon Valley Auto Group and finally as Los Gatos Luxury Cars, brands such as Bugatti and Lamborghini are now sold at 620 Blossom Hill Road. (AC.)

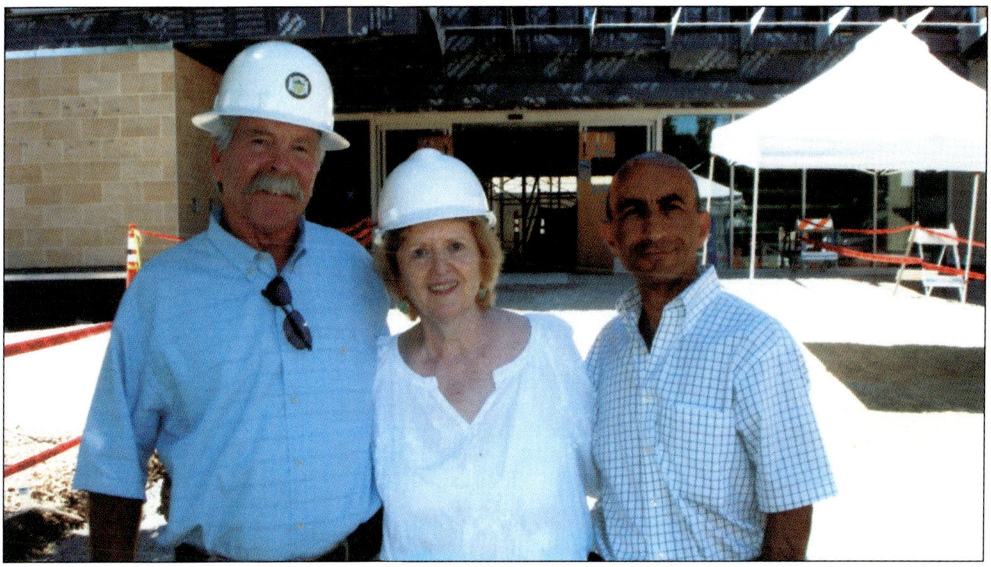

BUILDING THE DREAM. By the 1980s, the town had outgrown its library. During the decades that followed, the Friends of Los Gatos Library advocated for a new building. They steered through rocky shoals and opposition from some public officials until redevelopment money became available. Pictured are employees who helped spearhead the project. From left to right are project manager Bruce Smith, Library Director Peggy Conaway Bergtold, and Town Engineer Kevin Rohani. (AC.)

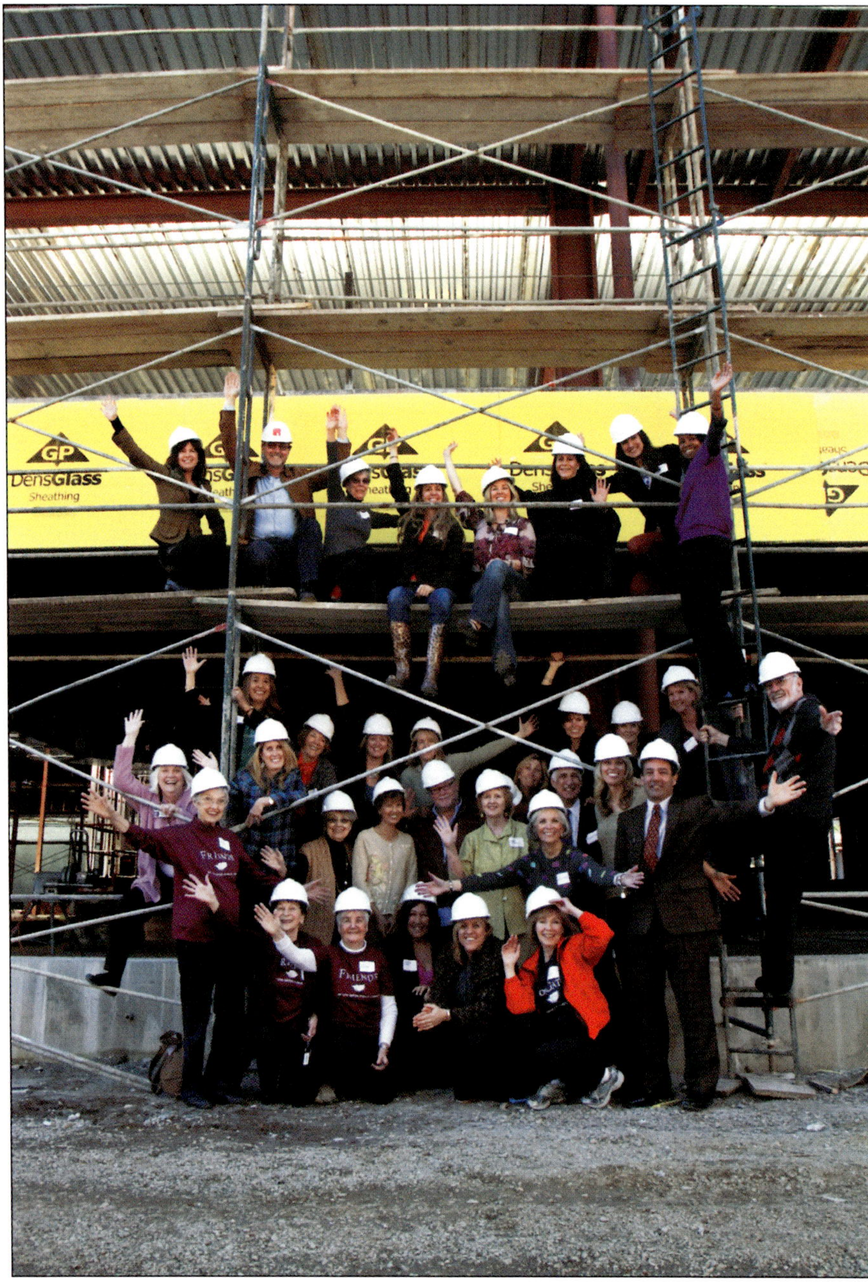

THE CAPITAL CAMPAIGN. The town budgeted $18.4 million for the new 30,250-square-foot library. The Friends of Los Gatos Library were asked to raise over $2 million for furniture, fixtures, and equipment to complete the new building. They accomplished that goal under the leadership of Sandy Decker, standing second from right in the second row with outstretched arms. This photograph, taken a year before the library opened on February 11, 2012, includes many members of the Friends group, each of whom contributed money to the capital campaign. In the first row, second from left, is Carol Hamilton, who served as president of the Friends throughout the long campaign in order to provide consistency and leadership for the organization. Approximately 60 volunteers participated in the successful fundraising campaign. (LGWT.)

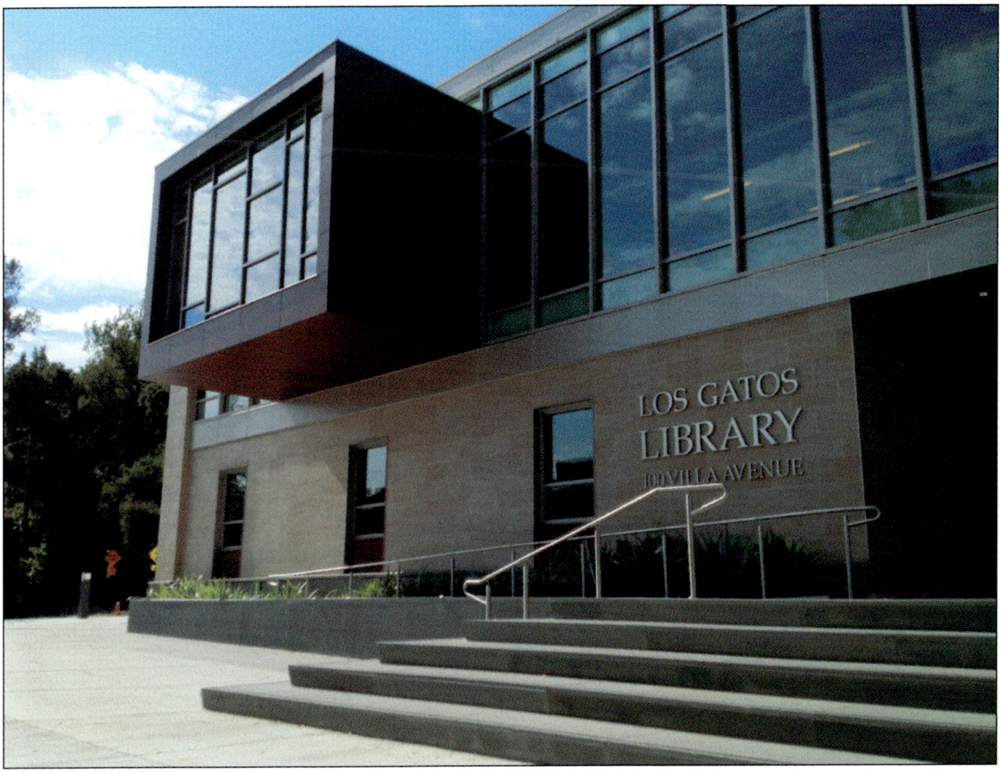

Library-As-Lantern. Noll & Tam Architects of Berkeley, California, depicted the library as a lantern in the woods, lighting the way to knowledge. The building is oriented to capture northern light, and the space was meticulously designed with a line of clerestory windows that bring additional daylight into the core of the building. The cantilevered bay window, shown above, pops out from the teen center. (BB.)

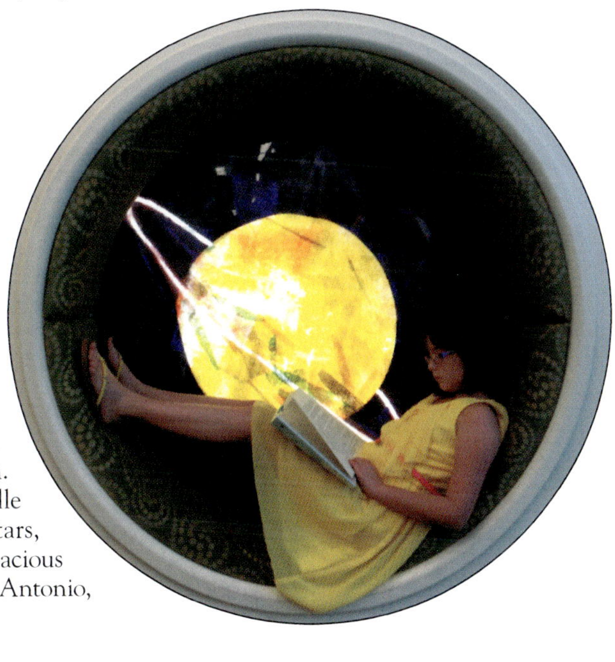

Nurdle Nooks. The new library is of modern design and blends nicely with the existing Civic Center. It is a warm and welcoming building and a great source of pride for the town. Artist Ben Phipps created 14 "Nurdle Nooks," representing planets and stars, from recycled plastic pellets for the spacious children's room. Sophie Peters, of San Antonio, Texas, demonstrates their use. (BB.)

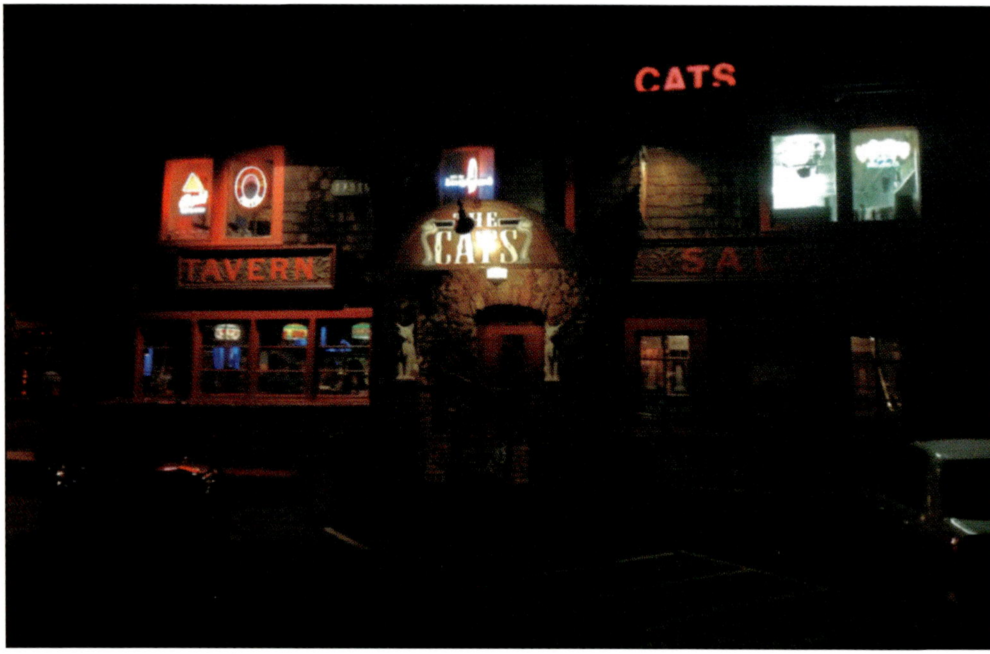

CATS RESTAURANT. The origin of the building that houses the Cats Restaurant & Tavern seems lost in time. The rustic, old landmark has housed a number of businesses in its history and has operated as a popular bar and restaurant since the 1940s. Diane Ogilvie owned the building for 30 years. Restored by Mark Edwards and his partners, the roadhouse now features famous BBQ and authentic Old West artifacts. (BB.)

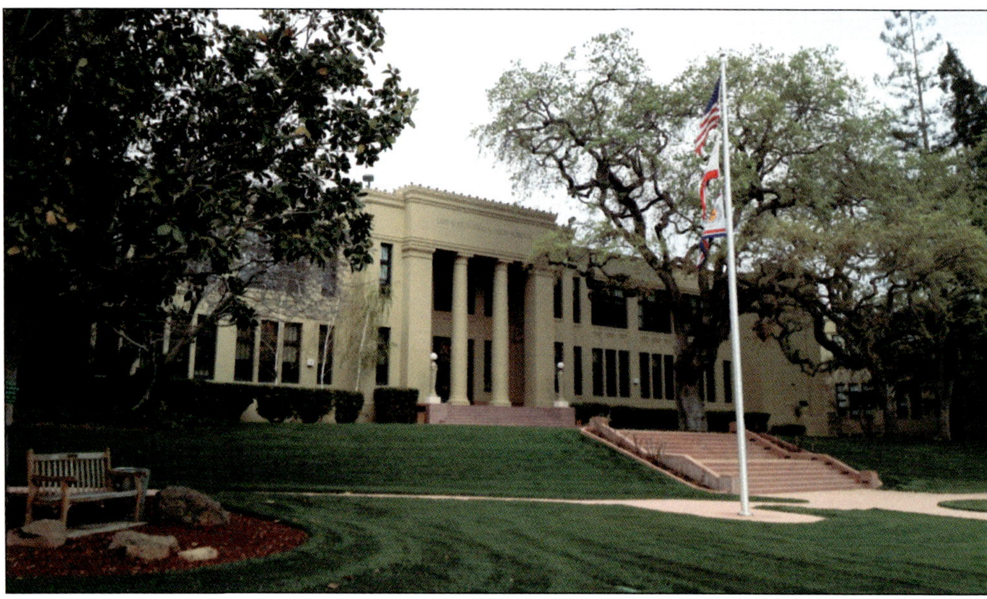

HOME OF THE WILDCATS. Los Gatos is proud of its high school. Its roots date to 1887, when Henry Meade Bland arrived at the elementary school on University Avenue and instituted a "graduate course" to prepare students for college entrance examinations. The high school evolved with a proud record of academic and athletic achievement. June graduation exercises are held on the front lawn. (BB.)

A 40-Year Tradition. Janice Benjamin's Indian Store was located on the first floor of Old Town from 1991 to 2007 before moving to West Main Street. The store was a treasure trove of pottery from the Hopi, Santa Clara, Acoma, and San Ildefonso, as well as American Indian fine art. After a remarkable 40 years in business, the shop closed in 2013. Benjamin is pictured with her husband, Ken. (Ken Benjamin.)

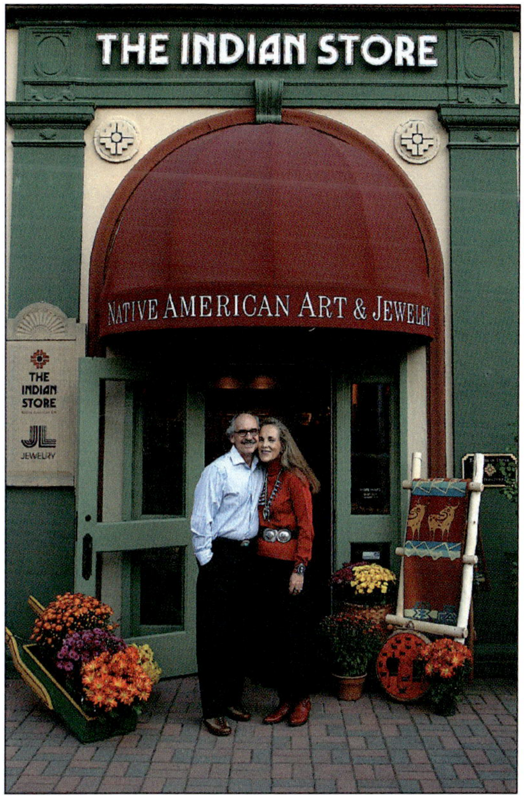

Let's Go to the Movies. When the Strand movie theater opened on November 18, 1916, 900 people showed up for 600 seats. Los Gatans have been going to the movies at 43 North Santa Cruz Avenue ever since, fires, earthquake and the Great Depression notwithstanding. Closed in October 2012 and reopened in May 2014, the historic venue underwent a spectacular restoration and now features the latest in luxury accommodations. (BB.)

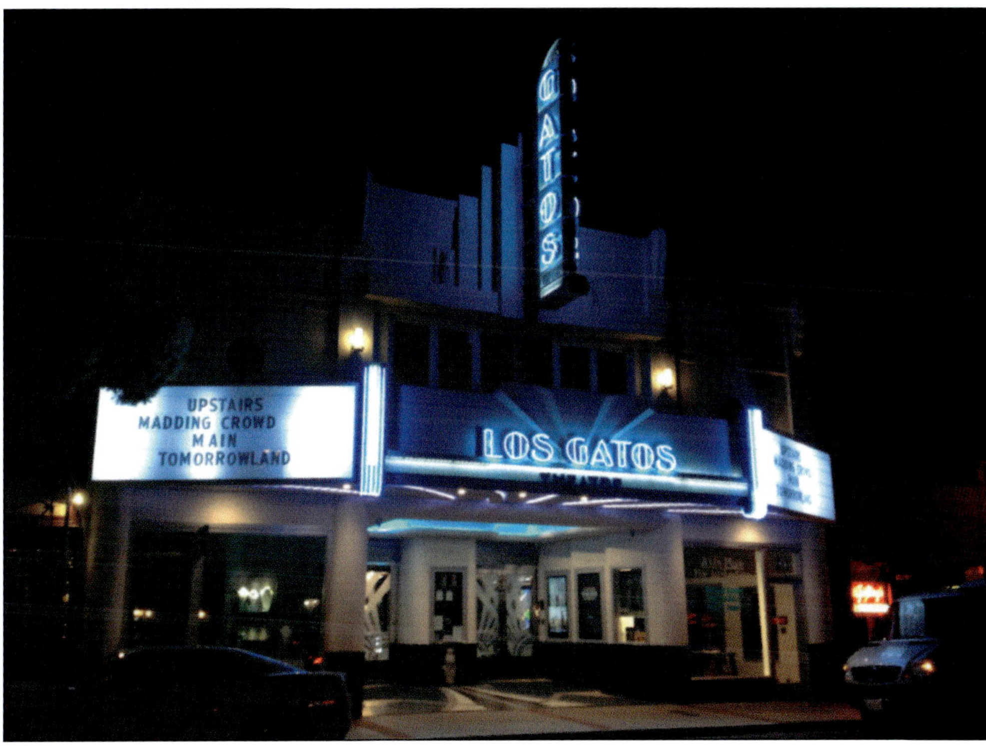

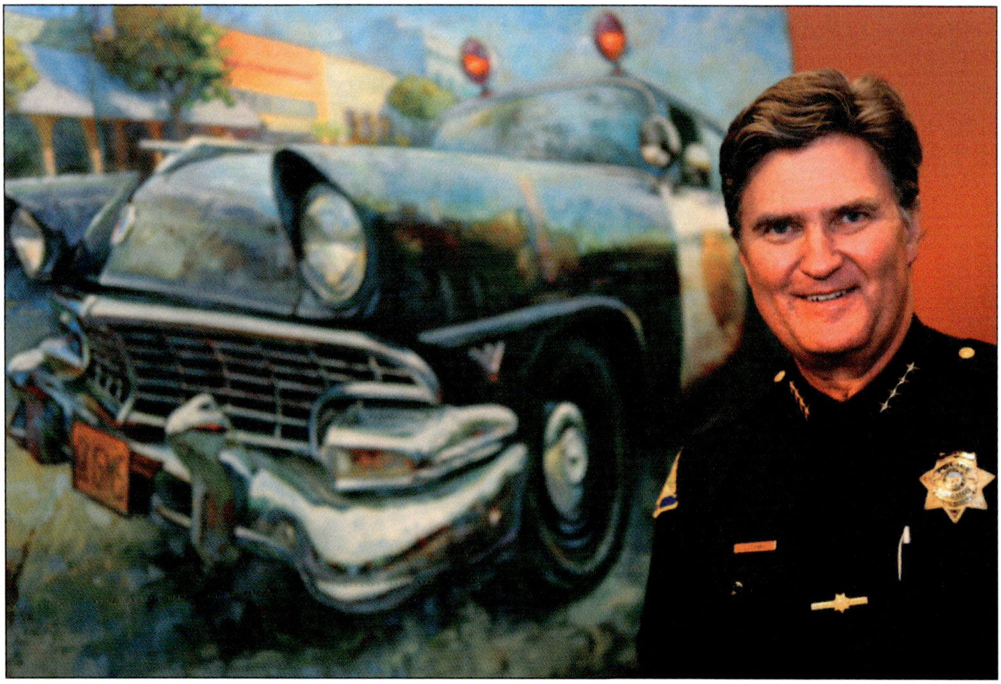

Chief Seaman. Scott Seaman was appointed chief of the Los Gatos–Monte Sereno Police Department in 2002 and served for 12 years. His retirement capped a noteworthy 39-year career in law enforcement. He believed in knowing the members of his community and cared for the welfare of youth. Chief Seaman is shown here in front of a painting by Gordon Smedt that hangs in the Police Operations building. (Scott Seaman.)

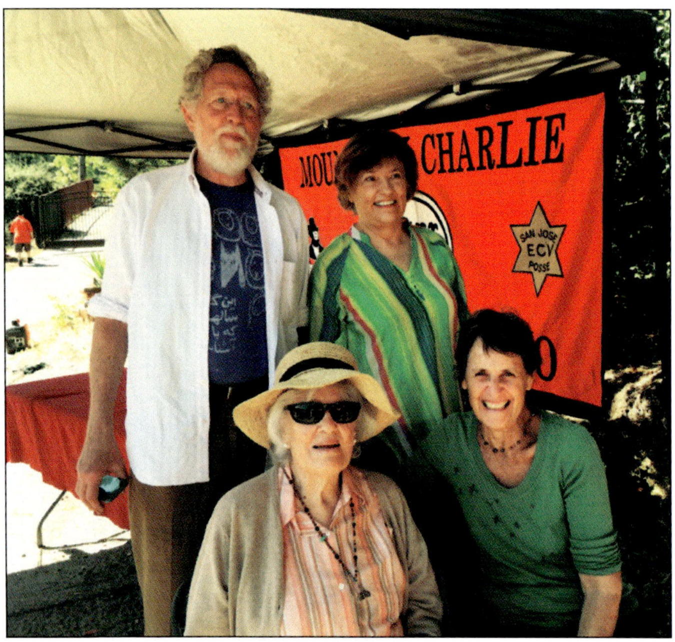

"Tash" at The Cats. To celebrate her 100th birthday, Katherine "Tash" Livingston (lower left) traveled to Los Gatos in June 2015, from Portland, Oregon, to witness the dedication of a plaque at her grandfather's estate, The Cats. "Tash" is the only surviving grandchild of Charles Erskine Scott Wood and his first wife, Nannie Moale Smith Wood. She is surrounded by her son, Bruce Livingston; her daughter Eliza Wood Livingston (upper right); and her niece, Sara Wood Smith (lower right). (AC.)

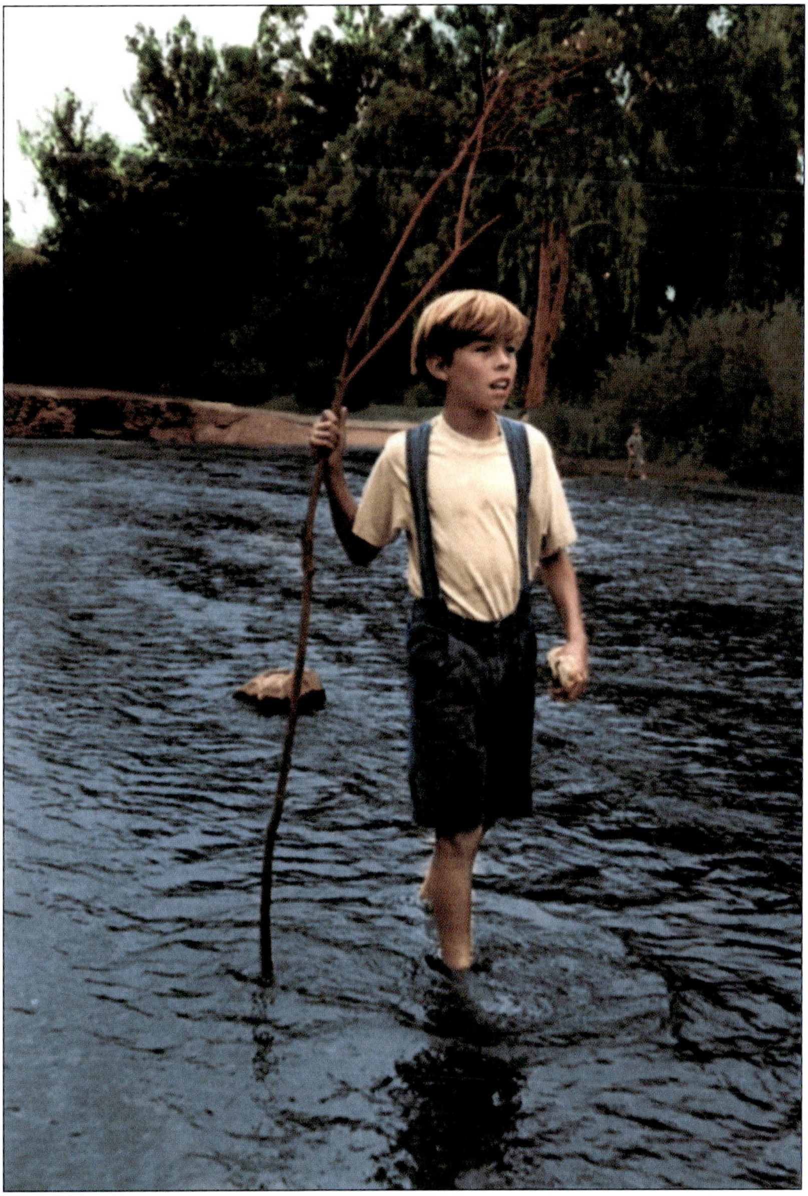

TIMELESS. From Ohlone Indians fishing for teeming salmon and speckled trout before the Yankees arrived, to children floating along in dappled sunlight on inner tubes in the days before the dam, the lovely and ever-living Los Gatos Creek is both beautiful and historical. Water from the creek drove the waterwheels at Forbes Mill. In the early 1900s, people set out picnic lunches on rocks that protruded into the stream and dined, creekside, between bold, bluff banks. A water carnival was held near Wrights, the trees hung with Chinese lanterns, while stringed instruments romanced the soft, summer air. In winter, the creek could jump its banks, water tumbling down the mountains toward the sea, taking out wooden bridges along the way. But when summer returned, the boys in town retreated to the Boogang, a crystal-clear swimming hole about a mile south of town. In 1992, Tony Landeros strolled along the creek like thousands of children before him. He might have collected tadpoles in a jar or just enjoyed the serenity nature provided. (LGWT; photograph by George Sakkestad.)

Discover Thousands of Local History Books Featuring Millions of Vintage Images

Arcadia Publishing, the leading local history publisher in the United States, is committed to making history accessible and meaningful through publishing books that celebrate and preserve the heritage of America's people and places.

Find more books like this at
www.arcadiapublishing.com

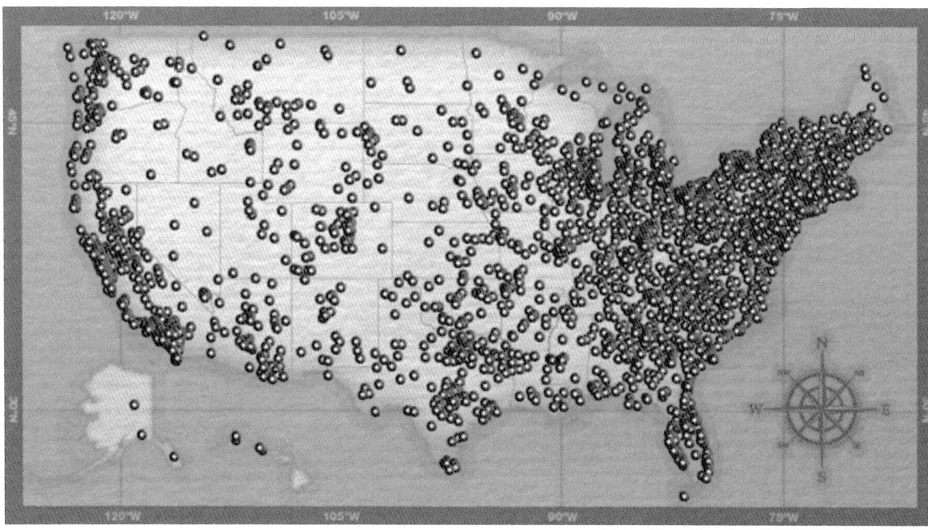

Search for your hometown history, your old stomping grounds, and even your favorite sports team.

Consistent with our mission to preserve history on a local level, this book was printed in South Carolina on American-made paper and manufactured entirely in the United States. Products carrying the accredited Forest Stewardship Council (FSC) label are printed on 100 percent FSC-certified paper.

MADE IN THE USA